THE
LAWYERS' GUIDE
TO
PERSONAL INJURY LAW

Jason Shapiro, Esq.

WingSpan Press

Printed in the United States of America

Published by WingSpan Press, Livermore, CA
www.wingspanpress.com

The WingSpan name, logo and colophon are the trademarks of WingSpan Publishing.

ISBN 978-1-59594-187-9

First Edition 2008

Library of Congress Control Number 2007936561

PREFACE

The Lawyers' Guide to Personal Injury Law is an instructional textbook for attorneys who want to become experts in the field of negligence law. The book provides a comprehensive analysis of the law in the various areas within the field – construction accidents, motor vehicle accidents, premises accidents, and more – and the numerous types of cases within each area. *The Lawyers' Guide to Personal Injury Law* details the many stringent legal requirements for successfully prosecuting each type of case, provides a multitude of strategic tips, and cautions of the various potential pitfalls to avoid. The book highlights the techniques and skills necessary at each stage of the litigation, including investigation, discovery, depositions, settlement negotiations, jury selection, and trial.

The Lawyers' Guide to Personal Injury Law concisely compiles a mountain of information – gleaned from many years of experience in the field, extensive legal research, and numerous seminars, books, journals, and articles – into one easy-to-use source. *The Lawyers' Guide to Personal Injury Law* thoroughly supplies the knowledge attorneys will need in order to effectively practice in the field of negligence and, ultimately, maximize monetary compensation for accident victims and their families.

ABOUT THE AUTHOR

Jason Shapiro is a trial attorney, lecturer, author, and the founder of Shapiro Law Offices. He is a *magna cum laude, Phi Beta Kappa* (top 1% of class) graduate of Tufts University and the University of Pennsylvania Law School, one of only five Ivy League law schools in the country. He is a longstanding member of the American Association for Justice (formerly the Association of Trial Lawyers of America), the New York State Trial Lawyers Association, and the Bronx County Bar Association, and is licensed to practice in multiple jurisdictions. He has devoted his practice to protecting the rights of accident victims and their families. Mr. Shapiro can be contacted at www.shapirolawoffices.com or 718-295-7000.

TABLE OF CONTENTS

DETAILED TABLE OF CONTENTS

CHAPTER 4: MOTOR VEHICLE ACCIDENTS – UNINSURED AND UNDER-INSURED MOTORIST COVERAGE 48

CHAPTER 1

GETTING STARTED: HAVING THE PROPER RESOURCES IN PLACE

There are a handful of resources which greatly aid personal injury attorneys in their practice. They are as follows:

• *Pattern Jury Instructions:* The *Pattern Jury Instructions* (published by West Publishing Company), commonly referred to as the "*PJI*", is essential to a personal injury practice. The *PJI* encompasses the charges (i.e., instructions) that the judge will read to a jury at the end of the case, should it fail to settle prior thereto. Hence, the plaintiff's attorney should always **start** with the *PJI* in order to know exactly what s/he must set out to prove. The *PJI* should be consulted at various stages of the case, including when deciding whether to accept or decline a particular case (i.e., will we be able to ultimately prove what is required?), prior to depositions, prior to jury selection, and prior to trial (or arbitration). There are often various pitfalls which will prevent a case, or a particularly helpful charge, from ever reaching a jury. Hence, the commentaries following the applicable charges should also be carefully consulted, as they discuss a plethora of litigated issues (and provide case law and citations) regarding each charge.

• *CPLR* and *New York Practice:* Every plaintiffs' personal injury attorney should have a copy of the *Civil Practice Law and Rules* (commonly referred to as the "*CPLR*"), as well as *New York Practice* by David Siegel (published by West Publishing Company). The *CPLR* sets forth the civil practice statutes, while *New York Practice* provides a detailed explanation of how these statutes apply to civil cases. Topics include jurisdiction, venue, statutes of limitations, parties, pleadings, motion practice, pretrial issues, trial, judgments, appeals, etc. *New York Practice* is an invaluable resource, particularly when engaged in motion practice.

• New York State Trial Lawyers Association (NYSTLA): There are many different bar associations throughout New York State. However, for plaintiffs' personal injury attorneys, the New York State Trial Lawyers Association (NYSTLA) is unmatched. NYSTLA provides many helpful services for plaintiffs' personal injury attorneys, and fights to protect the rights of plaintiffs (and, ultimately, the livelihood of plaintiffs' attorneys). NYSTLA also provides a listserv wherein personal injury attorneys (mostly plaintiffs' attorneys) can ask questions regarding their cases. The e-mails are circulated to hundreds of personal injury attorneys, with several informed responses to follow. This resource is invaluable, especially since plaintiffs' personal injury attorneys (unlike defense counsel) are typically sole practitioners or part of small firms.

• Saga Case Management Software: Utilizing the right case management program allows for efficiency which, in turn, allows for a greater case load (and, ultimately, more income). Presently, the best, and most popular, case management program is Saga (www.sagasys.com). Saga provides a way to store all necessary case information in an easy-to-use, organized manner. It also provides all necessary forms (including letters and pleadings) and minimizes wasteful time. The benefits associated with the Saga software **far** outweigh the cost. The program allows an office to cut its support staff in half, while improving service and providing tighter control over cases. Below is a summary of some of Saga's features:
  • organizes and tracks all case data, including a document manager for all outgoing and incoming documents;
  • automatically assembles form correspondence and pleadings, without the need to manually change the forms on each case;
  • sends alerts for upcoming deadlines and statutes of limitations;
  • tracks discovery and document exchange;
  • maintains a complete docket and calendar system, automatically uploading all court appearances from e-law;
  • automatically incorporates all case disbursements from QuickBooks into Saga, saving time and ensuring that all disbursements are repaid at the conclusion of each case;
  • provides a mass mailing merge; and
  • provides various management reports.

• *Verdict Search:* Plaintiffs' personal injury attorneys should subscribe to *Verdict Search.* This weekly magazine, published by American Lawyer Media, details recent personal injury cases that were either settled or reached a verdict. *Verdict Search* is generally used by plaintiffs' personal injury attorneys to determine case values. On a higher level, learning the residual effects of various types of injuries aids plaintiffs' attorneys in *maximizing* case value; it teaches plaintiffs' attorneys how to make the value of a case grow. Further, it allows plaintiffs' attorneys to familiarize themselves with various theories of liability.

   • Legal Research Program: Plaintiffs' personal injury attorneys should subscribe to a capable legal research program. Researching case law based upon the specific facts of the case can be critical at various stages of the proceedings, including:
   - deciding whether to accept or reject the case;
   - depositions;
   - motions for summary judgment motion; and
   - trial.

Westlaw is an excellent, easy-to-use source for legal research. The benefits reaped will be many times greater than the expense.

CHAPTER 2

MOTOR VEHICLE ACCIDENTS – NO-FAULT LAW

PART A: OVERVIEW

§ 2.01 Overview – Motor Vehicle Accidents – No-Fault Law

New York's no-fault insurance law was implemented to allow all victims of motor vehicle accidents to receive first-party benefits for their injuries (regardless of who is at fault); as a *quid pro quo*, tort liability was limited to only cases of serious injury. *Insurance Law (Ins. Law) §5101-5108: the "Comprehensive Motor Vehicle Insurance Reparations Act."* All motor vehicle liability insurance policies are required to provide basic first-party coverage. *Ins. Law §5103.* "First-party benefits" are payments to reimburse a person for "basic economic loss", which consists of loss of earnings, medical benefits, and certain miscellaneous expenses. The term "no-fault" is synonymous with "PIP" (or personal injury protection), which refers to the aforementioned first-party benefits.

PART B: EXTENT OF NO-FAULT COVERAGE

§ 2.02 Components of No-Fault Benefits

[1] Basic Economic Loss

Under New York's no-fault law, every motor vehicle liability insurance policy is required to cover an injured party's "basic economic loss" as a result of use or operation of a motor vehicle, subject to certain exclusions (see §§2.05, 2.06 below). Basic economic loss means up to $50,000 per person for a combination of medical expenses, loss of earnings, and miscellaneous expenses. This $50,000 in benefits is the maximum basic economic loss on a standard insurance policy. Basic economic loss also includes an option to purchase, for a premium, an additional $25,000 in no-fault coverage, known as optional basic economic loss (or OBEL). *Ins. Law §5102(a).*

[a] Medical Bills

As an element of "basic economic loss", no-fault insurance pays for all (subject to the monetary limitations above) medical bills incurred as a result of a motor vehicle accident. There is no time limit, as these benefits can be paid forever – so long as the treatment is related to the accident and remains medically necessary. *Ins. Law §5102(a)(1).*

[b] Loss of Earnings

As an additional element of "basic economic loss", no-fault insurance reimburses the claimant's loss of earnings for up to three years from the date of the accident. The claimant is entitled to 80% of his or her gross income, not to exceed a payment of $2,000 per month, up to the maximum in the insurance policy. *Ins. Law §5102(b)(1), Ins. Law §5102(a)(2).* Via an Additional Personal Injury Protection (APIP) endorsement in the insurance policy, the claimant may be able to recover up to $4,000 per month for loss of earnings. See below.

[1] Offsets to Prevent Double Recovery

No-fault insurance carriers may use payments made by New York State Disability, Social Security Disability, workers' compensation, and certain Medicare situations as offsets in order prevent double recovery. *See State Farm Mutual Motor Vehicle Insurance Companies v. Brooks,* 101 Misc.2d 704, 709, 421 N.Y.S.2d 1010, 1014 (Sup. Ct. Monroe Co. 1979), *rev'd* on other grounds, 78 A.D.2d 456, 435 N.Y.S.2d 419 (4th Dep't 1981) (deductions for Social Security, workers' compensation, and medical benefits intended to prevent double recovery); *Heitner v. GEICO,* 64 N.Y.2d. 834, 836, 486 NY.S.2d 933, 934 (1985) (no-fault policy to provide full compensation only to limits of basic economic loss). *See Ins. Law §5102(b).*

[2] Prompt Payment Required

First-party benefits are payable "as the loss is incurred" and are overdue if not paid within 30 days after the claimant supplies proof of the loss. The claimant is entitled to interest on overdue payments at a rate of 2% per month and may recover attorneys' fees incurred in collecting the claim. *Ins. Law §5106(a).*

[c] Miscellaneous Expenses

Certain miscellaneous expenses (e.g., housekeeper, taxi fares to see doctor, etc.) are also paid by no-fault insurance. The maximum miscellaneous coverage on the standard insurance policy is $25 per day, payable for up to one year after the accident. *See Ins. Law §5102(a)(3), 11 NYCRR §65.11(h).*

[2] Additional Personal Injury Protection

Via an additional personal injury protection (APIP) insurance policy endorsement (sometimes referred to as "extended PIP"), no-fault benefits can be increased beyond "basic economic loss", up to a maximum of $4,000 per month total. A review of the declarations page of the insurance policy will allow for a determination as to whether there is any such excess no-fault coverage.

Warning: No-fault payments made in excess of basic economic loss, which is generally $50,000 (unless OBEL was purchased to increase it to $75,000), will become a lien against the third-party claim. Hence, in such situations, the claimant's attorney must be sure to contact the no-fault insurance carrier prior to settling the third-party case. See chapter 8, §8.33[a].

---

[3] Death Benefit

No-fault insurance policies must also provide for the payment, as first-party benefits, to the estate of any covered person (other than an occupant of another motor vehicle or a motorcycle), of a death benefit of $2,000 for the death of such person as the result of use or operation of the motor vehicle. This accidental death payment is in addition to any first-party benefits payable for basic economic loss. *Ins. Law §5103(a)(4)*.

PART C: PRIORITY AMONGST MULTIPLE INSURANCE POLICIES

§ 2.03 Priority Amongst Various Motor Vehicle Insurance Policies

[1] Car Passenger

Where the claimant was a passenger in a motor vehicle accident, the insurance policy for the vehicle's owner is the primary no-fault provider; the passenger's own insurance policy, if s/he owns or leases a vehicle, is secondary. *Ins. Law §5103(a)(2)*. If the passenger does not own or lease a vehicle, the insurance of any resident-relative of the claimant is secondary. *Ins. Law §5103(a)(3)*. While the claimant is not entitled to a double recovery, s/he may seek additional benefits (e.g., OBEL or APIP) through the secondary insurance policy where the primary insurance policy does not afford such coverage.

[2] Bus Passenger

Where the claimant was a passenger on a bus (including a school bus), and was not an operator, owner or other employee of the bus, no-fault benefits are to be provided by the claimant's own insurance company, not that of the bus company. However, if the claimant is not covered by an insurance policy providing first-party benefits, nor is any relative in his or her household, then the no-fault benefits are to be provided by the bus' insurance company. *Ins. Law §5103(a)(1)*. See *Hill v. Metropolitan Suburban Bus Authority*, 157 A.D.2d 93, 97, 555 N.Y.S.2d 803, 806 (2d Dep't 1990) (bus passenger able to receive no-fault benefits from bus' insurer).

[3] Pedestrian / Bicyclist

Where the claimant was a pedestrian or bicyclist who was struck by a motor vehicle, the scenario is the same as the bus passenger situation discussed above; the insurance of the motor vehicle that struck the claimant is the primary no-fault provider. *Ins. Law §5103(a)(1),(2)*. Therefore, the claimant should proceed against the *same* insurance company for first-party (i.e., no-fault) benefits and the third-party negligence action.

Warning: In such a case, the claimant and the claimant's attorney must be ultra-cautious when dealing with the no-fault insurance carrier, for they may well attempt to use information obtained on the no-fault file to the claimant's detriment in the third-party negligence action.

Practice Tip: If multiple vehicles strike a pedestrian or bicyclist, the claimant should file a no-fault application with each vehicle's insurance carrier; they will have to apportion the no-fault benefits amongst themselves.

§ 2.04 Priority Amongst No-Fault and Workers' Compensation Benefits

Where the claimant is injured in a motor vehicle accident while in the course of employment, workers' compensation benefits are primary and no-fault benefits are secondary. *Ins. Law §5203(b), 11 NYCRR §65.15.*

Practice Tip: In such a situation, it is imperative that the claimant file an application for both workers' compensation benefits and no-fault benefits. Workers' compensation will only reimburse up to $400 per week (or 2/3 of the claimant's wages, whichever is less) in lost wages, whereas the claimant may earn significantly more than that. Thus, no-fault will then take effect, and will use the $400 per week as an offset.

Practice Tip: Drivers of livery cabs are often denied no-fault benefits on the ground that they are employees of the livery base (as opposed to independent contractors) and therefore covered by workers' compensation. Typically, where the driver is obtaining fares through a radio base, s/he is considered an employee (entitled to workers' compensation benefits); where s/he rents a car / medallion and picks up fares on the street (i.e., not radio-based), s/he is considered an independent contractor (entitled to no-fault benefits). Hence, where an injured livery cab driver's no-fault claim is denied, s/he must first proceed with a workers' compensation claim; once the claim is disallowed by the Workers' Compensation Board, s/he can then proceed through no-fault for benefits.

PART D: INCLUSIONS, LIMITATIONS, AND EXCLUSIONS

§ 2.05 No-Fault Inclusions

[1] MVAIC Benefits Where No Valid No-Fault Policy Exists

Where there are no valid insurance policies to provide no-fault benefits, a no-fault claim may be filed with Motor Vehicle Accident Indemnification Corporation (MVAIC). MVAIC is a not-for-profit corporation, capitalized by an assessment against all motor vehicle liability insurers in New York. *See Ins. Law §§5203, 5206, 5207.* No-fault benefits may be obtained from MVAIC. *Ins. Law §5221.* To qualify, the claimant must be a New York State resident (other than an insured, the owner of an uninsured motor vehicle, or his or her spouse when a passenger in that vehicle) or a resident of another state where recourse is afforded to residents of New York State of substantially similar character to that provided by MVAIC. *Ins. Law §5202(b).*

[2] Out-of-State Vehicle

With respect to accidents occurring within New York State, no-fault coverage is deemed in effect on an out-of-state vehicle. This applies even if the insurance policy issued on the vehicle did not provide for no-fault coverage – so long as the insurer of the out-of-state vehicle is authorized to transact, actually transacts, or is under the control of an insurer authorized to transact or which transacts, business in New York. *See Ins. Law §5107.*

[3] Out-of-State Accident

No-fault benefits, via a New York State issued insurance policy, must also be payable to (or on behalf of) New York State residents injured in motor vehicle accidents outside of New York State. *See Ins. Law §5103(a)(3).*

§ 2.06 No-Fault Exclusions

[1] Vehicles Excluded from No-Fault Coverage

No-fault coverage only pertains to "motor vehicles", as defined by New York State's Insurance Law. For purposes of the no-fault law, "motor vehicle" does not include:

- motorcycles and all-terrain vehicles;
- electrically-driven devices operated by a person with a disability (e.g., wheelchair);
- vehicles which run only upon rails (e.g., train);
- snowmobiles;
- fire and police vehicles, other than ambulances;
- farm equipment;
- tractors used exclusively for agricultural purposes, or for snow plowing other than for hire; or
- self-propelled caterpillar or crawler-type equipment while being operated on the contract site.

See VTL §§125, 311; Ins. Law §5102(f).

Practice Tip: Even though motorcycles are excluded from no-fault coverage, liability insurance coverage on a motorcycle must provide for payment of no-fault benefits to people, other than the motorcycle's occupant(s), injured as a result of the use or operation of the motorcycle within New York. *Ins. Law §5103(f)*. Thus, where a pedestrian or bicyclist is struck by a motorcycle, s/he can obtain no-fault benefits through the motorcycle's insurance policy.

[2] Individuals Excluded from No-Fault Coverage

An insurer may exclude the following from no-fault coverage:

- person who intentionally causes his or her own injury;

- person injured as a result of operating a motor vehicle while intoxicated or drug impaired;
- person injured while committing a felony;
- person injured while racing;
- person injured while operating or occupying a stolen vehicle;
- person owning an uninsured vehicle who is injured by that vehicle; and/or
- mechanic injured while servicing that vehicle.

Ins. Law §5103(b).

Practice Tip: An underage, unlicensed driver is nonetheless entitled to no-fault benefits.

PART E: DEALING WITH NO-FAULT INSURER

§ 2.07 Filing No-Fault Application

[1] 30-Day Deadline

The claimant must file the no-fault application (also referred to as an NF-2) with the appropriate no-fault insurance carrier within 30 days after the date of the accident. *See 11 NYCRR §65-1.1, 2.4 (Regulation 68).*

Warning: If the no-fault application is not received in a timely manner and is therefore denied, a "soft tissue injury" claimant may be unable to proceed with a third-party negligence action. In essence, the denial will often preclude necessary treatment and testing, such as MRIs and future surgery. As a result, the claimant may be unable to prove s/he sustained a "serious injury" under the Insurance Law. See chapter 3, §§3.04, 3.13[1], 3.18.

Practice Tip: Sending the no-fault application via certified mail, return receipt requested, will provide proof of timely filing.

[2] Completing No-Fault Application

In completing the no-fault application, the claimant must be mindful that the injuries may grow. Unless there is some type of "catch-all" with respect to the injuries claimed (e.g., "and various other parts of the body"), the insurance carrier may refuse to pay for treatment or procedures relating to an injury not specifically delineated on the application.

Warning: The claimant should also be aware that the defendant in the third-party action will eventually gain access to the no-fault file, which may include a copy of the application. Hence, the description of how the accident occurred, along with the description of the injuries, should be completed with that in mind.

§ 2.08 No-Fault Examinations Under Oath

Insurance carriers have the right to demand that a claimant be produced for an examination under oath (EUO) in an effort to identify fraud and violations of New York State law in submissions of claims for reimbursement. There are particular rules to be followed by the insurer, notably that they are not to treat the applicant as an adversary and that they are not to demand verification of the facts unless there is good reason to do so. *See 11 NYCRR §65.15(a)(2), (3). Rules for Settlement for First-Party Benefits.* Failure to attend the EUO will likely result in a denial of the entire no-fault claim. Further, the claimant can demand that the EUO be held in the county where the claimant resides. *See 11 NYCRR §3.5(d).*

> **Practice Tip:** The claimant's attorney should request, in writing, the specific reason why the EUO is being sought. The insurer is required to clearly inform the claimant of the insured's position regarding the disputed matter. *See 11 NYCRR §65.15 (a)(5).* Learning the reason will allow the attorney to better prepare the client and properly defend the examination.

> **Warning:** The EUO should be limited to questions regarding the facts of the occurrence (such as the time, place, occupants of vehicle, etc.) and treatment (i.e., to determine whether the healthcare providers' bills are proper), but should not delve into other areas such as liability. Increasingly, insurers are using EUOs as a way of obtaining an additional deposition of a claimant, for use in the third-party negligence action.

§ 2.09 No-Fault Independent Medical Examinations

The claimant will a receive notice in the mail to attend an examination by the no-fault carrier's physician, referred to as an independent medical examination ("IME"). The purpose of the examination is to determine whether any further treatment is medically necessary. A no-fault insurer cannot discontinue payment on outstanding bills even though maximum medical improvement has been reached. The claimant need only establish that the treatment continues to be necessary. *Hobby v. CNA Insurance*, 267 A.D.2d 1084, 1085, 700 N.Y.S.2d 346 (4th Dep't 1999). The harsh reality, though, is that the IME physicians will invariably conclude that further treatment is not necessary. This will result in the denial of future benefits (regarding the area of expertise of the particular physician).

§ 2.10 Claimant's Options Following No-Fault Denial

[1] No-Fault Arbitration or Lawsuit

Following the no-fault IME, the claimant will most likely be denied further no-fault benefits. The claimant may challenge the no-fault denial by demanding a no-fault arbitration or by commencing an action in court. Typically, arbitration is the preferred method, as it is cheaper, quicker, and less time-consuming. See §2.12 below.

> **Warning:** If the claimant challenges a denial, it may have a negative impact upon the third-party negligence case due to *collateral estoppel*. That is, if it is determined that further treatment was not medically necessary, the plaintiff will be precluded from offering evidence of future treatment (including future surgery) in the third-party negligence action. Therefore, the claimant / plaintiff should not contest any no-fault denial until the third-party negligence action is concluded.

> **Practice** Tip: One should not challenge a no-fault denial while treatment is ongoing because the decision will only apply to past denials and does not preclude the insurance company from denying future benefits.

[2] Healthcare Provider Lien

Following a no-fault denial, the claimant's medical providers may agree to continue treatment if allowed to place a lien on the third-party negligence action. That means that the medical provider will be paid out of the proceeds of the settlement of the third-party action. The medical provider will send a written lien (signed by the claimant) to the claimant's attorney to sign, acknowledging that the attorney will honor said lien upon the conclusion of the case. See chapter 8, §8.34.

> **Practice Tip:** If the claimant is going to allow one or more healthcare liens on the file (or is going to pay the healthcare provider out-of-pocket), the claimant must see to it that the healthcare providers continue to timely submit the bills to the no-fault carrier, and continue to receive denials on them; this will preserve the claimant's no-fault arbitration rights, allowing him or her to attempt to recoup the money paid on account of the lien (or paid out-of-pocket). Only the bills which are timely submitted and then denied can be challenged. Hence, it is good practice for the claimant's attorney to incorporate such language into the lien letter prior to signing. The attorney should also add that the physician will bill the patient at the no-fault fee schedule rates.

[3] Assigning Benefits to Healthcare Provider

Following a no-fault denial, certain healthcare providers will continue to treat the claimant without a lien. These providers will generally require an assignment of benefits, allowing them to proceed to a no-fault arbitration (or court action) on behalf of the claimant. In this scenario, the claimant does not have to worry about paying the bills, as the healthcare provider is assuming the risk. This is not the norm, but it is permitted by certain healthcare providers.

§ 2.11 Proceeding With No-Fault Arbitration

[1] Demanding Arbitration

The claimant may demand arbitration by simply checking off a box on the back of a denial of claim form, and sending it in with a nominal fee (which will ultimately be reimbursed by the insurer where the claimant is successful). The claimant should attach all bills, denial of claim forms, and all documentary evidence s/he intends to rely on (e.g., physician's records, operative report, etc.). The respondent (i.e., no-fault insurance company) will have 30 days to submit a written opposition. At the no-fault arbitration, an arbitrator will decide whether the medical bills should be paid by the no-fault insurance carrier. The claimant may similarly arbitrate loss of earnings claims and miscellaneous expense claims which have been timely submitted but denied. The statute of limitations to challenge a no-fault denial is six years from the date of the denial, as it is a contractual action based upon the insurance policy. *CPLR §213.*

> **Warning:** The claimant / plaintiff's attorney should be sure that the retainer agreement expressly states that no-fault representation, including any no-fault arbitrations / hearings, is not included. If, at the conclusion of the third-party action, the claimant / plaintiff wishes to proceed with a no-fault arbitration, s/he should be referred to a no-fault specialist (that is, it is usually not economically feasible for a plaintiff's personal injury attorney).[1]

[2] Standing to Arbitrate

For the claimant to proceed with the no-fault arbitration, s/he will need a release of lien along with a waiver and consent executed by the healthcare provider, unless the claimant paid the healthcare provider directly and is simply seeking reimbursement. In the event the healthcare provider has an assignment of rights (as opposed to a lien), the arbitration is filed in the name of the healthcare provider – by the healthcare provider or its attorney. The healthcare provider cannot have both an assignment of rights and a lien on the file.

[3] Goal of No-Fault Arbitration

Once the claimant establishes that the post-denial bills were timely submitted (and subsequently denied), the goal at the no-fault arbitration is to prove that the post-denial treatment was medically necessary and causally related to the accident; this should be done through a recent medical affirmation and/or reports. *See Hobby v. CNA Insurance,* 267 A.D.2d 1084, 1085, 700 N.Y.S.2d 346 (4th Dep't 1999). Similar proof must be submitted to support a loss of earnings claim, as well.

A lack of medical necessity defense is only properly interposed when the claim denial form, and any other documentation submitted within the 30-day claim determination period, set forth a factual basis and medical rationale sufficient to establish the absence

---

1   Attorneys' fees for no-fault representation are paid by the insurer and are *capped* at 20% of the amount of first-party benefits, plus interest thereon, subject to a maximum of $850. *11 NYCRR §§ 65-4.6, 65-4.7 (Regulation 68-D).*

of medical necessity. Further, even if the defense is timely asserted, an IME report that is conclusory in nature and lacking a detailed basis and medical rationale for the denial of benefits is insufficient.

[4] Itemized Medical Bills

The claimant must have an itemization of medical bills (with proper no-fault billing codes and a no-fault fee schedule), along with an affirmation from the physician that s/he has not received any of the fees from a collateral source. The healthcare provider is required to utilize the no-fault fee schedule, and cannot hold the claimant – and hence the no-fault provider – liable for the balance of the fee if it is beyond the no-fault fee schedule.

[5] No-Fault Arbitration Brief and Presentation

Prior to the no-fault arbitration, a brief should be submitted (at the time of filing of the arbitration demand) which includes *prima facie* entitlement to the benefits sought; this is done by submitting proof of mailing of bills in a timely manner from each healthcare provider (or affidavits of service, evidence of standard office practices or procedures, or an admission by the insurer that it timely received the bills). Further, narrative reports or medical affirmations – from each physician whose bills were denied – expressing causal relationship and medical necessity must be submitted. The claimant's attorney should also include the following: an itemization of bills, waivers from healthcare providers as to bills which the claimant has already paid (e.g., paid out of settlement), a copy of the general release and closing statement from the third-party negligence action (which can help support the claim of causality and medical necessity), and a copy of any satisfactions of liens. No-fault arbitrations are generally very informal. The claimant's attorney should proceed in narrative form, as the arbitrator is unlikely to require actual testimony. A written decision generally arrives within 30 days of the hearing. An appeal to a master arbitrator may be made within 21 days after the mailing of the decision. *11 NYCRR §§ 65-4.10 (Regulation 68-D).*

CHAPTER 3

MOTOR VEHICLE ACCIDENTS – THIRD-PARTY CLAIMS

PART A: OVERVIEW

§ 3.01   Overview – Motor Vehicle Accidents – Third-Party Claims

Motor vehicle accident cases include representation of injured drivers, passengers, pedestrians, motorcyclists, and bicyclists. As with any type of accident case, there are three main categories to evaluate: liability, damages, and insurance coverage.

Proving liability in a motor vehicle accident case is sometimes a rather simple task – such as where the plaintiff was a passenger, or was the driver of a rear-ended vehicle. Other types of motor vehicle accident cases can pose more difficult liability issues, including intersection accidents and pedestrian knockdown cases.

In a motor vehicle accident case, unlike any other type of negligence case, the plaintiff must be able to prove that s/he sustained a "serious injury" as defined in *Insurance Law §5102(d)*. Otherwise, s/he will be precluded from receiving *any* compensation over and above that which is afforded by no-fault coverage. Failure to meet the "serious injury" threshold will result in the dismissal of the case.

Availability of sufficient insurance coverage is a major factor in motor vehicle accident cases, whereas in other types of accident cases – such as premises liability, construction accidents, medical malpractice, and products liability cases – there is usually sufficient insurance coverage for even very serious injuries and large economic losses.

PART B: ELEMENTS OF MOTOR VEHICLE ACCIDENT CAUSE OF ACTION

§ 3.02   Defendant's Failure to Use "Reasonable Care"

[1] "Reasonable Care" – In General

When operating a motor vehicle, the driver's conduct must be that of reasonable care or ordinary prudence. *See Siegel v. Sweeney*, 266 A.D.2d 200, 201, 697 N.Y.S.2d 317, 318 (2d Dep't 1999) (motorist entering intersection with green light in his or her favor must nonetheless exercise reasonable care). Voluntary intoxication and involuntary infirmities (e.g., age and physical handicaps) do not affect the reasonableness standard. The infirmity will only affect a defendant's liability if a causal relationship can be established between the infirmity and the accident. *See Polley v. Polley*, 11 A.D.2d 121, 123, 202 N.Y.S.2d 425, 428 (1st Dep't 1960), *aff'd*, 9 N.Y.2d 1006, 218 N.Y.S.2d 672 (defendant-motorist's failure to wear prescription eyeglasses – as required by his driver's license – at the time of the accident, did not affect his liability, absent showing of causal connection).

[2] Reasonable Speed

The operator of a motor vehicle must drive at a reasonable rate of speed under the circumstances. *Vehicle & Traffic Law (VTL) §1180(a)*. The defendant does not need to be driving in excess of the posted speed limit in order to be found negligent. *See Bagnato v. Romano*, 179 A.D.2d 713, 714, 578 N.Y.S.2d 613, 614 (2d Dep't 1992) (where defendant was driving below speed limit but had not reduced speed at intersection where crash occurred, whether his failure to decelerate constituted negligence was question for jury). An operator must drive at an appropriately reduced speed when: approaching and crossing an intersection or railway grade crossing, traveling around a curve, approaching a hill or traveling on a narrow or winding road, and when any special hazard exists with respect to pedestrians or other traffic because of the weather or highway conditions. *VTL §1180(e)*.

[3] Control of Vehicle

An operator of a vehicle must exercise reasonable care to keep the vehicle under reasonable control at all times. *Woolley v. Coppola*, 179 A.D.2d 991, 992, 578 N.Y.S.2d 729, 730 (3d Dep't 1992) (even in emergency situation, driver under duty to act reasonable in light of emergency). Where a driver loses control of his or her vehicle and breaches the reasonableness standard, s/he will be held liable for any resulting injuries. However, if a sudden emergency develops which causes the driver to lose control of the vehicle, it may not constitute negligence if the emergency was not the fault of the driver. *Malatesta v. Hopf*, 163 A.D.2d 651, 653, 557 N.Y.S.2d 994, 996 (3d Dep't 1990).

[4] Proper Lookout

An operator of a motor vehicle must maintain a proper lookout, remaining observant while driving in order to see dangerous or hazardous conditions. *Bolta v. Lohan*, 242 A.D.2d 356, 661 N.Y.S.2d 286, 287 (2d Dep't 1997) (driver negligent where accident occurred because of failure to see that, which through proper use of senses, should have been seen). The operator of a motor vehicle is expected to observe everything in plain view. However, a driver is not expected to anticipate the unforeseeable, the unlawful, or the negligent conduct of another. *See Villa v. Vetuskey*, 50 A.D.2d 1093, 1094, 376 N.Y.S.2d 359, 364 (4th Dep't 1975) (where motorist has right-of-way at intersection, he may assume that others who do not have right-of-way will slow down or stop to let him pass safely).

[5] Maintenance of Vehicle's Equipment

The owner and operator of a motor vehicle must maintain the vehicle's equipment and replace it when necessary. A vehicle must be equipped and maintained for use on public highways in such a way that it does not become a dangerous instrumentality. *See VTL §§375, 376.* A violation of a safety equipment statute is not negligence *per se*. Rather, proof is required that the defect was the proximate cause of the injury and that the operator or owner of the vehicle discovered, or should have discovered, that there was a defect in the equipment which could result in injury if not repaired. *See Breese v. Hertz Corp.*, 25 A.D.2d 621, 622, 267 N.Y.S.2d 703, 705 (1st Dep't 1966) (truck driver had notice of defect which he should have corrected before continuing on his trip).

[6] Violation of Statute, Ordinance, or Code

The violation of a statute or ordinance may constitute negligence *per se*, give rise to absolute liability, or constitute *prima facie* evidence of negligence. The distinction between negligence *per se* and absolute liability is that the comparative negligence defense is available only in the case of negligence *per se*, but not where absolute liability is imposed. *See Harris v. Moyer*, 255 A.D.2d 890, 680 N.Y.S.2d 351, 352 (4th Dep't 1998) (defendant's guilty plea to failing to yield right of way did not establish negligence as a matter of law, allowing for apportionment of 25% of liability to other driver).

A violation of a statute will constitute negligence *per se* when the statute defines a standard of care to be applied to a particular situation, and that standard has not been met. *See Dlal v. City of New York*, 262 A.D.2d 596, 692 N.Y.S.2d 468, 470 (2d Dep't 1999) (failure to wear prescription eyeglasses in violation of restriction on license was negligence *per se* pursuant to *VTL §509[3]*).

A violation of a statute will impose absolute liability when the statute defines a standard of care to be applied in a particular situation, and that standard has not been met. *See Dean v. Baumann*, 39 A.D.2d 138, 332 N.Y.S.2d 665 (3d Dep't 1972), *aff'd*, 32 N.Y.2d 756, 344 N.Y.S.2d 950 (1972) (violation of *VTL §1174(a)*, prohibiting overtaking school bus stopped with red visual signal, resulted in absolute liability).

A violation of a code or ordinance will provide some evidence for the jury to consider, and will not rise to the level of negligence *per se*. *See Nielsen v. New York*, 38 A.D.2d 592, 328 N.Y.S.2d 698 (2d Dep't 1971), appeal dismissed, 30 N.Y.2d 568, 330 N.Y.S.2d 787 (1972) (municipal code requiring city streets to be clean from debris was ordinance, not statute, and therefore violation did not result in negligence *per se*).

[7] *Res Ipsa Loquitur*

The doctrine of *res ipsa loquitur* acts as an exception to the rule that the mere happening of an accident is not evidence of negligence. Under the doctrine of *res ipsa loquitur*, the plaintiff's case may reach the jury without direct evidence of negligence. *See Cebula v. Bonime*, 92 A.D.2d 856, 459 N.Y. S.2d 847 (2d Dep't 1983) (where car left road and collided into tree killing all witnesses, inference of negligence arose).

§ 3.03 Proximate Cause

[1] Proximate Cause – In General

In order for the driver of a motor vehicle to be held liable for the plaintiff's injuries, the driver's conduct must have caused those injuries. In general, a defendant will be liable only when his or her negligence is a proximate, rather than remote, cause of the plaintiff's injuries. *Quiquin v. Fitzgerald*, 146 A.D.2d 894, 897, 536 N.Y.S.2d 874, 876 (3d Dep't 1989). Even where the defendant's negligence is based on a statutory violation, the violation must be the proximate cause of the damages sustained by the plaintiff. *See Albano v. Brooklyn Union Gas Co.*, 733 N.Y.S.2d 110, 111 (2d Dep't 2001) (violation of traffic regulations could not result in imposition of liability due to failure to establish proximate cause between violations and accident).

[2] Foreseeable Injuries

The driver of a motor vehicle is liable for the plaintiff's injuries only where the injuries were a foreseeable consequence of the driver's act or omission. A reasonable person under similar circumstances must have been able to foresee a risk of harm to the plaintiff. *See Gladstone v. State of New York*, 18 N.Y.2d 987, 278 N.Y.S.2d 222 (1966) (contingency too remote to be reasonably anticipated).

A defendant may be relieved of liability for a plaintiff's injuries if a subsequent intervening act which could not have been reasonably anticipated breaks the causation chain. Whether the third-party's negligent act or omission absolves the defendant of liability depends on whether the act or omission was foreseeable. *See Golding v. Farmer*, 273 A.D.2d 834, 837, 710 N.Y.S.2d 212, 213 (4th Dep't 2000) (superseding cause not found, thereby not relieving defendant of negligence).

[3] Emergency Situation

A driver with an emergency which s/he did not create will not be held liable for failure to exercise the best judgment in that emergency, but is merely required to do what might be reasonably expected of the average prudent motorist under similar circumstances. *Kuci v. Manhattan and Bronx Surface Transit Operating Authority*, 88 N.Y.2d 923, 924, 646 N.Y.S.2d 788 (1996) (emergency doctrine should have been charged to jury where bus suddenly swerved to avoid car alleged to have cut off bus).

The fact that a driver might have been able to prevent the accident will not result in liability if the driver exercised what seemed to have been his or her best judgment under the circumstances. *See Borst v. Sunnydale Farms, Inc.*, 258 A.D.2d 448, 489, 685 N.Y.S.2d 269, 270 (2d Dep't 1999) (defendant not liable because he reasonably responded to emergency situation and nothing supported plaintiff's contention that defendant could have taken other evasive measures). Courts will often use the terms "emergency doctrine" and "unavoidable accident" synonymously. *See Sears v. Doviak*, 306 A.D.2d 681, 682, 760 N.Y.S.2d 278, 279 (3d Dep't 2003) (emergency doctrine absolved defendant of liability). The emergency doctrine does not apply where the party seeking to invoke it created or contributed to the emergency. *Sweeney v. McCormick,*

159 A.D.2d 832, 833, 552 N.Y.S.2d 707, 708 (3d Dep't 1990) (defendant precluded from invoking emergency doctrine where defendant contributed to emergency).

§ 3.04 No-Fault Threshold
[1] "Serious Injury" Threshold

In motor vehicle accident cases, claims for non-economic losses (e.g., pain and suffering) are required to have resulted in a "serious injury" as defined in *Insurance Law §5102(d)*. *See Manessis v. Command Bus Co.*, 251 A.D.2d 556, 673 N.Y.S.2d 930 (2d Dep't 1998) (although defendant was found 100% responsible for accident, jury found that plaintiff did not sustain "serious injury" pursuant to *Insurance Law §5102(d)* and, therefore, was awarded no damages).

Pursuant to *Insurance Law §5102(d)*, "serious injury" means a personal injury which results in:

- death;
- dismemberment;
- significant disfigurement;
- a fracture;
- loss of a fetus;
- permanent loss of use of a body organ, member, function, or system;
- permanent consequential limitation of use of a body organ or member;
- significant limitation of use of a body function or system; or
- a medically determined injury or impairment of a non-permanent nature which prevents the injured person from performing substantially all of the material acts which constitute such person's usual and customary daily activities for not less than 90 days during the 180 days immediately following the occurrence of the injury or impairment.

See §§3.13, 3.18 below.

[2] Exceptions to Proving "Serious Injury"
[a] Exceptions – In General

There are rare situations where a plaintiff in a motor vehicle accident case does not have to prove "serious injury" in order to receive compensation for non-economic losses. The requirement to prove "serious injury" only exists where the plaintiff and defendant are *both* "covered persons" under no-fault law. See sections [b] and [c] below.

[b] Motorcyclist-Plaintiff

A motorcyclist-plaintiff is not a "covered person" and, therefore, does not have to prove "serious injury" in a negligence action against another driver. *See Ins. Law §§5103(a)(1),(2),(3), 5104(a)(b)*. *See Carbone v. Visco*, 115 A.D.3d 948, 497 N.Y.S.2d 524 (4th Dep't 1985). See chapter 2, §2.06.

[c] Defendant Not Covered Person

Where the defendant is not a "covered person" under no-fault law, the plaintiff will not be required to prove "serious injury". An example of this is where the defendant is *not* a motor vehicle driver or owner – such as a motor vehicle accident case against a municipal defendant (e.g., involving a road defect). In such a scenario, the plaintiff is not required to meet the no-fault "serious injury" threshold in the case against the municipal defendant.

[3] Threshold for Economic Losses

Tort recovery for economic loss is only allowed if the loss is in excess of no-fault compensation. *See Ins. Law §5104(a).* See chapter 2, §2.02.

PART C: MOTOR VEHICLE ACCIDENT INTAKE

§ 3.05 Gathering Information at Motor Vehicle Accident Intake

[1] Liability

The best way to preliminarily assess liability with respect to a motor vehicle accident is by examining the police accident report (known as the MV-104A). Sometimes, though, the prospective client is not yet in possession of the police accident report at the time of the intake. The attorney should first determine the prospective client's role in the accident – driver, passenger, pedestrian, motorcyclist, or bicyclist. The attorney should also obtain the prospective client's version of the accident. Additional information such as citations issued, witnesses, traffic control devices, weather conditions, skidding, and vehicle(s) leaving the road is relevant. See §§3.11, 3.12 below for further details in terms of evaluating liability.

[2] Damages

In assessing damages, the attorney should preliminarily determine whether the injuries are already sufficient to meet the "serious injury" threshold – such as where the prospective client has sustained a fracture and/or undergone surgery. If not, the attorney will usually be in a much better position to fairly assess the damages in the case six months post-accident – after reviewing the objective test results (MRIs), the extent of the medical treatment, the amount of time lost from work, and determining whether surgery was performed or is necessary. *See Ins. Law §5102(d).* The attorney should also determine whether the prospective client was wearing a seatbelt (if applicable), as failure to have done so can decrease the value of the case. *See VTL §1229-c.* See §3.13[4] below. See also chapter 10, §10.21[7].

[3] Insurance Coverage Issues

A very important factor in assessing a potential motor vehicle accident case is the availability of sufficient insurance coverage. A preliminary assessment of the potential insurance policy limits of the tortfeasor(s) should be made at the time of intake (if possible).

Practice Tip: The attorney can often have a good idea as to whether or not the insurance coverage will be lacking by carefully reviewing the police accident report. If the tortfeasor's vehicle is a commercial vehicle or a new, expensive vehicle, there is likely significant insurance coverage. Where the tortfeasor's vehicle is old or the insurance code is "999" (i.e., Assigned Risk), the insurance coverage may well be minimal.

Thereafter, in the event the insurance coverage is lacking – where there is either no insurance or inadequate insurance coverage – it must be determined whether the prospective client has any uninsured / under-insured motorist policies which afford additional coverage. The insurance issues can take time to fully assess. See §3.14 below for further details in terms of evaluating insurance coverage. See chapter 4 for a comprehensive review of uninsured / under-insured motorist coverage.

[4] Venue

A preliminary assessment should be made at the time of intake as to the potential choices of venue. These include any county in which the plaintiff or any of the defendants reside on the date of commencement of the lawsuit. *See CPLR §503. See also CPLR §§504, 505* regarding venue considerations where there is a municipal defendant. The accident report is a good place to start. Venue considerations may even impact whether the case is one the attorney wishes to accept. See §3.15[6] below.

[5] Statutes of Limitations and Conditions Precedent to Lawsuit

In general, the statute of limitations in a motor vehicle accident case is three years. *CPLR §214.* Where a potential defendant is a governmental entity (e.g., motor vehicle accident with a police vehicle), a notice of claim must generally be filed within 90 days of the date of the accident and a lawsuit must be commenced within one year and 90 days from the date of the accident. *See General Municipal Law §50-e* and chapter 7, §§7.03, 7.10. The attorney should be aware of the shortened statute of limitations periods associated with wrongful death cases (two years from the date of death or the applicable statute of limitations period, whichever is shorter). *See CPLR §§210, 215.* The attorney should also be aware that the statute of limitations periods (but not notice of claim time limitations) for infants (i.e., under 18 years of age) is automatically tolled during the infancy. *See CPLR §208.*

§ 3.06 Deciding to Accept, Reject, or Investigate Motor Vehicle Accident Case

The attorney will have to consider liability, damages, insurance coverage, venue, and the statute of limitations in determining whether to accept, reject, or investigate a motor vehicle accident case. At the time of the motor vehicle accident intake, there may well be several factors still unknown. Whether the prospective client's injuries will be able to meet the "serious injury" threshold is often not yet known. The attorney will often be unable to fully assess the client's injuries until six months post-accident –

following treatment, objective testing (such as MRIs), and possibly surgery. Insurance coverage issues generally take time to sort out, as well.

Practice Tip: Since it typically takes some time to comprehensively assess all the relevant factors, it is generally best to have the client sign a retainer agreement which states that the attorney is accepting the motor vehicle accident case "subject to investigation". This will allow some time to determine the extent of insurance coverage, and whether the client will be able to meet the "serious injury" threshold. Obviously, where liability is poor, the attorney will usually want to reject the case at intake.

---

§ 3.07 Retainer Agreement in Motor Vehicle Accident Case

[1] Motor Vehicle Accident Retainer Agreement – In General

If the attorney decides to accept the motor vehicle accident case, the client must sign a retainer agreement. A motor vehicle accident retainer agreement should set forth the contingency fee; the standard fee (and maximum allowed contingency fee in a non-medical malpractice personal injury case) is 33 1/3% of the net recovery. The retainer agreement should set forth the fact that disbursements such as fees for court costs, process servers, medical records, investigators, experts, and all other costs associated with the case are to be reimbursed at the conclusion of the case. The *net* recovery is then used to compute the attorney's contingency fee. The retainer agreement should also make clear that all liens are the sole responsibility of the client, and are to be paid out from the client's share of the proceeds. The motor vehicle accident retainer agreement should also explicitly list liens such as no-fault (e.g., APIP), workers' compensation, Medicaid, Medicare, Department of Social Services, and medical liens as the client's responsibility.

[2] Scope of Representation in Motor Vehicle Accident Retainer Agreement

The motor vehicle accident retainer agreement should expressly exclude representation for no-fault, workers' compensation, New York State Disability, and appellate work. It should clearly state that the attorney is being retained to represent the plaintiff for a third-party negligence claim and/or uninsured / under-insured motorist claims only.

The retainer agreement should also state that the law firm is accepting the case subject to investigation. This will allow the attorney to terminate the agreement at any time prior to litigation, for any reason such as a determination that liability is poor or the client's inability to meet the "serious injury" threshold (e.g., where the MRI results are negative). It will often take six months to determine whether the client will be able to meet the "serious injury" threshold.

[3] Executing Authorizations

At the same time the client signs the retainer agreement, s/he should also sign several sets of authorizations to obtain medical records, no-fault records, employment records, and workers' compensation records (if applicable). This will allow the attorney to obtain copies of the records, and to send authorizations to the tortfeasor's claims representative regarding evaluation, and possible settlement, of the case.

[4] Filing OCA Retainer Statement

After becoming retained, a retainer statement must be promptly filed with the Office of Court Administration (OCA). A self-addressed stamped postcard should be included for OCA to stamp the retainer number which must then be used on the closing statement at the conclusion of the case. In the event the retainer statement is not timely filed, an attorney's affirmation setting forth the reason for lateness along with a request that the retainer statement be filed *nunc pro tunc*, should be included.

§ 3.08 Discussing No-Fault Law with Client

The client should be informed of the essence of no-fault law in terms of the first-party benefits s/he is entitled to receive regardless of fault, as well as the threshold requirement of proving "serious injury". *Ins. Law §5102(a),(d).*

Practice Tip: The client should be educated as far as what will be required in order to meet the "serious injury" threshold, in terms of documented treatment, results of objective testing (such as MRIs), and the inability to perform usual and customary daily activities in at least 90 of the first 180 days following the accident.

---

§ 3.09 Discussing Client's Right to Reimbursement for Loss of Earnings

The client should be informed of his or her right to have no-fault, workers' compensation, and/or NYS Disability provide reimbursement for loss of wages. Typically, no-fault will pay for loss of wages. See chapter 2, §2.02[b]. However, where the client was involved in an accident in the course of his or her employment, workers' compensation takes precedence as the primary coverage; thus, no-fault only pays over and above workers' compensation payments, if necessary. See chapter 2, §2.04.

NYS Disability will pay up to 26 weeks (six months) of benefits to a worker who is disabled due to a non-work related injury. The injured party must miss at least 2 weeks of work in order to apply for NYS Disability. The maximum benefit paid by NYS Disability is $170 per week or 40% of the loss of wages, whichever is less. The no-fault carrier will take an offset with respect to any payments made by NYS Disability. See chapter 2, §2.02[b][1].

§ 3.10 Discussing Prompt Filing of Documentation

The client should be informed of the need to promptly file the no-fault application, as well as the MV-104 (for drivers) and, where applicable, a NYS Disability claim, workers' compensation claim, uninsured / under-insured motorist claim, MVAIC claim, and/or a notice of claim.

PART D: EVALUATING LIABILITY IN MOTOR VEHICLE ACCIDENT CASE

§ 3.11 Gathering Information to Evaluate Liability in Motor Vehicle Accident Case

[1] Police Accident Report

In evaluating liability in a motor vehicle accident case, the best place to start is the police accident report, known as the MV-104A. While the police officer's description of the accident, unless based upon first-hand observation by the officer, is generally not admissible at trial, the officer's record of statements made by the driver(s) is admissible. Further, much can be learned by looking at the areas of impact on each car, as documented on the police accident report. The police accident report also includes the weather conditions and whether any traffic citations were issued.

Warning: If the plaintiff's attorney is faced with the task of having to prove something contrary to the police accident report, it will generally be a difficult challenge. It will not be easy to convince an insurance claims representative to offer money on a case where the police accident report paints the plaintiff as the responsible party, notwithstanding the fact that some of the entries may be inadmissible. The damages and insurance coverage should be assessed to determine how much time and money should be spent attempting to prove liability.

The police accident report can be obtained at the police precinct that responded to the accident. It usually takes a few days for the police accident report to be ready, and is generally available at the precinct for only 30 days following the accident. Thereafter, a certified copy of the police accident report, which may well be needed at the time of trial, can be obtained from the Department of Motor Vehicles in Albany, New York, but not until 180 days after the accident. To obtain a certified copy of the police accident report, DMV Form 198-c must be completed and mailed, along with a nominal fee, to the DMV, Public Services Bureau, Empire State Plaza, Albany, NY 12228. See www.nysdmv.com. There are also various companies, such as First Advantage ADR (www.fadv.com), that will obtain the records for a nominal fee.

[2] MV-104 of Driver(s)

Where a motor vehicle accident results in property damage greater than $1,000 *or* any personal injury, each driver is required to file an MV-104 (i.e., the driver's own version of the accident report) with the Department of Motor Vehicles in Albany within ten days after the accident. The MV-104 of each driver can be obtained from the Department of Motor Vehicles in Albany, as well.

Practice Tip: The tortfeasor's MV-104 can be quite useful, for it is often completed before any attorneys are involved. It can be used to obtain contradictions from the defendant at his or her deposition, as well as to expose the defendant's contradictions at trial. The plaintiff's attorney should also make sure to have a copy of the plaintiff's MV-104 in order to properly prepare the plaintiff for his or her deposition.

[3] Witness Statements

The police accident report sometimes includes the name and telephone number of eyewitnesses to the accident. Where liability is not clear-cut, these witnesses should be contacted immediately. The prospective client should also provide the names, phone numbers, and addresses of any witnesses to the accident, including other people in his or her car. The attorney must assess the severity of the injuries, the amount of available insurance coverage, and whether liability is questionable, in deciding whether it is cost-effective to employ a private investigator to obtain statements from the witnesses.

[4] Photographs

Photographs of the accident scene (e.g., those depicting the fact that the defendant had a stop sign and the plaintiff did not) can also be helpful. Photographs of the areas of damage to the vehicle(s) can also help better assess, and ultimately prove, liability.

Warning: Sometimes a photograph that helps prove liability also hurts the plaintiff's "serious injury" claim (i.e., where little damage is depicted). Hence, the plaintiff's attorney must use proper discretion.

[5] Property Damage Assessment

The percentage of fault the insurance carriers assess in terms of property damage (i.e., with respect to paying for the repairs to the vehicle[s]) can also help later on when attempting to settle the bodily injury claim. The plaintiff's attorney should retain a copy of the tortfeasor's insurer's letter setting forth its assessment of fault.

Example: The property damage claims examiner for the tortfeasor's insurer determines that the tortfeasor was 90% at fault and therefore pays for 90% of the value of the damage to plaintiff's vehicle. Later, the bodily injury claims examiner from the same insurance company states that s/he feels liability is a 50/50 proposition. The plaintiff's attorney should utilize the 90% finding by the property damage claims representative to the plaintiff's advantage while negotiating the bodily injury claim.

§ 3.12 Evaluating Liability in Various Types of Motor Vehicle Accident Cases

[1] Passenger

There is generally no better liability case than that of a passenger in a motor vehicle accident. Thus, in evaluating the case of a passenger, liability attributable to the defendant(s) is generally assumed to be 100%.

Warning: A bus or train passenger injured as a result of sudden jerking of the bus or train faces a much more difficult liability situation. *See PJI §2:165,* see chapter 7, §7.24[2].

A passenger is not responsible for the actions of the driver. A passenger must, however, use reasonable care for his or her own safety. By entering a vehicle where the driver is under a known disability such as intoxication, *see Bergeron v. Hyer*, 55 A.D.2d 1001, 1003, 391 N.Y.S.2d 767, 769 (4th Dep't 1997), or sleepiness, *see Purchase v. Jeffrey*, 33 A.D.2d 620, 304 N.Y.S.2d 619, 620 (3d Dep't 1969), a passenger can be held comparatively negligent. If so, the jury must then decide whether the negligence was a proximate cause of the injuries.

Practice Tip: An added benefit of a passenger-plaintiff is that the insurance coverage of all cars involved in the accident is available to be pursued (as opposed to a driver-plaintiff who, obviously, cannot pursue the liability coverage of the vehicle s/he was driving).

[2] Driver – Rear-End Collision

Where the driver-plaintiff's car was rear-ended by another vehicle, liability attributable to the offending vehicle is also generally considered to be 100%. *See Lopez v. Minot*, 258 A.D.2d 564, 685 N.Y.S.2d 469, 470 (2d Dep't 1999) (when moving vehicle collides with rear of stopped vehicle, *prima facie* liability exists unless driver of moving vehicle can rebut inference of negligence). Following too closely is prohibited. *VTL §1129.*

There are, however, viable defense arguments such as sudden stopping by the plaintiff (including skidding) or that the plaintiff cut in front of the defendant, thereby causing the collision. A sudden stop or decrease in speed without first giving an appropriate signal to the driver immediately behind, when there is an opportunity to do so, is strictly prohibited. *VTL §1163(c).* Further, where a vehicle skids due to a driver's failure to use reasonable care (e.g., driving too fast or not paying attention), *prima facie* negligence is established against the skidding vehicle. *See Pfaffenbach v. White Plains Express Corp.*, 17 N.Y.2d 132, 269 N.Y.S.2d 115 (1966) (proof of skidding which causes vehicle to deviate from its normal course of travel establishes *prima facie* negligence).

Practice Tip: In general, it will be difficult for a defendant to dispute liability where s/he rear-ended the plaintiff's vehicle. A rear-ended driver-plaintiff who was *stopped* – in traffic, at a traffic light, or at a stop sign – at the time of the accident will have better success with a motion for summary judgment on the issue of liability.

[3] Driver – Intersection Collision

[a] Uncontrolled Intersection Case

At an uncontrolled intersection, a driver approaching the intersection is required to yield the right of way to a vehicle which has already entered the intersection. Where two vehicles enter the intersection at approximately the same time, the vehicle on the left is required to yield the right of way to the vehicle on the right. *VTL §1140.*

[b] Controlled Intersection Case

Where an intersection is controlled by a traffic signal, a driver is required to obey the instructions of the traffic control device unless otherwise directed by a traffic or police officer. *VTL §1110.* Where a vehicle enters an intersection against a red light, the driver is negligent. When the light is green, the driver has the right to assume a red light for the cross traffic. However, the driver must still use reasonable care under the circumstances. *VTL §1111.*

A vehicle approaching a stop sign is required to stop at the stop line or, if none exists, before entering the crosswalk. *VTL §1172.* After coming to a stop, the vehicle is required to yield the right of way to approaching vehicles. Approaching vehicles are still required to use reasonable care and not to proceed recklessly into the intersection. *VTL §1142.* Obligations to stop under *VTL §§1172* and *1142* do not apply where the stop sign is not in a proper position and sufficiently legible to be seen by an ordinary observant person (*VTL §1110[b]*), unless the driver knew or should have known that the sign was there. *New v. Cortright*, 32 A.D.2d 576, 299 N.Y.S.2d 43 (3d Dep't 1969). Where the obligations to stop do not apply, *VTL §1140* (concerning uncontrolled intersections) applies.

[c] Evaluation of Intersection Accidents for Settlement Purposes

In evaluating intersection collision accidents, it is important to know which directions of travel were controlled by a traffic control device such as a stop sign, yield sign, or traffic light. Where neither vehicle had a traffic control device (regarding their respective directions of travel), liability is generally evaluated as a 50/50 proposition – meaning the plaintiff's damages will have to be discounted by 50% in terms of valuing the case. The same applies where both drivers were confronted with similar traffic control devices at the intersection. Witness accounts can be crucial in these types of cases, such as in determining which vehicle ran the red light. The plaintiff's attorney must determine early-on whether the case warrants the expense of an investigation, based upon the extent of the injuries and the likely extent of insurance coverage.

Practice Tip: The discounted (for comparative negligence) value of the case may still exceed the policy limits of the defendant(s). Hence, the plaintiff's comparative negligence may not affect the overall settlement value where the insurance coverage is limited.

Where only one driver's direction of travel possessed a traffic control device (such as a stop sign), most of the fault will be attributed to the vehicle with the traffic control device. However, there will be questions as to whether the other vehicle was speeding, failed to keep a proper lookout, or failed to slow down when approaching the intersection.

[4] Driver – Left-Turn Case

A "left-turn case" – where a vehicle, turning left at an intersection across oncoming traffic, collides with a vehicle passing through the intersection from the opposite direction – is a common type of motor vehicle accident case. Turns are not supposed to be made unless and until such movement can be made with reasonable safety, and the appropriate signal is given. *VTL §1163(a).*

Practice Tip: In evaluating a left-turn case, the two sides will generally agree that the vehicle turning left across traffic is 70-80% at fault for failure to use reasonable care. The other vehicle – the one proceeding straight – is thus usually assessed 20-30% of the blame for speeding, failing to slow down at the intersection, and/or failing to keep a proper lookout.

[5] Driver – Authorized Emergency Vehicle

Authorized emergency vehicles are allowed to proceed through a red light or stop sign after slowing down, as may be necessary for safe operation. *VTL §1104.* The drivers of such vehicles are only liable for reckless disregard, not simply lack of due care under the circumstances. *VTL §1104(e), Saarineen v. Kerr,* 84 N.Y.2d 494, 497, 620 N.Y.S.2d 297, 298 (1994) (recklessness required). It takes more than a "momentary lapse in judgment" to satisfy the reckless disregard test. *Id.*

[6] Pedestrian Knockdown Case

[a] Pedestrian Crossing Street

When a pedestrian is crossing within a crosswalk, whether marked or unmarked, the driver is required to yield the right of way to the pedestrian. If, however, a pedestrian tunnel or overpass is provided at the point where the pedestrian is crossing, the pedestrian is required to yield the right of way to the vehicles. Further, a pedestrian is prohibited from suddenly leaving the curb or other place of safety and walking or running in front of the path of a vehicle which is so close that it is impractical for the driver to yield. *VTL §1151.*

When a pedestrian is crossing outside the crosswalk, the pedestrian is required to yield the right of way to all vehicles on the roadway. *VTL §1152.* Crossing outside the crosswalk is not prohibited and is not negligence as a matter of law. Whether the plaintiff exercised reasonable care under the circumstances is a question for the jury. *See Chandler v. Keene*, 5 A.D.2d 42, 43, 168 N.Y.S.2d 788, 791 (3d Dep't 1957) (four-year-old plaintiff struck and killed by defendant's vehicle); *see also Franco v. Zingarelli*, 72 A.D.2d 211, 217, 424 N.Y.S.2d 185, 189 (1st Dep't 1980) (crossing at point other than intersection does not, as a matter of law, require finding of negligence on pedestrian's part).

> **Practice Tip:** Pedestrian knockdown cases often involve injuries that are quite serious. Even where not extremely serious, injuries sustained by a pedestrian are generally valued greater than a normal motor vehicle accident case, by virtue of the fact that a human being was struck by a moving vehicle. Liability, however, can be a major hurdle in pedestrian accident cases. Witness statements may be vital to the case.

[b] Pedestrian Walking Along Roadway

Where there are no sidewalks, a pedestrian is required, when practicable, to walk only on the left side of the roadway or its shoulder facing traffic approaching from the opposite direction. Upon the approach of any vehicle, the pedestrian is required to move as far left as practicable. *VTL §1156(b).*

[c] Bicyclist Along Roadway

Every driver of a motor vehicle is required to use due care to avoid colliding with a bicyclist and should sound his or her horn when necessary. *VTL §1146.* A bicyclist, other than in the City of New York, is required to ride near the right-hand curb or to use the right-hand shoulder when safe to do so, so as to prevent undue interference with the flow of traffic. *VTL §1234(a). See also NYC Traffic Rules §402(e); see also PJI §2:76A.* Bicyclists are granted all the rights, and are subject to all of the duties, that apply to drivers of motor vehicles. *Redcross v. State*, 241 A.D.2d 787, 660 N.Y.S.2d 211 (3d Dep't 1997).

PART E: EVALUATING DAMAGES IN A MOTOR VEHICLE ACCIDENT CASE

§ 3.13 Gathering Information to Evaluate Damages in Motor Vehicle Accident Case

[1] "Serious Injury" Threshold

The *quid pro quo* for entitlement to "no-fault benefits" is that an injured party's injuries must (except in extremely rare circumstances) rise to a certain level (known as the "serious injury" threshold) in order to successfully pursue a negligence lawsuit arising out of a motor vehicle accident. In short, a motor vehicle accident victim cannot, except in extremely limited circumstances, successfully bring a third-party negligence action unless s/he can prove that s/he sustained a "serious injury" under the Insurance Law. *See Ins. Law §5102(d).* The serious threshold categories are enumerated earlier in the chapter in §3.04[1] above.

Practice Tip: In meeting the "serious injury" threshold in a "soft-tissue injury" motor vehicle accident case, three things ("the three Ts") must be examined: treatment (must occur for a minimum of 90 to 180 days immediately following the accident), testing (positive MRI results are essential), and time off from work (with 90 to 180 days following the accident being very helpful to the case). Essentially, it is difficult to assess whether a potential "soft tissue injury" plaintiff will be able to meet the "serious injury" threshold until evaluating the case six months post-accident.

[2] Obtaining Medical Records

Determining the extent of the injuries is obviously quite important. All of the medical records relating to the accident, and those relating to prior injuries to the same body parts, should be quickly obtained. This includes the ambulance call report, emergency room records, hospital records, physicians' records, physical therapy records, diagnostic testing records (such as MRI reports), and operative reports. The attorney should also check the ambulance call report, emergency room records, and other medical records to see if there are any entries which state that the client was not wearing a seatbelt, as well as entries regarding liability (i.e., how the accident occurred, the speed of the vehicles, etc.). See chapter 10, §10.04 regarding the admissibility of entries in various medical records.

Practice Tip: In a motor vehicle accident case, the plaintiff's attorney may wish to purchase a copy of the no-fault file. Typically, all of the medical records are included, since the medical providers must submit the records in order to be paid. Ordering the no-fault file may be much less burdensome than ordering records from each medical provider individually.

[3] Photographs

Photographs depicting injuries (such as bruises, scars) and/or medical devices (such as casts or external fixation devices) should be taken right away. This will allow a jury, several years later, to appreciate the extent of the plaintiff's injuries. Further, photographs depicting heavy damage to the vehicle(s) can help buttress the "serious injury" claim.

[4] Seatbelt Defense

VTL §1229-c(3) requires the use of a seatbelt by an operator and any front-seat passenger 16 years of age or older. Where the insurance claims representative raises the seatbelt defense (i.e., the plaintiff failed to wear an available, functioning seatbelt, and would not have sustained the injuries had s/he done so), s/he must be made aware that the plaintiff's attorney has a strong understanding of the defense – including the difficulties of proving all of the elements. See chapter 10, §10.21[7] for a more detailed discussion. *See also PJI §§2:87, 2:87.1, and 2:87.2.*

Warning: As far as settlement negotiations are concerned, insurance claims representatives typically attempt to discount the value of the plaintiff's case by 50% where it is clear that a front-seat passenger plaintiff was not wearing a seatbelt and the injuries would not have been sustained otherwise.

PART F: EVALUATING INSURANCE COVERAGE IN MOTOR VEHICLE ACCIDENT CASE

§ 3.14 Gathering Information to Evaluate Insurance Coverage in Motor Vehicle Accident Case

[1] Identifying Insurance Carrier(s)

The name of the tortfeasor's insurance carrier can be obtained by matching the insurance code on the police accident report with the list of insurers (www.ins.state.ny.us/dmvindex.htm) or by searching the license plate number on the Department of Motor Vehicles' website (see www.nydmv.state.ny.us/dialin.htm). When the police accident report lists the vehicle's insurance code as 999, this means the insurance was obtained through Assigned Risk. In such a case, the plaintiff's attorney should go to www.aipso.com/ny (or call 866-694-6084) to ascertain the name of the insurance carrier.

Practice Tip: A Department of Motor Vehicles search of the registration and the vehicle identification number (VIN) may lead to additional addresses (for venue purposes) and additional owners (whose names do not appear on the accident report). See §3.15[6] below.

[2] Determining Insurance Coverage Limits of Tortfeasor's Vehicle

Once the identity of the tortfeasor's insurance carrier is ascertained, the plaintiff's attorney may obtain the insurance coverage limits of the tortfeasor's vehicle by sending the insurance carrier a letter pursuant to *Insurance Law §3420(f)(2)(a)*.

Practice Tip: While the purpose of *Insurance Law §3420(f)(2)(a)* is to allow the claimant to know early-on whether there is a potential SUM claim (see chapter 4, §4.04[1] for full discussion), it can be utilized as a tool for the plaintiff's attorney to simply determine the extent of the insurance coverage on the tortfeasor's vehicle.

Once litigation is commenced, the defendant is required, upon demand pursuant to *CPLR §3101(f)*, to disclose all insurance coverage information, including all excess and umbrella coverage. *See CPLR §3101(f)*.

The minimum motor vehicle insurance policy limits in New York State are 25/50 (i.e., $25,000 per claimant up to a maximum of $50,000 per accident) and 50/100 where a death is involved. *See 11 NYCRR §60-1.1.* Tow trucks must carry combined single limits of $300,000 or more for bodily injury and wrongful death. *VTL §311(4)(a).* Passenger buses licensed by the NYS Department of Transportation must carry minimum limits of 100/300 for bodily injury; in reality, most passenger buses have policies of $1,000,000 or more. All New York City Taxi & Limousine Commission (TLC) taxis – including NYC liveries, yellow cabs, and first-class car services – are required to have a minimum of 100/300 policy. Neighborhood car services can carry 25/50 minimum limits.

[3] Considering Joint and Several Liability in Motor Vehicle Accident Cases

Motor vehicle accident cases provide complete joint and several liability. *CPLR §1602(6)* provides an exception to *CPLR §1601*'s limitation on joint and several liability with respect to the non-economic portion of claims. This means that the plaintiff simply needs to hold the "deep pocket" defendant responsible for at least 1% of the fault for that defendant to be liable for *all* of the plaintiff's damages (i.e., *including* pain and suffering), less any offset for the plaintiff's comparative negligence. See chapter 8, §8.24.

Practice Tip: Joint and several liability afforded in motor vehicle accident cases is often a great help to the passenger-plaintiff, who is likely to gain complete access to the insurance policies of all vehicles involved; however, where there is a rear-end collision, it may be difficult to prove that the rear-ended vehicle was even 1% at fault. For a driver-plaintiff to be able to utilize joint and several liability to his or her benefit, there must be multiple tortfeasor-defendants involved in the action (e.g., at least a three-car accident).

Example: P is a passenger in vehicle A, and there is a collision between vehicle A ($25,000 insurance policy, but 95% at fault) and vehicle B ($100,000 insurance policy, but only 5% at fault). Vehicle A and vehicle B are each responsible for the entire amount of P's damages (including pain and suffering). Hence, if P is awarded $125,000 for her pain and suffering, A's insurance carrier will pay $25,000 and B's insurance carrier will pay $100,000. See chapter 8, §8.24 regarding settling with one, but not all, defendants.

[4] Determining Whether Excess Insurance Coverage Exists

[a] Ascertaining Whether Driver Has Policy, in Addition to Owner

Companies such as Medlegal Research Group (www.medlegalresearchgroup.com, 800-253-9022) or MEA Services (www.measervicesinc.com, 800-330-3340) can provide information regarding insurance coverage of *drivers* (i.e., where the driver is not the owner of the vehicle).

Practice Tip: Where the driver has his or her own insurance policy (i.e., in addition to the vehicle owner's policy), the plaintiff can pursue the coverage as excess coverage, over and above the coverage on the vehicle s/he was driving.

[b] Ascertaining Whether Owner or Driver Has Excess / Umbrella Policy

Companies such as Medlegal Research Group and MEA Services (see above) can provide information regarding excess or umbrella insurance coverage – which defendants and insurance carriers are often untruthful about. The plaintiff's attorney, in any case with significant damages, should place the excess / umbrella insurance carrier(s) on notice immediately; this will avoid a possible disclaimer for lack of timely notice.

[5] Vicarious Liability

[a] Motor Vehicle Owner

Pursuant to *VTL §388(1)*, the owner of a motor vehicle is vicariously liable for the acts of the driver, so long as driving with permission, express or implied. *See PJI §§2:245 - 2:251.*

As of August 2005, however, a federal statute immunizes leasing companies and car rental companies from vicarious liability – unless the accident occurred outside of the period of the rental / lease or there is negligence or criminal wrongdoing on the part of the owner (e.g., negligent maintenance or negligent entrustment). *See 49 U.S.C. §30106.* Negligent entrustment would apply where the vehicle is leased or rented to an incompetent, inexperienced, or reckless person, notwithstanding the fact that the defendant knew or should have known.

[b] New York City TLC Taxi Medallion Owners

Even if not the driver or owner of the cab, the owner of the taxi medallion (i.e., the yellow cab license which is the actual metal medallion affixed to the car for public display) is vicariously liable for the acts of the driver pursuant to the TLC rules. *See NYC Administrative Code §19-530; see Karlin v. H&L Maintenance*, 97 Civ. 2551 (E.D.N.Y. 1997) (medallion owner vicariously liable).

As discussed in §3.14[2] above, all New York City Taxi &Limousine Commission (TLC) taxis – including NYC liveries, yellow cabs, and first-class car services – are required to carry a minimum of 100/300 policy. The license plate numbers of New York City Taxi & Limousine Commission (TLC) livery cabs generally begin with the letter "T" and end with the letter "C", making it easy to recognize such vehicles by simply reviewing the police accident report.

Practice Tip: In the event the injuries are very serious, the plaintiff's attorney may wish to pursue the taxi medallion – which certainly has value. The plaintiff's attorney should notify the TLC of the case in order to verify ownership of the medallion, and to ensure that the taxi and medallion are not leased, refinanced, or sold. Then, in the event of a judgment in excess of the insurance policy limits, the plaintiff's attorney can force a sale of the medallion (e.g., by the sheriff).

[c] Employer

Where a driver was driving in the course of his or her employment, the employer is vicariously liable. The employer's liability rests upon the doctrine of *respondeat superior*. *See Bank v. Rebold,* 69 A.D.2d 481, 419 N.Y.S.2d 135 (2d Dep't 1979).

[6] Uninsured / Under-insured Motorist Coverage

Where the injured party was involved in a motor vehicle accident with an uninsured or under-insured vehicle (i.e., there is insufficient insurance coverage to fully compensate the injured party for his or her injuries) *and* the host vehicle, the injured party, or a resident-relative / spouse has its own motor vehicle insurance policy, a timely claim should be made through such insurance company for uninsured / under-insured motorist coverage. The declarations page of all potential uninsured / under-insured motorist policies should be obtained in order to determine whether such a claim is possible. See chapter 4 for a comprehensive discussion.

[7] Determining Whether MVAIC Claim Required

Where the tortfeasor's vehicle was uninsured (e.g., where the tortfeasor's car was stolen, or where there was a hit and run) and the injured party does not have access to an uninsured motorist policy (see section above), s/he should file a timely claim with Motor Vehicle Accident Indemnification Corporation (MVAIC). See chapter 4, §§4.05[2], 4.08.

Practice Tip: Filing a claim with MVAIC can also help ascertain insurance information; if there is valid insurance coverage, MVAIC will return the application to the claimant's attorney, providing the appropriate insurance company's information.

PART G: LITIGATING MOTOR VEHICLE ACCIDENT CASE

§ 3.15 Preparing Motor Vehicle Accident Complaint

[1] Required Elements of Motor Vehicle Accident Complaint

A complaint based on a motor vehicle accident must allege the following:

- the defendant(s) owned the vehicle(s);
- the defendant(s) operated the vehicle(s);
- the defendant-driver was driving with the vehicle owner's permission;
- plaintiff's status at the time of the accident, such as passenger, pedestrian, or driver;
- the date, approximate time, and place of the accident;
- the defendant's negligence caused the accident; and
- the plaintiff's damages exceed the no-fault threshold.

[2] Alleging No-Fault Threshold Satisfied

In a motor vehicle accident action by one "covered person" against another "covered person" – the vast majority of motor vehicle accident cases – the complaint must allege that the "no-fault" threshold has been met pursuant to *Insurance Law §5102*. An action for non-economic loss will not be available unless the plaintiff has sustained a "serious injury" as defined in *Insurance Law §5102(d)*. Thus, the plaintiff's attorney must plead that the plaintiff has sustained a "serious injury", in accordance with *Ins. Law §5102(d)*. An action for basic economic loss will not be available; an action for economic loss may be brought where the economic loss exceeds basic economic loss. *Ins. Law §5104(a)*. The plaintiff's attorney should plead that plaintiff's economic losses were in excess of basic economic loss as defined in *Insurance Law §5104(a)*. See chapter 2, §2.02.

[3] Pleading Applicability of Joint and Several Liability

A motor vehicle accident complaint must allege that the action falls within the exception set forth in *CPLR §1602(6)*. This exception allows for joint and several liability, meaning that if a defendant is 1% at fault, s/he is responsible for 100% of the non-economic damages (as well as the economic losses in excess of basic economic loss), subject to any offset for comparative negligence. In general, this exception is applicable in the case of a passenger (i.e., in an accident involving at least two vehicles) or a driver (i.e., in an accident involving more than two vehicles).

> **Example:** P is a passenger in a two-car accident. If a vehicle with a $25,000 insurance policy is held 99% responsible and a vehicle with a $1,000,000 policy is held 1% responsible, P will be afforded $1,025,000 in liability coverage for damages (including pain and suffering). *CPLR §1602(6)*.

[4] Determining Who To Sue

Potential defendants include:
  - drivers of all vehicles involved in the accident;
  - owners of all vehicles involved in the accident;

> **Practice Tip:** Registered owners are vicariously liable for negligent use or operation of the vehicle by any person using or operating the vehicle with the owner's permission, express or implied. *See VTL §388*. Under *VTL §388*, the liability of the owner and driver are joint and several. See §3.14[5][a] above.

  - employer(s) of driver(s);

> **Practice Tip:** Where a driver was driving in the course of his or her employment, the employer is vicariously liable. The employer's liability rests upon the doctrine of *respondeat superior*. *See Bank v. Rebold*, 69 A.D.2d 481, 419 N.Y.S.2d 135 (2d Dep't 1979). See §3.15[5][b] above.

  - New York City Taxi & Limousine Commission taxi medallion owner; and

Practice Tip: New York City Taxi & Limousine Commission taxi medallion owners are vicariously liable for the acts of the driver pursuant to the TLC rules. *See NYC Administrative Code §19-530.* See §3.14[5][c] above.

- governmental entity (e.g., municipality).

Practice Tip: Where the injuries are severe and insurance coverage (including uninsured / under-insured motorist coverage) is limited, a claim may have to be brought against a municipality. Examples include a road defect or lack of stop sign. Proving liability in such a case, though, is extremely difficult.

[5] Jurisdiction

Pursuant to *VTL §§253* and *254*, non-New York resident owners and operators of motor vehicles involved in accidents within New York State may be served via the Secretary of State, and are subject to the jurisdiction of the courts of the State of New York. *See VTL §§253, 254.*

[6] Choosing Best Venue

The plaintiff's attorney may choose to properly venue the case in any county within the New York State where either the plaintiff or any defendant maintains a residence on the date of commencement of the lawsuit. *CPLR §503.*

Practice Tip: Choosing the most plaintiff-friendly venue can be the most important decision the plaintiff's attorney makes through the course of the case.

Practice Tip: A Department of Motor Vehicles search of the registration and the vehicle identification number (VIN) may lead to additional addresses (for venue purposes) and additional owners (whose names do not appear on the accident report). See §3.14[1] above.

There are additional venue considerations with respect to corporations and municipalities, as set forth in *CPLR §§503, 505.* See chapter 7, §7.07. See also chapter 5, §§5.04[3], 5.05[4] below.

§ 3.16 Preliminary Conference in Motor Vehicle Accident Case

It is usually the defendant who demands most of the discovery in a motor vehicle accident case. The defense typically seeks authorizations to obtain plaintiff's medical records, no-fault records, medical records relating to plaintiff's prior motor vehicle accidents and prior lawsuits (i.e., where plaintiff alleges injuries to the same part or parts of the body s/he previously injured), employment records, W-2s and income tax records (if there is a claim for lost earnings).

In every motor vehicle accident case, the plaintiff should serve disclosure demands on the defendant, pursuant to *CPLR §3101*, seeking the following:

- insurance information regarding the owner(s), driver(s), driver's employer (where accident occurred in the course of employment), and any other defendant(s), including excess and umbrella policies;
- photographs (of the accident site, as well as photographs depicting the damage to the vehicles);
- names and addresses of witnesses (to the accident, as well as the property damage of the vehicles, and the plaintiff's condition);
- accident reports (MV-104A);
- defendant's MV-104[2];
- estimates, invoices, bills, and receipts regarding property damage to the vehicle(s);
- name and address of the towing company and auto body repair shop;
- car rental agreement or lease agreement, if applicable;
- defendant's cellular phone records around the time of the accident;
- defendant's trip sheet, in the case of a taxi driver;
- name and address of the medallion owner, in the case of a yellow taxi;
- surveillance films of the plaintiff;
- statements of plaintiff (written or recorded); and
- expert witness information.

These demands should be served on the defendant(s) as soon as the answer is received, and a provision should be written into the preliminary conference order requiring the defendant to respond to these demands. The plaintiff is absolutely entitled to all of the aforementioned information, other than expert witness disclosure, prior to the commencement of depositions. *See Tai Tran v. New Rochelle Hospital*, 99 N.Y.2d 383, 389, 756 N.Y.S.2d 509, 513 (2003) (*CPLR §3101*'s full disclosure requirement gave plaintiff right to obtain any surveillance material on demand, prior to depositions).

> **Practice Tip:** Where the injuries are of the "soft-tissue" nature, the plaintiff's attorney may attempt to shorten the time limits (via the preliminary conference order) for making a motion for summary judgment (which, pursuant to *CPLR §3212,* is 120 days from the filing of the note of issue).

In a case involving extremely serious injuries, the plaintiff's attorney may want to have the preliminary conference order require the defendant to preserve the vehicle and make it available for inspection by the plaintiff's experts (e.g., accident reconstruction expert and/or seatbelt expert). See chapter 11, §11.02 for a motor vehicle accident preliminary conference checklist.

---

2   The plaintiff may seek a copy of the defendant's MV-104, if having difficulty obtaining it. *See Rodriguez v. Middle Atlantic Auto Leasing, Inc.,* 78 A.D.2d 629, 432 N.Y.S.2d 709 (1st Dep't 1980) (defendant required to provide copy of MV-104 or affidavit that defendant searched files and is not in possession of the MV-104).

§ 3.17 Examinations Before Trial in Motor Vehicle Accident Case
[1] Preparing Plaintiff for Examination Before Trial
[a] Liability

The most important part of the motor vehicle accident case is generally the plaintiff's examination before trial testimony. As such, properly preparing the plaintiff to testify cannot be overlooked. The plaintiff should be educated as to the law of the particular case, and what needs to be proven. Plaintiff's counsel should review (with the plaintiff) the police accident report, MV-104s of all drivers, witness statements, and any photographs. The plaintiff should be prepared to answer questions regarding:

- the date, time, location, and day of week of the accident;
- a description of the accident;
- weather and lighting conditions;
- where coming from and going to (i.e., was plaintiff in a rush to get somewhere?);
- where looking immediately prior to the accident;
- attempts to avoid the accident (horn, brakes, swerve);
- why plaintiff failed to avoid the accident;
- vision, including whether wearing required eyeglasses or contact lenses;
- distractions, such as cell phones, eating, drinking, reading, smoking, reaching for a map, and talking in the car;
- proper maintenance of the vehicle, including whether the brakes, tires, lights, horn, and steering were functioning properly;
- the speed limit, speed of the vehicles at impact, and the speed of the vehicles at different points approaching the accident;
- time, speed, and distance questions (see §3.17[2][b]);
- the application of the brakes (light, medium, or heavy) and skidding (which is evidence of lack of control) of either vehicle;
- conversations regarding the accident, including with driver(s) and passenger(s) of either vehicle, police, ambulance personnel, emergency room staff, medical providers, spouse, and other friends / relatives; and

Practice Tip: It is vital that the plaintiff be consistent with respect to each conversation s/he may have had regarding the accident. To the extent the plaintiff does not recall the specific conversation(s), s/he should not guess. The more conversations s/he attempts to recount regarding the accident, the more inconsistencies will result. Further, recounting details of such conversations can generally only help the defense (i.e., admissions), for they are generally inadmissible if offered by the plaintiff (i.e., buttressing).

- the law as it applies to the specific case (e.g., stop sign case or pedestrian case), pursuant to the applicable *PJI* charges.

See chapter 11, §11.08 for a checklist.

[b] Damages

Regarding damages, the plaintiff should be familiarized with what is stated or shown in relevant documents, including the bill(s) of particulars, ambulance call report, emergency room records, operative reports, all other medical records, photographs (of the vehicles and the injuries), damage estimates, and repair bills of the vehicles. The plaintiff must also be prepared for a possible seatbelt defense (which also requires knowledge of what the police accident report, as well as the aforementioned documents, state in that regard). Finally, the plaintiff must be educated as to the law of the case (i.e., as stated in the pattern charges in the *PJI*). *See PJI §§2:88A - 2:88G* regarding the "serious injury" threshold. Discussed below are the general topics which should be covered while preparing the plaintiff for his or her deposition in a motor vehicle accident case. See chapter 11, §11.08 for a checklist of topics.

[1] Inability to Perform Usual and Customary Daily Activities

Where the plaintiff's injuries are of the "soft-tissue" nature (i.e., no fractures or surgeries), s/he must be prepared as to the high level of proof required under the law. In short, the plaintiff with only "soft-tissue" injuries must aim to prove, at a minimum, that for at least 90 of the first 180 days after the accident, s/he could not perform substantially all the acts constituting his or her usual and customary daily activities. *Ins. Law §5102(d)*. The plaintiff must be made aware that the first six months post-accident are crucial to the case.

The plaintiff will be asked quality of life questions, contrasting his or her normal daily activities before the accident versus after the accident. Typical areas of inquiry on this issue include:

- activities the plaintiff could no longer perform, or could only perform with restriction, for some time after the accident (e.g., working, sleeping, dressing, brushing teeth / hair, showering, walking, sitting, standing, navigating stairs, exercising, socializing, sexual relations, cooking, cleaning, engaging in sexual relations, performing hobbies, gardening, etc.);
- the plaintiff's inability to resume work / modified duty;
- how the plaintiff traveled to and from doctors' offices;
- trips / vacations taken by the plaintiff since the accident;
- changes in the plaintiff's weight (with the inference being the plaintiff's weight would have increased if inactive);
- the plaintiff's memberships to gyms (i.e., was s/he unable to go as a result of the accident?);
- whether the plaintiff needed to hire a caretaker or outside help to clean; and
- the plaintiff's use of stairs (e.g., walk-up apartment).

[2] Photographs Depicting Damage to Vehicles

The plaintiff should be made aware that defense counsel may show him or her photographs depicting little, if any, damage to the vehicle(s). The plaintiff must be cautioned that testifying that photographs fairly and accurately depict the damage to the vehicle(s) will ensure the admissibility of the photographs at the time of trial. Such photographs can be fatal to the plaintiff's case at trial. The plaintiff's attorney must be sure to review the photographs with the plaintiff prior to the deposition.

[3] Impact and Damage to Vehicles

The plaintiff should be prepared to answer questions about the accident which bear on the issue of damages, such as:

- the amount of damage to the vehicles;
- the location of the impact on the vehicles;
- whether the plaintiff's vehicle moved as a result of the impact;
- the force of the impact (light, medium, or heavy);
- whether the plaintiff's body made contact with any part of the inside of the car;
- whether the plaintiff was wearing a seatbelt, as well as being able to describe the seatbelt (i.e., as coming across the shoulder and lap *or* just the lap);
- whether air bag(s) deployed; and
- whether the vehicle was able to be driven from the accident scene or was towed.

[4] Pain and Suffering

In the event the plaintiff meets the "serious injury" threshold, s/he will be compensated for any past pain and suffering, as well as any future pain and suffering. The plaintiff should be prepared to answer questions regarding:

- type of pain / description, and whether the pain has increased, decreased, or remained the same over time (and quantifying the pain);
- whether s/he is presently in pain;
- medications taken, as well as dosages, refills, doctors who prescribed them, and pharmacies that filled the prescriptions;
- loss of consciousness and bleeding at the scene of the accident;
- length of time confined to hospital, home, and bed;
- surgeries undergone (as well as future surgeries); and
- residual effects, such as loss of range of motion, scarring, deformities, etc.

[5] Treatment

The plaintiff should be prepared to answer questions regarding his or her treatment, such as:

- whether the plaintiff left the accident scene via ambulance;
- whether the plaintiff was treated at the hospital;
- the names and locations of each healthcare provider s/he treated with;

- the length and frequency of treatment;
- the identity of the person who referred the plaintiff to each healthcare provider;
- the number of times the plaintiff was treated by the doctor;
- the length of the visits to healthcare providers, the type of treatment received, and whether the treatment changed (such as following MRI results);
- the complaints made to each doctor, the examinations administered, the diagnostic testing performed (and the results);
- the medical equipment / assistive devices (e.g., braces, bandages, casts, crutches, canes, walkers, wheelchairs, etc.) prescribed;
- the reason for gaps in treatment (if any);
- the reason treatment ended and whether the plaintiff was prescribed (and performs) a home exercise program;
- whether the plaintiff is still undergoing treatment, the last time s/he visited the doctor, and date of the next scheduled doctor's appointment; and
- whether the plaintiff underwent surgery, and whether a doctor has recommended or discussed future surgery as an option.

[6] Prior and Subsequent Accidents and Injuries

The insurance companies have access to a system whereby they can find out about any prior claims the plaintiff has made.[3] The plaintiff should be prepared to answer questions about any prior accidents or treatment relating to the part(s) of the body claimed to have been injured in the present case. Questions relating to prior injuries to the same part of the body will be asked.

> **Practice Tip:** It is important that the plaintiff testify truthfully about the existence of documented priors. However, where applicable, it is also important to relate the fact that the prior condition was not as significant as the defense may believe, and it had not been a problem for a long time.

The plaintiff should also be prepared to answer questions regarding whether s/he re-injured himself / herself after the accident.

[7] Economic Losses / Out-of-Pocket Expenses

The plaintiff should be prepared to testify about the loss of earnings (including lost pension, annuities, health insurance, sick / vacation days, etc.), non-reimbursed medical bills, and any other non-reimbursed monies the plaintiff had to expend as a result of the accident (e.g., co-payments, hiring of cleaning service, etc.). In a motor vehicle accident case, though, the plaintiff will only be entitled to collect money for economic losses to the extent they are greater than "basic economic loss" (except in

---

3   The plaintiff's attorney may want to run his or her own search on the client, so as not to be caught "off guard" later on. For a nominal fee, a search can be made through Insurance Services Offices, 545 Washington Boulevard, Jersey City, NJ, (800) 888-4476. www.iso.com.

rare instances, such as a motorcycle accident). *Ins. Law §5102(a).* See chapter 2, §2.02 and §3.04 above.

[c] Derivative Plaintiff

When the injured party's spouse (or parent, in the case of an infant-plaintiff) is also named as a plaintiff in the action (i.e., derivative claim), the derivative plaintiff will also be required to testify at a deposition. Both spouses should be prepared to testify as to how the accident has affected the marriage. Testimony may include the plaintiff's inability to perform housework (including cooking, cleaning, gardening, food shopping, etc.), problems with sex life, trouble caring for children, and other marital discord. *See PJI §§2:315 - 2:318.*

The derivative plaintiff must also be prepared to answer questions about the accident and the accident scene (where s/he has personal knowledge), whether s/he is aware of any photographs, conversations with the plaintiff about how the accident occurred (which are admissions and, therefore, not hearsay if offered by the defendant), and the status of plaintiff's injuries.

Warning: Derivative claims are often more harmful than beneficial for the plaintiff's case. The derivative plaintiff's cause of action is generally not factored into settlements, while the derivative plaintiff's testimony may well be detrimental to the plaintiff's case. Such claim should be discussed with the plaintiff and, to the extent s/he agrees to not proceed with a derivative cause of action, s/he should sign-off on it via a waiver. *See Wingate, Russotti & Shapiro, LLP v. Friedman, Khafif & Associates*, 41 A.D.3d 367 (1st Dep't 2007) (failure to bring derivative action on behalf of spouse can result in discharge for cause).Where the plaintiff's spouse is not named in the lawsuit, s/he will rarely be subpoenaed for a deposition.

[2] Conducting Motor Vehicle Accident Examination Before Trial

[a] Preparing to Question Tortfeasor(s)

The plaintiff's attorney should review the law of the particular case (via the *Pattern Jury Instructions)* to determine precisely what s/he wants to prove. Reviewing documents such as the police accident report, the MV-104s of all drivers, photographs of the accident scene and the vehicles, witness statements, and the insurance coverage limits of the vehicles is essential. Proving certain things, such as the defendant's speeding, skidding, vehicle leaving the road, failure to keep a proper lookout, and/or failure to obey a traffic control device, can be dispositive of the case. See §3.19 below.

Practice Tip: Where there are multiple defendant-drivers, the plaintiff's attorney should attempt to place more of the fault on the driver with the larger insurance policy.

[b] Time, Speed, and Distance Questions

Attorneys can really score points at trial due to time, speed, and distance questions in motor vehicle accident cases. When compared to the witness' testimony of what rate of speed s/he was traveling, inevitably there will be great contradiction.

> **Practice Tip:** After a simple mathematical conversion, the jury can be told that the witness was lying. The mathematical conversion to keep in mind is that 1 mile per hour = 1.5 feet per second. Some judges will take judicial notice of this fact (e.g., 30 m.p.h. = 45 feet / second).

Responses to time and distance questions can also be used to show that the witness was or was not within the speed limit. An example of time and distance questions is as follows: How far is it from point A to point B? How long did it take you to travel from point A to point B? If the witness responds by saying, "I don't know," the questioner should ask, "Was it more or less than…?" to attempt to box the witness in. The witness must also be asked what speed s/he was traveling at various points in time immediately leading up to the accident.

[c] Outlining Examination Before Trial Areas

The attorney should have an outline of the questions s/he will be asking. There are many *pro forma* motor vehicle accident questions which should be asked in all motor vehicle accident cases. The attorney must also be prepared to ask questions regarding the specific type of case at hand. Utilizing the *Pattern Jury Instructions* to prepare for the deposition is essential. See chapter 11, §11.05 for a checklist of *pro forma* topics.

§ 3.18 "Serious Injury" Threshold Motion for Summary Judgment

[1] Defending "Serious Injury" Threshold Motion – In General

Through the course of a "soft-tissue" motor vehicle accident case (e.g., sprains and strains, whiplash, etc.), the defense may well make a motion for summary judgment on the issue of damages. If the motion is granted, the case is dismissed. It is therefore imperative that the plaintiff's attorney evaluate the case and determine whether it meets the "serious injury" threshold requirements, prior to commencing a lawsuit. Otherwise, the plaintiff's attorney may spend years of work, in addition to advancing thousands of dollars in disbursements, only to have the case dismissed.

The motor vehicle accident plaintiff ultimately must meet at least one of the "serious injury" threshold categories (i.e., at trial) in order to be able to be awarded any money. In defending a motion for summary judgment on damages (i.e., "serious injury" threshold), the plaintiff must show that, at the very least, a genuine issue of fact exists as to whether the plaintiff meets at least one of the below-listed categories.

[2] Meeting at Least One of the "Serious Injury" Threshold Categories

[a] Death

Death resulting from a motor vehicle accident constitutes a "serious injury". *Ins. Law §5102(d)*. A death resulting from a motor vehicle accident injury allows for the award of pain and suffering on the personal injury case. *Ins. Law §5104(a)*. Such is the case even where the injury alone would have been insufficient to meet the "serious injury" threshold had decedent survived. *See Ruvolo v. Frobin*, 85 A.D.2d 504, 444 N.Y.S.2d 461 (1st Dep't 1981).

[b] Dismemberment

Dismemberment is generally defined as the loss of a limb. An example of a dismemberment is an amputation. "Dismemberment" overlaps the "permanent loss of use" category and is generally more difficult to prove.

[c] Fracture

A fracture resulting from a motor vehicle accident constitutes a "serious injury" under the no-fault law. *Ins. Law §5102(d)*. A dentist's description of a chipped tooth as a fracture did not satisfy the "serious injury" threshold. *See Epstein v. Butern*, 155 A.D.2d 513, 547 N.Y.S.2d 374 (2d Dep't 1989). Under certain circumstances, however, a chipped tooth may satisfy the "serious injury" threshold. *See Kennedy v. Anthony*, 195 A.D.2d 942, 600 N.Y.S.2d 980 (3d Dep't 1993) (fracture was undeniable, and called for prompt repair and immediate treatment). While a deviated septum does not constitute a "serious injury", *see Ives v. Correll*, 211 A.D.2d 899, 621 N.Y.S.2d 179 (3d Dep't 1995), a fracture of nose cartilage may be deemed a fracture for purposes of satisfying the "serious injury" threshold. *See Gonzalez v. Brayley*, 199 A.D.2d 1013, 605 N.Y.S.2d 585 (4th Dep't 1993).

[d] Significant Disfigurement

A significant disfigurement resulting from a motor vehicle accident constitutes a "serious injury" under the no-fault law. *Ins. Law §5102(d)*. A disfigurement, generally a scar, is significant if a reasonable person viewing the plaintiff's body in its altered state would regard the condition as unattractive, objectionable, or as the object of a pity or scorn. *See Waldron v. Wild*, 96 A.D.2d 190, 468 N.Y.S.2d 244 (4th Dep't 1983). *See also Cushing v. Seeman*, 247 A.D.2d 891, 668 N.Y.S.2d 791 (4th Dep't 1998).

[e] Loss of Fetus

A loss of a fetus resulting from a motor vehicle accident constitutes a "serious injury" under no-fault law. *Ins. Law §5102(d)*. A medical affidavit is necessary to establish causation. No cause of action is available, however, for the unborn fetus.

[f] Permanent Loss of Use

The permanent loss of use of a body organ, member, function, or system constitutes a "serious injury" under the no-fault law. *Ins. Law §5102(d)*. To qualify as permanent loss of use, the plaintiff needs to establish that the loss is total. *See Geloss v. Monster*, 289 A.D.2d 746, 734 N.Y.S.2d 340 (3d Dep't 2001). *See also Licari v. Elliot*, 57 N.Y.2d 230, 455 N.Y.S.2d (1982).

[g] Permanent Consequential Limitation

A permanent consequential limitation of use of a body organ or member constitutes a "serious injury" under the no-fault law. *Ins. Law §5102(d)*. Whether a limitation of use is consequential relates to a medical significance; it also involves a comparative determination of the degree or qualitative nature of the injury based on the normal function, purpose, and use of the body part. *See Toure v. Avis Rent-A-Car Systems, Inc.*, 98 N.Y.2d 345, 746 N.Y.S.2d 865 (2002). The medical opinion must be based on objective medical evidence. A medical expert must prove the extent or degree of limitation via a quantitative assessment of the plaintiff's limitation or a qualitative assessment of the plaintiff's condition. *Id*. The limitation must be significant or important, as well as permanent, in order to qualify as a "serious injury" under this category. *See Countermine v. Galka*, 189 A.D.2d 1043, 593 N.Y.S.2d 113 (3d Dep't 1993).

[h] Significant Limitation of Use

A significant limitation of use of a body function or system resulting from a motor vehicle accident constitutes a "serious injury" under the no-fault law. *Ins. Law §5102(d)*. A significant limitation of use need not be permanent, *see Oberly v. Bangs Ambulance Inc.*, 96 N.Y.2d 295, 727 N.Y.S.2d 378 (2001), although a permanent injury is not excluded from the meaning. *See Preston v. Young*, 239 A.D.2d 729, 657 N.Y.S.2d 499 (3d Dep't 1997). However, a showing of medical significance is required, involving a comparative determination of the normal function, purpose, and use of the body part. *Toure v. Avis Rent-A-Car Systems, Inc.*, 98 N.Y.2d 345, 746 N.Y.S.2d 865 (2002). The medical opinion must be based on objective medical evidence. A medical expert must prove the extent or degree of limitation via a quantitative assessment of the plaintiff's limitation or a qualitative assessment of the plaintiff's condition. *Id*. The limitation must be more than minor, mild, or slight. *See Decker v. Stung*, 243 A.D.2d 1033, 633 N.Y.S.2d 448 (3d Dep't 1997) (20% impairment not a significant limitation). The doctor's findings generally must be based on a recent examination of the plaintiff, *see Grossman v. Wright*, 268 A.D.2d 79, 707 N.Y.S.2d 233 (2d Dep't 2000), and any significant gap in treatment must be explained. *Id*. However, a finding by the plaintiff's physician that the injuries are permanent absolves the plaintiff of the "based on recent exam" requirement. *Toure v. Avis Rent-A-Car Systems, Inc.*, 98 N.Y.2d 345, 746 N.Y.S.2d 865 (2002). The previously determined permanence is an adequate explanation for any gap in treatment. *Id*.

[i] 90 in 180

Where the plaintiff sustained a "medically-determined injury or impairment of a non-permanent nature that prevented him or her from performing substantially all of the material acts that constituted his or her usual and customary daily activities for at least 90 of the first 180 days immediately following the accident," this constitutes a "serious injury" under the no-fault law. *Ins. Law §5102(d)*.

Where the plaintiff resumes daily activities, the "serious injury" threshold may be satisfied under this category if the ability to perform those activities remained substantially impaired. *See Judd v. Walton,* 259 A.D.2d 1016, 703 N.Y.S.2d 845 (4th Dep't 1999) (plaintiff's return to work within statutory period did not preclude finding of serious injury).

The plaintiff must submit medical evidence supporting the disability for the requisite time period. *Decker v. Stung*, 243 A.D.2d 1033, 663 N.Y.S.2d 448 (3d Dep't 1997). The medical expert's conclusions must be based on objective medical evidence. *See Toure v. Avis Rent-A-Car Systems, Inc.*, 98 N.Y.2d 345, 746 N.Y.S.2d 865 (2002). Mere mention of an MRI report without establishing the actual findings in the report is insufficient to meet the "serious injury" threshold. *Id.* Rather, an affirmation from the radiologist as to the findings is necessary.

[3] Opposing "Serious Injury" Threshold Motions

The plaintiff's attorney must do the following in order to establish, *prima facie*, that the plaintiff sustained a "serious injury":

- establish the exact nature of the plaintiff's injuries by *objective* medical proof in admissible form;
- determine how the injury qualifies as a "serious injury" under at least one of *Insurance Law §5102(d)*'s definitions (see §3.18[2] above); and
- affirmatively establish that the injuries and resulting limitations are *causally related* to the motor vehicle accident in question, after careful consideration of all possible pre-existing conditions and prior injuries.

Further, with respect to the categories that are not clear-cut (and, hence, the ones typically at issue in a motion for summary judgment), the plaintiff (i.e., through his or her physician) must offer a reasonable explanation for terminating (or having a prolonged gap in) treatment (e.g., patient reached maximum medical improvement, further treatment would have been palliative in nature, patient given home exercise program). *See Pommells v. Perez,* 4 N.Y.3d 566, 797 N.Y.S.2d 380 (2005). *See also Francouvig v. Senekis Cab Corp.*, 41 A.D.3d 643, 838 N.Y.S.2d 635 (2d Dep't 2007) (gap in treatment adequately explained by plaintiff who stopped treating because no-fault cut her off and she could not afford to pay for further treatment). A defendant cannot make out a *prima facie* case on a "serious injury" threshold motion where the defendant's physician fails to offer an opinion regarding the 90 in 180 category. *Hoxhan v. McEachern*, 42 A.D.3d 433, 840 N.Y.S.2d 89 (2d Dep't 2007).

§ 3.19 Making Motion for Summary Judgment in Motor Vehicle Accident Case

The plaintiff should make a motion for partial summary judgment (i.e., on the issue of liability) when applicable. Besides removing the issue of liability from the case, a successful motion for summary judgment will entitle the plaintiff to interest from the date of the liability decision in plaintiff's favor. *CPLR §5002. See Van Nostrand v. Froehlich*, 44 A.D.3d 54, 844 N.Y.S.2d 293 (2d Dep't 2007) (plaintiff entitled to interest from the date of liability decision through the damages verdict, even though question of "serious injury" was at issue until damages trial; this is the rule in all but the Fourth Department which holds that interest does not accrue until a finding of "serious injury", *see Ruzycki v. Baker*, 301 A.D.2d 48, 750 N.Y.S.2d 680 [4th Dep't 2002]). A motion for summary judgment on the issue of liability must be considered in the following types of motor vehicle accident cases:

- rear-end collision, *see Macauley v. Elrac*, 6 A.D.3d 584, 775 N.Y.S.2d 78 (2d Dep't 2004) (defendant's attempt at non-negligent explanation "conclusory and speculative" and insufficient to rebut inference of negligence);
- single-car collision (passenger-plaintiff);
- cross-over / car leaving road case, *see Pfaffenbach v. White Plains Express Corp.*, 17 N.Y.2d 132, 269 N.Y.S.2d 115 (1966);
- stop sign case, *see Jenkins v. Alexander*, 9 A.D.3d 286, 780 N.Y.S.2d 133 (1st Dep't 2004) (driver with right-of-way has no duty to watch and avoid driver who might fail to stop at stop sign); *see Friedberg v. Citiwide Auto Leasing, Inc.*, 22 A.D.3d 522, 801 N.Y.S.2d 770 (2d Dep't 2005) (summary judgment granted even where driver stopped at stop sign, but thereafter failed to yield right-of-way); *see also VTL §§1172, 1142(a)*;
- yield sign case, *see VTL §1142*;
- red light case, *see VTL §§1110 and 1111*;
- left-turn case, *see Torro v. Schiller*, 8 A.D.3d 364, 777 N.Y.S.2d 915 (2d Dep't 2004) (violation of *VTL §1141* sufficient for summary judgment where opponent of motion failed to raise triable issue of fact as to other driver's negligence); and
- dozing driver case, *see PJI §2:85A*.

To be cautious, the plaintiff should also make a *prima facie* showing of "serious injury" in making a motion for summary judgment on the issue of liability, although liability is unrelated to the issue of "serious injury". *Reid v. Brown*, 308 A.D.2d 331, 332, 764 N.Y.S.2d 260 (1st Dep't 2003) (granting summary judgment on liability does not include any finding that "serious injury" threshold satisfied). *See also Abbas v. Cole*, 44 A.D.3d 31, 840 N.Y.S.2d 388 (2d Dep't 2007). The plaintiff can also make a motion for summary judgment on the issue of "serious injury" (e.g., fracture).

Warning: The risk in making a motion for summary judgment on the issue of liability is that the defendant may make a cross-motion for summary judgment (to dismiss plaintiff's case) on the issue of "serious injury".

CHAPTER 4

MOTOR VEHICLE ACCIDENTS – UNINSURED AND UNDER–INSURED MOTORIST COVERAGE

PART A: OVERVIEW

§ 4.01 Overview – Uninsured Motorist (UM) and Supplementary Uninsured / Under-insured Motorist (SUM) Coverage

Uninsured motorist and under-insured motorist coverage protect victims of motor vehicle accidents where compensation is not otherwise available. Every motor vehicle insurance policy issued in the State of New York contains a mandatory uninsured motorist (UM) endorsement which provides the "insured" (see §§4.02, 4.03 below) with minimal insurance coverage to pursue, for bodily injury or death, where the tortfeasor's vehicle was "uninsured". *Ins. Law §3420(f)(1).* Thus, where the tortfeasor was uninsured, the injured claimant can still be compensated for pain and suffering to the same extent as if the tortfeasor's vehicle possessed the minimum New York State liability coverage (25/50, or 50/100 where death occurs) by pursuing a first-party claim against the UM insurer. *Id.*

For an additional premium, supplementary uninsured / under-insured motorist (SUM) coverage may be purchased on a motor vehicle insurance policy. *See 11 NYCRR §60-2.3 (Regulation 35-D).* SUM provides insurance coverage in the case where the offending vehicle was *either* uninsured *or* under-insured (i.e., the amount of the tortfeasor's coverage is inadequate to fully compensate the injured party for his or her injuries). SUM coverage generally provides limits of at least $100,000 per person and $300,000 per accident, but cannot be greater than the liability coverage on its policy. Where SUM coverage is purchased, the SUM endorsement on the insurance policy trumps the mandatory uninsured motorist (UM) endorsement in the case of an uninsured motorist claim. *11 NYCRR §60-2.3(e).* The two endorsements, however, are quite similar.

UM and SUM benefits, like no-fault benefits, are first-party benefits. The insurer stands in the shoes of the uninsured or under-insured tortfeasor. *See Nationwide Mut.*

Life Ins. Co. v. Holbert, 39 Misc.2d 78, 241 N.Y.S.2d 589 (Sup. Ct. Broome Co. 1962). Entitlement to uninsured motorist (UM or SUM) benefits and under-insured motorist (SUM) benefits, just as in a third-party lawsuit, is established upon a showing of the uninsured / under-insured tortfeasor's negligence, and the claimant's damages (including proving "serious injury"[4]). *See Ins. Law §3420(f)(1); 11 NYCRR §60-2.3 (f) III (3).*

Where the tortfeasor has no insurance and the injured claimant does not have a UM or SUM policy to pursue, a claim may be made to the Motor Vehicle Accident Indemnification Corporation (MVAIC). MVAIC provides minimum New York State insurance policy limits for the injured party to pursue.

PART B: ASSESSING UNINSURED AND UNDER-INSURED MOTORIST COVERAGE

§ 4.02 Determining Whether Claimant Covered by UM / SUM Policies

[1] Vehicle Occupied by Claimant

Uninsured / under-insured motorist coverage on the vehicle the claimant was occupying at the time of the accident is available to the claimant. *See Regulation 35-D at 11 NYCRR §60-2.3(f)(a)(2).*

> **Example:** The claimant can seek uninsured or under-insured benefits through his or her employer's insurance policy where, for example, the accident occurred in a company car and the tortfeasor's liability policy limits were less than the claimant's employer's uninsured / under-insured limits.

[2] Claimant's Own Insurance Policy

Uninsured / under-insured motorist coverage on the claimant's own vehicle is also available to the claimant. This vehicle may or may not have been the vehicle the claimant was occupying at the time of the accident.

[3] Insurance Policies of Resident-Relatives / Spouse

The named insured and, while residents of the same household, the spouse and the relatives of either, are insured under the UM and SUM endorsements of the insured's policy. *See Regulation 35-D at 11 NYCRR §60-2.3(f)(a); 11 NYCRR §60-1.1(c); Interboro Mutual Indemnity Ins. Co. v. Johanessen*, 273 A.D.2d 237, 238, 704 N.Y.S.2d 445 (2d Dep't 2000) (resident-relative of policyholder insured person for purposes of uninsured motorist benefits).

---

4   *See Meegan v. Progressive Ins. Co.*, 838 N.Y.S.2d 749 (4th Dep't 2007). However, the Second Department in *Raffelini v. State Farm Mut. Auto Ins. Co.*, 36 A.D.3d 92, 823 N.Y.S.2d 440 (2d Dep't 2006) held that in an under-insured claim (in a common-law action against claimant's own liability insurer, i.e., after exhausting the tortfeasor's insurance policy), the claimant need not prove "serious injury", for *Insurance Law §3420(f)(2)'s* omission of the "serious injury" requirement regarding SUM claims is meaningful. This matter will ultimately have to be reconciled by the Court of Appeals.

> **Example:** P is a passenger in a single-car accident. Unbeknownst to P, the vehicle s/he was in did not have a valid insurance policy in effect on the date of the accident. However, P's mother, whom P lives with but was not involved in the accident, has an insurance policy with respect to her own vehicle. On that policy, P's mother has $100,000 worth of SUM coverage. P is thus insured under his or her mother's policy for up to $100,000.

Residency requires at least some degree of permanence and intention to remain. *New York Central Mutual Fire Ins. Co. v. Bonilla*, 269 A.D.2d 599, 704 N.Y.S.2d 819 (2d Dep't 2000) (no residency found where claimant lived at three different addresses in two-year period).

§ 4.03 Priority Amongst Various Uninsured / Under-insured Motorist Policies

The claimant has a potential uninsured or under-insured motorist claim under more than one policy. Stacking, or proceeding against all possible uninsured / under-insured motorist carriers for the full amount of their respective uninsured / under-insured motorist coverages afforded under their policies, is not permitted. The uninsured / under-insured motorist coverage which takes first priority is that of the vehicle the claimant was occupying (*see Regulation 35-D at 11 NYCRR §60-2.3III[7]*); second priority is claimant's own insurance policy (*see Regulation 35-D at 11 NYCRR §60-2.3III(8)[a]*); third priority is a policy of a resident-relative / spouse (*see Regulation 35-D at 11 NYCRR §60-2.3III(8)[c]*). Each uninsured / under-insured motorist policy must be exhausted successively. *See Regulation 35-D at 11 NYCRR §60-2.3III(9).* If a lesser-in-priority insurance policy has lower limits (such as #3 in the example below), that policy cannot be properly pursued. The claimant can only utilize a lesser-in-priority uninsured / under-insured policy to the extent it has greater limits than each of the greater-in-priority policies.

> **Example:** First priority (insurance policy on friend's car which claimant was occupying) = $50,000; second priority (claimant's own insurance policy) = $100,000; third priority (insurance policy in household) = $50,000. The claimant can only recover, at most, the amount of the highest insurance policy. In this example, that is $100,000 ($50,000 from #1 and $50,000 from #2).

§ 4.04 Notice of Claim

[1] Requesting Policy Limits of Offending Vehicle

Insurance Law §3420(f)(2)(A) requires the insurer of the offending vehicle to disclose its liability insurance policy limits within 45 days after written request. Further, the time to make an uninsured / under-insured claim, discussed below, is tolled during the period in which the insurer fails to disclose its limits as requested.

See Ins. Law §3420(f)(2)(A). Thus, it is imperative that the claimant's attorney make this written request promptly.

[2] Time Requirement

A timely written notice of a claim by the claimant is required prior to applying for uninsured / under-insured benefits. This is accomplished by sending a letter (certified mail, return receipt requested, preferably) to the uninsured / under-insured claims department of the insured's insurance company. *See Transportation Ins. Co. v. Pecoraro*, 270 A.D.2d 851, 852, 705 N.Y.S.2d 155, 156 (4th Dep't 2000) (where policy specifies notice must be in writing, other forms will not suffice). The claimant's attorney must do so "within 90 days or as soon as practicable" with respect to a UM claim, or "as soon as practicable" with respect to a SUM claim. *See Regulation 35-D at 11 NYCRR §60-2.3(e)III(2); See Unwin v. New York Central Mutual Fire Ins. Co.*, 268 A.D.2d 669, 700 N.Y.S.2d 580, 582 (3d Dep't 2000) ("as soon as practicable" requires notice be given "within a reasonable time under the circumstances").

In the case of a disclaimer of coverage by the offending vehicle's insurer, the time to provide the notice of claim to the uninsured / under-insured insurance carrier does not begin to run until the date of the disclaimer – rather than the date of the accident.

> **Practice Tip:** Notice of claim letters should be sent out to any insurer through which an uninsured or under-insured claim may be made (e.g., host vehicle's insurance carrier, claimant's own insurance carrier, and resident-relatives' insurance carriers).

[3] Demonstrating Due Diligence Where Delay Occurs

Where substantial delay occurs, the claimant must demonstrate due diligence in ascertaining the insurance status of the offending vehicle. *Rekemeyer v. State Farm Mutual Insurance Company*, 7 A.D.2d 955, 777 N.Y.S.2d 551 (3d Dep't 2004) (burden of proof on insured to provide admissible evidence excusing delay). The insured-claimant is required to demonstrate that s/he was diligent in attempting to ascertain the insurance status of the offending vehicle. *Id.*

[4] Good Faith Basis for Asserting Claim

Simply sending notice of a "potential (UM / SUM) claim", devoid of any real good faith basis, is insufficient because that potential exists in the vast majority of motor vehicle accident cases. *American Cas. Ins. Co. v. Silverman*, 271 A.D.2d 528, 705 N.Y.S.2d 676, 677 (2d Dep't 2000) (hypothetical letter insufficient to notify insurer of intention to make claim). Similarly, notice of a no-fault claim does not satisfy the notice requirement. *In the Matter of Metropolitan Property and Casualty Company v. Mancuso*, and *Nationwide Insurance Co. v. DiGioachino*, 931 N.Y.2d 487, 112, 693 N.Y.S.2d 81, 86 (1999).

[5] Notice of Intention to File MVAIC Claim

A notice of intention to file a MVAIC claim must be served on MVAIC within 180 days of the date of the accident. *Ins. Law §5208(a)(1).* See §4.08[3][a] below.

§ 4.05 Statutes of Limitations

[1] UM and SUM Claims

Claims asserted against an insurer exist solely by way of the insurance contract. Thus, such claims are governed by a six-year statute of limitations. *CPLR §213.* The claimant's cause of action does not accrue until s/he possesses the legal right to be paid and the ability to enforce the right in court. Thus, for example, the right to payment under an under-insured motorist claim does not accrue until after the tortfeasor's liability coverage is fully exhausted by payment. *See Continental Ins. Co. v. Richt,* 253 A.D.2d 818, 819, 677 N.Y.S.2d 634, 635 (2d Dep't 1999) (cause of action does not accrue until claimant possesses legal right to be paid).

[2] MVAIC Claims

The statute of limitations to file a lawsuit against MVAIC is the same as in any motor vehicle negligence claim. Generally, the statute of limitations is three years from the date of the accident, or two years from the date of death in a wrongful death case. *See Hickman v MVAIC,* 75 N.Y.2d 975, 556 N.Y.S.2d 506 (1990) (petitioner entitled to toll limitations period to commence wrongful death action against MVAIC during period court was considering petitioner's application for leave to file late notice of intention to make claim).

PART C: UNINSURED MOTORIST CONTEXT

§ 4.06 Purpose of Uninsured Motorist Coverage

The purpose of uninsured motorist insurance coverage is to compensate victims of motor vehicle accidents where compensation is not otherwise available. No liability insurance policy may be issued unless it contains a mandatory uninsured motorist (UM) endorsement which provides coverage up to $25,000 per person and $50,000 per accident (or 50/100 where death occurs). *Ins. Law §3420 (f)(1), 1995 Laws, ch. 305, "Uninsured Motorist Endorsement – New York".* If, for an additional premium, an insurance policy contains supplementary uninsured / under-insured motorist (SUM) coverage, the SUM coverage will apply to the uninsured motorist situation, taking precedence over the mandatory UM endorsement. *See 11 NYCRR §60-2.3(e).* The UM and the SUM endorsement are essentially the same (with respect to uninsured motorist claims), with minor variations, except that the SUM coverage provides greater policy limits. UM coverage applies to accidents that occur in New York State (or in another state, so long as it has a similar mandated minimum UM coverage). *Ins. Law §3420(f)(1).* SUM coverage applies so long as the accident occurred in the United States (or in one of its possessions / territories) or Canada. *11 NYCRR §60-2.3(e)(III).*

§ 4.07 Determining Whether Tortfeasor's Motor Vehicle Uninsured

[1] Any *One* Tortfeasor Uninsured

In order to have a potential uninsured motorist claim, it first must be determined whether the tortfeasor's vehicle is uninsured. Where there are multiple tortfeasors / defendants and any *one* qualifies as an uninsured motorist, the claimant may properly bring an uninsured motorist claim.

[2] Vehicle Stolen or Used Without Owner's Permission

A vehicle which is stolen or used without the owner's express or implied permission is deemed uninsured. *See 11 NYCRR §60-2.3(f)(c)(1), Ins. Law §3420(f)(1)*. However, where the tortfeasor's vehicle was driven by someone other than the owner, there is a strong presumption of permissive use pursuant to *Vehicle & Traffic Law §388. See General Accident Ins. Co. v. Bonefont*, 277 A.D.2d 379, 380, 716 N.Y.S.2d 596 (2d Dep't 2000) (very strong presumption of permissive use exists). This presumption can, however, be rebutted. The filing of a police report can be used to rebut the presumption of permissive use.

> **Practice Tip:** The claimant should demand arbitration against the uninsured motorist carrier as soon as there is a permissive use issue. Where there is a third-party action pending and the defendant denies permissive use either in the answer, a response to a notice to admit, or at an examination before trial, an uninsured motorist arbitration demand should be made. Once the demand for arbitration is made, the uninsured motorist insurance carrier will likely bring a petition to stay the arbitration. The two insurance companies will litigate the issue via a framed-issue hearing (i.e., a quick trial on the issue of permissive use) and the judge will determine which claim is viable and which one is not (as between the first-party and third-party claims). The claimant should not wait for the trial in the third-party action before demanding the uninsured motorist arbitration, as potentially years of time, effort, and interest will be wasted.

[3] Vehicle Unregistered

An unregistered vehicle is uninsured. *11 NYCRR §60-2.3(f)(c)(1), Ins. Law §3420(f)(1)*. Unregistered vehicles automatically fall within the statutory meaning of "uninsured", whether or not they are actually insured.

[4] Tortfeasor's Insurance Policy Cancelled or Not Renewed

Where the tortfeasor's vehicle did not have valid insurance coverage on the date of the accident, the vehicle is considered uninsured, *see Ins. Law §3420(f)(1)*, so long as the stringent cancellation requirements were complied with. *See VTL §313. See also American Home Assurance Co. v. Chin*, 269 A.D.2d 24, 708 N.Y.S.2d 453 (2d Dep't 2000) (notice of cancellation not in compliance with *VTL §313* held ineffective and invalid). Under New York law, an insurance policy cannot be retroactively canceled as against an innocent third-party, even where fraud or misrepresentation in procuring the insurance policy exists. *Integon Ins. Co. v. Goldson*, 300 A.D.2d 396, 751 N.Y.S.2d 527 (2d Dep't 2000) (retroactive cancellation of automobile insurance policy based upon fraud by insured not permitted in New York unless claimant participated in fraud).

[5] Conditions Precedent Where Hit and Run by Unidentified Vehicle

In order to be able to utilize uninsured motorist coverage in regard to a hit and run by an unidentified vehicle, certain conditions precedent must be met, as follows:

- Identity Unascertainable: The claimant must be unable to ascertain the identity of the driver *and* owner of the "hit and run" vehicle. *See 11 NYCRR §60-2.3(f)(d)(2), Franke v. MVAIC*, 53 A.D.2d 614, 384 N.Y.S.2d 20 (2d Dep't 1976).

- Physical Contact: There must have been physical contact, direct or indirect, with the claimant or claimant's vehicle by a vehicle driven by a person whose identity is unascertainable. *See Ins. Law §§3420(f)(3), 5217; see also 11 NYCRR §60-2.3(f)(c)(2).* If not (e.g., where claimant was cut-off and swerved into a pole), the uninsured motorist claim will be barred. If one vehicle starts a "chain reaction" and is not identified, direct contact with that car is not required so long as contact somehow existed with another car as a result. *See Allstate Ins. Co. v. Killakey*, 78 N.Y.2d 325, 574 N.Y.S.2d 927 (1991) (indirect contact with claimant's vehicle sufficient).

- Promptly Report to Police: The claimant, or somebody on the claimant's behalf, must report the accident to the police, a peace officer, or the Commissioner of Motor Vehicles within 24 hours or as soon as reasonably possible. *See 11 NYCRR §60-2.3(f)(c)(2).* Otherwise, an uninsured motorist claim will be barred.

- Sworn Statement: A sworn statement setting forth all the elements necessary for this claim must (as set forth above) be sent to the UM carrier within 90 days of the date of the accident. *See 1995 Laws, ch. 305, "Uninsured Motorist Endorsement – New York".* The 90-day limitation has been eliminated with respect to the SUM endorsement, *see 11 NYCRR §60-2.3(f)(c)(2)(I),* although it is better practice to send it out within the 90-day time period nonetheless. The statement must set forth that the claimant has a cause of action arising out of such incident for damages against a person whose identity is unascertainable, as well as the facts thereof. *Id. See Matter of Allstate v. Estate of Aziz*, 17 A.D.2d 460, 793 N.Y.S.2d 138 (2d Dep't 2005).

- Inspection of Vehicle: At the request of the insurer, the claimant must make the vehicle (which the insured person was occupying at the time of the accident) available for inspection. *See 11 NYCRR §60-2.3(f)(c)(2)(I).*

[6] Tortfeasor's Liability Disclaimed or Coverage Denied

Where the tortfeasor's insurance carrier disclaims liability or denies coverage with respect to a third-party negligence claim, the UM or SUM insurance carrier will determine whether the disclaimer was made in a timely manner as required by *Insurance Law §3420(d)*. An example is where there is a lack of cooperation by the insured, resulting in the denial of coverage by his or her insurance company.

Disclaimer notices are required to notify both the "insured" and the injured of the disclaimer in writing. *See Ins. Law §3420(d)*. Although the claimant's attorney is required to provide timely notice to the UM or SUM insurance carrier for the uninsured claim to proceed, the failure to do so may be overcome if neither the claimant nor the claimant's attorney received a timely disclaimer from the third-party tortfeasor's insurance carrier. *See Wasserheit v. New York Central Mutual Fire Ins. Co.*, 271 A.D.2d 439, 705 N.Y.S.2d 638 (2d Dep't 2000) (four-month delay held unreasonable as matter of law).

> **Practice Tip:** Where the third-party insurance carrier disclaims liability or denies coverage, the claimant's attorney should simply demand an uninsured motorist arbitration against the UM or SUM insurance carrier. The UM or SUM insurance carrier will then litigate the insurance issue with the third-party carrier, while the claimant's attorney avoids all the legal work necessary in bringing a declaratory judgment action.

> **Practice Tip:** A demand for an uninsured motorist arbitration should be made even in the case where there are two defendants in the third-party action – where one is providing coverage and the other is disclaiming. The uninsured motorist demand will ultimately provide a resolution to the insurance issue, for the UM or SUM insurance carrier will bring a petition to stay the arbitration on the grounds that the disclaimer is invalid. In such an instance, the plaintiff / claimant's attorney must be cognizant of the uninsured motorist coverage limits versus the third-party coverage limits and argue accordingly at the framed-issue hearing.

[7] Tortfeasor's Insurance Carrier Insolvent

Depending on the specific facts (as discussed below), an injured party may be able to properly bring an uninsured motorist claim where the tortfeasor's insurance carrier is insolvent. Where an injured policy holder is entitled to insurance coverage through a UM endorsement (but not SUM coverage from his or her own insurer), and the alleged tortfeasor's insurer has paid into the New York Public Motor Vehicle Liability Security Fund ("PMV Fund") but has been declared insolvent after the underlying accident, the injured policyholder's recourse is not against his or her own insurer for UM coverage; rather, the injured policyholder's recourse is against the PMV Fund via the superintendent. *See Ins. Law Article 74*. An insured who has purchased SUM coverage may seek benefits upon the insolvency of the tortfeasor's insured, and need not proceed against the PMV Fund. *See Eagle Ins. Co. v. Hamilton*, 4 A.D.3d 355, 773 N.Y.S.2d 68 (2d Dep't 2004), *recalled and vacated*, 16 A.D.3d 498, 791 N.Y.S.2d 605 (2d Dep't 2005); *see also American Manufacturers Mut. Ins. v. Morgan*, 296 A.D.2d 491, 745 N.Y.S.2d 726 (2d Dep't 2002). Where the insolvency is of a non-New York insurer which did not contribute to the PMV Fund, the vehicle is deemed uninsured. *See Taub v. MVAIC*, 31 A.D.2d 378, 298 N.Y.S.2d 212 (1st Dep't 1969).

[8] Out-of-State Policy with Less Than NYS Minimum Policy Limits

Where the offending vehicle in an accident occurring within New York State is covered for less than the New York minimum coverage requirements (by an insurer not authorized to do business in New York), the tortfeasor is deemed uninsured. *Neals v. Allstate Ins. Co.*, 34 A.D.2d 265, 311 N.Y.S.2d 315 (2d Dep't 1970). However, where the insurer is authorized to conduct business in New York State, it must provide liability coverage (for the NYS accident) equal to the New York State minimum insurance policy limits.

§ 4.08 MVAIC Claim

[1] MVAIC – In General

A person who is injured in an accident involving an uninsured motor vehicle and is not covered under an uninsured motorist endorsement (i.e., UM or SUM) may bring a claim against Motor Vehicle Accident Indemnification Corporation (MVAIC). *Matter of St. John*, 105 A.D.2d 530, 481 N.Y.S.2d 787 (3d Dep't 1984); *see MVAIC Act, Ins. Law §§5201-5225*. MVAIC is a non-profit corporation that is capitalized by an assessment against all insurers writing motor vehicle liability policies in New York State. *See Ins. Law §§5203, 5206, 5207.* MVAIC provides a minimum required policy ($25,000 per claimant up to a maximum of $50,000 per accident; and $50,000 for death of one person and $100,000 for death of more than one person) for a claimant to pursue. *Ins. Law §5210.* A MVAIC claim is available for the same reasons in which an uninsured motorist claim is available – the only difference being that a MVAIC claim is only available where the claimant does not have access to any uninsured motorist coverage. *See Ins. Law §§3420(f)(1), 5201.* To bring a claim against MVAIC, the claimant must be a New York State resident (or be a resident of another state that provides recourse similar to MVAIC). *Ins. Law §5202(b).*

[2] MVAIC Exclusions

Pursuant to *Ins. Law §5201, t*he following are excluded from MVAIC coverage:

- injuries or death of a person driving in violation or suspension of driving privileges;
- claims against persons not liable under law;
- accidents caused by government vehicle(s); and
- hit and run claims that fail to meet the statutory requirements for such claims (see §4.07[5] above).

[3] Conditions Precedent to Lawsuit Against MVAIC
[a] Notice of Intention to File MVAIC Claim

A notice of intention to file a MVAIC claim must be served on MVAIC within 180 days of the date of the accident (or within 180 days of an insurance company's denial of coverage or disclaimer of liability). *Ins. Law §5208(a).* A claimant may seek court leave to file a late notice of intention within one year after the commencement of the filing period. *Ins. Law §5208(c).* A notice of intention to file a MVAIC claim must be sent to MVAIC (in triplicate)[5], along with a MVAIC no-fault form (timely), and a copy of the police accident report. The notice of intention requires the claimant to provide the names and dates of birth of all household members (i.e., so MVAIC can determine whether there is a valid insurance policy, such as a UM or SUM policy, to pursue instead of MVAIC).

[b] MVAIC Statement Under Oath

MVAIC may investigate any claim. *See Ins. Law §§5206, 5208.* Often MVAIC sends a representative / investigator to the claimant's home (or attorney's office) to take a written statement from the claimant. Questions generally focus on attempting to find a valid insurance policy (of tortfeasor, claimant, or claimant's resident-relatives / spouse), in order to disclaim MVAIC coverage. Questions regarding liability and damages are generally asked, as well.

[4] Commencing Lawsuit Against MVAIC

Once the conditions precedent are complied with, permission must be asked of the New York State Supreme Court for leave to sue MVAIC. In doing so, a notice of petition and a petition for leave to sue (under *Ins. Law §5102*) are necessary.

Practice Tip: When dealing with a hit-and-run accident with a known uninsured defendant, the plaintiff's attorney may wish to first sue the owner and driver; then, the plaintiff's attorney can notify MVAIC of the lawsuit via certified mail, return receipt requested (along with a copy of the pleadings), and demand that they appear and answer for the defendant(s). If they choose not to, a default judgment will undoubtedly be entered against the owner / operator. If payment is not made within 30 days, an application can then be made to have MVAIC, as a joint and several tortfeasor, make payment on the judgment.

---

[5] Assigning Claim to MVAIC

As a condition to payment of a settlement, the claimant must assign his or her claim (against the financially irresponsible motorist) to MVAIC, which is then subrogated to all of the claimant's rights against the financially irresponsible motorist. *Ins. Law §5213.*

---

5   MVAIC, 110 William Street, 19th Floor, New York, New York 10038, www.mvaic.com, (646) 205-7800.

PART D: UNDER-INSURED MOTORIST CONTEXT

§ 4.09 Purpose of Under-insured Motorist Coverage

Where the claimant's damages exceed the amount of the tortfeasor's insurance coverage, the claimant will attempt to exhaust the tortfeasor's coverage and then proceed against the SUM insurance carrier for under-insured motorist coverage, if available. The claimant's attorney will need a "tender" (of the insurance policy) letter from the third-party insurance carrier in order to proceed with the SUM claim.

> **Example:** Where the tortfeasor in a third-party claim only has a $25,000 liability policy, but the claimant has a $100,000 SUM policy, the claimant can attempt to collect up to $75,000 (i.e., $100,000 less the $25,000) from the SUM carrier. To be entitled to seek the additional coverage through the SUM carrier, however, the claimant must first exhaust the tortfeasor's entire policy.

SUM coverage applies so long as the accident occurred in the United States (or in one of its possessions / territories) or Canada. *11 NYCRR §60-2.3(e)(III)*.

§ 4.10 Determining Whether Under-insured Motorist Coverage is Triggered

The claimant's liability insurance coverage limits must be greater than the tortfeasor's liability coverage in order to trigger under-insured motorist coverage (because SUM limits can never be greater than the liability limits on the same policy). *See Ins. Law §3420(f)(2)(A), Liberty Mutual Ins. Co. v. D'Antonio*, 266 A.D.2d 393, 697 N.Y.S.2d 532 (2d Dep't 1999). Otherwise, there cannot be an under-insured claim. The claimant must ascertain the limits of the tortfeasor's insurance coverage in order to make an under-insured motorist claim. Where a request is made to the tortfeasor's insurance carrier for the insurance coverage limits, the carrier is required to provide such information within 45 days. *Ins. Law §3420 (f)(2)(A)*.

§ 4.11 Determining Whether Offsets Exist

Once insurance coverage is triggered, the claimant's SUM coverage limits will determine the amount of SUM coverage available to the claimant. The available SUM coverage is offset by the amount the claimant has already received from the third-party tortfeasor(s). *See Regulation 35-D at 11 NYCRR §60-2.3(a)(2), III(5)(h)*.

> **Example:** Suppose the claimant is in a two-car accident where the tortfeasor's insurance carrier tenders its 25/50 policy, and the claimant has 100/300 liability coverage and 100/300 SUM coverage. Under-insured motorist benefits are triggered because the claimant's liability coverage is greater than the tortfeasor's. While the claimant's SUM coverage is $100,000, it is reduced by the $25,000 the claimant has already received. Therefore, the total available SUM coverage is $75,000.

§ 4.12 Providing SUM Carrier Notice of Legal Action

As a condition precedent to SUM insurance coverage, the claimant or claimant's attorney is required to "immediately" provide the SUM insurer with a copy of the summons and complaint and other legal papers served in connection with the underlying lawsuit against the tortfeasor in order to protect the insurance company's subrogation rights as against the tortfeasor. *Regulation 35-D* at *11 NYCRR §60-2.3(e)III(4)*. Failure to do so may preclude the claimant from obtaining coverage through the SUM policy. *Nationwide Mut. Ins. Co. v. Charles*, 275 A.D.2d 324, 325, 712 N.Y.S.2d 578, 579 (2d Dep't 2000) (nine month delay in sending summons and complaint violated Notice of Legal Action condition of insurance policy and vitiated coverage).

> **Practice Tip:** Enforcement of the Notice of Legal Action provision requires a timely notice of disclaimer by the insured. *See Hess v. Nationwide Mut. Ins. Co.*, 273 A.D.2d 689, 690, 709 N.Y.S.2d 701, 703 (3d Dep't 2000) (untimely disclaimer will be held invalid); *see also McEachron v. State Farm Insurance Company*, 295 A.D.2d 685, 742 N.Y.S.2d 925, 926 (3d Dep't 2002) (lengthy delay without reasonable explanation will be unreasonable as a matter of law).

§ 4.13 Exhausting of Primary Coverage

The claimant must exhaust the insurance policy of a single tortfeasor before proceeding with an under-insured claim. *See Regulation 35-D* at *11 NYCRR §60-2.3 III(9)*.

> **Example:** Where the third-party insurance carrier offers the claimant $24,999 of a $25,000 policy, acceptance by the claimant would bar an under-insured motorist claim (unless the remainder of the policy was already paid out to other claimant[s]).

> **Practice Tip:** Once one tortfeasor's insurance policy is exhausted (or at least tendered), the plaintiff's attorney must analyze the situation and decide whether to pursue another tortfeasor or the under-insured motorist coverage, depending on which policy provides greater additional coverage.

The SUM insurance carrier will require proof of exhaustion. That is, the claimant's attorney must provide a copy of the tortfeasor's declarations page and an affidavit from the tortfeasor (provided by his or her insurance company) that there is no excess or umbrella coverage applicable to the case.

§ 4.14 Receiving Consent to Settle

With respect to an under-insured motorist claim, the claimant's attorney must obtain the SUM insurance carrier's permission prior to settling with the third-party tortfeasor. *See Regulation 35-D* at *11 NYCRR §60-2.3 III(10)*. The claimant's attorney cannot simply send a general release to the tortfeasor's insurance company – even if they have tendered their policy. Otherwise, the claimant and the claimant's attorney may be violating the subrogation rights of the SUM carrier (discussed below). *See Regulation 35-D at 11 NYCRR §60-2.3 III(13), Friedman v. Allstate Insurance Co.*, 268 A.D.2d 558, 703 N.Y.S.2d 198 (2d Dep't 2000) (failure to obtain written consent from under-insured carrier precluded insured from asserting claim for under-insured motorist benefits).

The SUM insurance carrier must either consent to the settlement *or* advance the amount of the tortfeasor's insurance policy offered within 30 days (plus 5 additional days for mailing); otherwise, the SUM carrier is deemed to have consented to the settlement. *Id. See also State Farm Mut. Auto Ins. Co. v. Callisto*, 255 A.D.2d 876, 680 N.Y.S.2d 39, 40 (4th Dep't 1998). Thus, if the SUM carrier consents, the claimant may proceed with the under-insured motorist claim. If, however, the SUM carrier does not consent because it wants to utilize its subrogation right to pursue a lawsuit against the tortfeasor (i.e., because s/he has substantial assets), the SUM carrier is required to: (i) advance the money offered by the tortfeasor's insurance carrier to the claimant's attorney and (ii) take an assignment of the claim. *See Regulation 35-D at 11 NYCRR §60-2.3 III (10).*

> **Example:** L is the liability insurance carrier, U is the under-insured motorist insurance carrier. L tenders its policy. The claimant needs U's permission to settle the case. In a reasonable time, U must consent to the settlement or pay the claimant and take an assignment of the claimant's third-party negligence claim.

PART E: UNINSURED OR UNDER-INSURED MOTORIST ARBITRATION

§ 4.15 Demanding Arbitration

The claimant may commence an uninsured or under-insured action by either filing a lawsuit or demanding arbitration. The claimant may choose between suing or demanding arbitration only when there is SUM coverage; when there is only UM coverage, and hence the limits are 25/50, the claimant's only option is to demand arbitration. *See Regulation 35-D at 11 NYCRR §60-2.3 III(12).*

> **Practice Tip:** Demanding arbitration is usually preferable because it is much quicker, less costly, much less time-consuming, and the decision cannot be appealed.

The demand for arbitration must be served on the American Arbitration Association (AAA) via certified mail. *See CPLR Article 75.* The AAA will provide the claimant's attorney with the required forms, upon request.

§ 4.16 Petitions to Stay Arbitration

[1] 20-Day Rule

The UM / SUM insurance carrier may bring a petition to stay the arbitration. *See CPLR Article 75*. The UM / SUM insurance carrier must move to stay the arbitration within 20 days from receipt of the demand for arbitration or it shall be precluded from doing so. *CPLR §7503(c)*. The demand for arbitration must mention the insurer's right to seek a stay within 20 days of receipt of the notice, pursuant to *CPLR §7503(c)*. The 20 days is a statute of limitations and, hence, a court cannot extend it. If the demand for arbitration incorrectly identifies the applicable insurance policy, it is deemed an improper demand and, thus, the insurer is not bound by the 20-day limitation. If the insurance carrier fails to obtain a stay, the claimant may proceed to arbitration.

> **Practice Tip:** Where the claimant's attorney, shortly after the accident, sends the UM/SUM carrier a certified letter claiming no-fault benefits and UM/SUM benefits, plus a statement stating that "claimant intends and provides this notice of intention to demand arbitration," this is sufficient notice for which the carrier only has 20 days to bring a motion to demand a stay. *GEICO v. Castillo-Gomez*, 34 A.D.3d 477, 824 N.Y.S.2d 159 (2d Dep't 2006) (carrier precluded from asserting that tortfeasor was uninsured because clock started with claimant's attorney's initial demand letter, which complied with all the statutory requirements).

[2] Exception to 20-Day Rule

The only exception to the 20-day rule is where the application to stay is based on the ground that no agreement to arbitrate exists. *See Matarasso v. Continental Casualty Co.*, 56 N.Y.2d 264, 451 N.Y.S.2d 703 (1982).

> **Example:** Assume a claimant ("C") makes a claim against her mother's SUM policy on the ground that her mother is a resident-relative. Where the SUM carrier claims that C's mother is not a resident-relative of C's (i.e., either they did not live together or they are not relatives), a stay can be sought after the 20-day period on the ground that no agreement to arbitrate exists.

[3] Permanent Stay Versus Temporary Stay

The claimant's insurance carrier may seek a permanent stay (alleging, for example, an improper uninsured motorist claim) or a temporary stay (seeking for time to complete some limited discovery). Usually, the insurance carrier will ask for a permanent stay and, in the alternative, a temporary stay. See §4.16[5] below.

[4] Burden of Persuasion

An insurer seeking to stay arbitration has the burden of proof (e.g., proving that the offending vehicle was insured at the time of the accident). *See Transportation Ins. Co. v. Phillips*, 248 A.D.2d 392, 669 N.Y.S.2d 860 (2d Dep't 1998). Once a *prima facie* case of insurance coverage is established, *see Brogan v. New Hampshire Ins. Co.*, 250 A.D.2d 562, 673 N.Y.S.2d 156 (2d Dep't 1998) (*prima facie* case of insurance coverage established via submission of police accident report or DMV records), the burden shifts to the claimant to produce evidence to the contrary; the claimant then must offer proof that the vehicle was never insured or that such insurance coverage was canceled. *Id.*; *Travelers Property Cas. Co. v. Schoenheimer*, 676 N.Y.S.2d 902 (Sup. Ct. N.Y. Cty. 1998).

[5] Discovery Demands

Pursuant to the insurance contract, insurers are entitled to a statement by the claimant (either a tape recorded telephone statement or an examination under oath), a physical examination of the claimant, and authorizations to obtain relevant medical records.

Sometimes a petition to stay arbitration will be brought by the insurance carrier in order to obtain discovery. In the petition to stay the arbitration, the insurance carrier often asks the court, to the extent the permanent stay is not granted, to require the respondent (i.e, the claimant) to submit to the discovery (namely the examination under oath and the independent medical examination). *See Allstate Ins. Co. v. Baez*, 269 A.D.2d 392, 702 N.Y.S.2d 878 (2d Dep't 2000) and *Peerless Ins. Co. v. McDonough*, 269 A.D.2d 398, 702 N.Y.S.2d 880 (2d Dep't 2000) (arbitrations temporarily stayed allowing insured to obtain discovery).

The respondent / claimant can oppose late discovery demands on the ground that the insurance carrier waived its right to discovery by waiting for the arbitration demand to request same. *See Interboro Mut. Indemnity Co. v. Pardon*, 270 A.D.2d 266, 704 N.Y.S.2d 834 (2d Dep't 2000) (insurer waived right to discovery because it failed to utilize opportunity prior to commencement of proceeding within which to seek discovery).

§ 4.17 Arbitration Brief

Prior to the arbitration (at least 10 days prior), the claimant's attorney should prepare an arbitration brief to serve on his or her adversary (i.e., the UM / SUM insurance carrier's attorney) and the arbitrator. Once the case proceeds to arbitration, the only issues for the arbitrator to consider are liability and damages. That is, the issue as to whether or not the case was properly brought pursuant to the UM / SUM endorsement of an insurance policy is no longer an issue at the time of the arbitration. If the case proceeds to arbitration, the claimant already prevailed on the UM / SUM issue.

Practice Tip: The arbitration brief should include: a cover sheet, a table of contents, a brief statement of facts, a liability section, a damages section (including injuries, treatment, results of objective testing, surgeries, photographs, lost time from work, loss of earnings, liens, and the amount of damage to the vehicles, if significant), and a conclusion (which should be rather simple, but should include a demand). Accident reports, medical records and reports, photographs, and any other relevant documentation which supports the plaintiff's claims should be annexed as exhibits.

CHAPTER 5

PREMISES LIABILITY

PART A: OVERVIEW

§ 5.01 Overview – Premises Liability

Premises liability is a term that encompasses a wide-range of negligence cases. A premises liability case emanates from an accident, and resulting injury, which occurs on someone's premises. In this chapter, various types of premises liability cases are discussed in depth, including the following:

- slip / trip and fall accidents, in general;
- sidewalk accidents;
- snow and ice accidents;
- transient substance (e.g., fruit, debris, water, oil) accidents;
- lead-paint poisoning;
- sports-related accidents;
- negligent service of alcohol;
- negligent security / intentional torts; and
- dog bites.

PART B: ELEMENTS OF PREMISES LIABILITY CAUSE OF ACTION

§ 5.02 Examining Elements of Premises Liability Cause of Action

[1] "Reasonable Care" Standard

In premises liability cases, liability of an owner or possessor of land is measured by the single standard of "reasonable care under the circumstances." *Basso v. Miller*, 40 N.Y.2d 233, 241, 386 N.Y.S.2d 564, 568 (1976) (setting forth standard). *Basso* abolished the common-law rule that the duty owed by an owner or possessor of land varied depending on the plaintiff's status as licensee, invitee, or trespasser. *Peralta v. Henriquez*, 100 N.Y.2d 139, 760 N.Y.S.2d 741 (2003). The jury may, however, factor the plaintiff's status into its evaluation of the "reasonableness" of the defendant's conduct. *Basso v. Miller*, 40 N.Y.2d 233, 240, 386 N.Y.S.2d 564, 573 (1976).

Exception: Infants (i.e., under 18 years of age) are held to the standard of conduct of a reasonably prudent child of the same age, sex, experience, and knowledge. *See PJI §§2:48-2:49.*

[2] Prerequisites for Liability in Premises Liability Case

In proving liability in a premises liability case, the plaintiff's attorney must initially be able to establish that, on the date of the accident, the target defendant(s):

- owned;
- controlled;
- occupied;
- maintained; or
- made "special use" of the premises.

See Portaro v. Tillis Inv. Co., 304 A.D.2d 635, 757 N.Y.S.2d 606, 607 (2d Dep't 2003); *see also Warren v. Wilmorite, Inc.*, 211 A.D.2d 904, 621 N.Y.S.2d 184 (3d Dep't 1995) (liability for dangerous condition on property generally predicated upon ownership, occupancy, control, or "special use" of the property). Occupancy and control of the premises are the key prerequisites for liability. *See Morrone v. Chelnik Parking Corp.*, 268 A.D. 2d 268, 701 N.Y.S.2d 48, 49 (1st Dep't 2000) (landlord entitled to summary judgment because lessee was responsible for maintenance and repair, and landlord maintained no control over premises).

The plaintiff's attorney must also be able to identify the dangerous or defective condition which caused the accident.

[3] Required Elements for Liability in Premises Liability Case

Once the prerequisites for liability are established, the plaintiff's attorney's task is to prove at least one of the following:

- The defendant *created* the dangerous or defective condition, *see Peralta v. Henriquez*, 100 N.Y.2d 139, 145, 760 N.Y.S.2d 741, 745 (2003) (defendant's creation of dangerous condition may relieve plaintiff's obligation of proving notice of that condition);
- The defendant had *actual notice* of the dangerous or defective condition;
- The defendant had *constructive notice*, meaning that the defendant *should have known*, of the dangerous or defective condition;
- The defendant *violated an applicable statute, code, or ordinance.* See §5.02[4] below; and/or
- The doctrine of *res ipsa loquitur* applies to the case. See §5.02[5] below.

THE LAWYERS' GUIDE TO PERSONAL INJURY LAW

Practice Tip: The plaintiff's attorney should attempt to prove as many of the above elements as possible. If the case does not fall into at least one of the above categories, it will generally not be worthy of pursuit. However, if the plaintiff's attorney can, at a minimum, create an issue of fact regarding one or more of the required elements (along with proximate cause), a motion for summary judgment can be defeated. *See CPLR § 3212(b).* This will allow for a potentially significant settlement or verdict.

[4] Violation of Statute, Code, or Ordinance

The violation of a statute may give rise to absolute liability, constitute negligence *per se*, or constitute *prima facie* evidence of negligence. The distinction between absolute liability and negligence *per se* is that the comparative negligence defense is available only in the case of negligence *per se*, but not where absolute liability is imposed. *See Lopes v. Rostad,* 45 N.Y.2d 617, 412 N.Y.S.2d 127 (1978). A violation of a statute will constitute negligence *per se* when the statute defines a standard of care to be applied to a particular situation, and that standard has not been met. *See Schmidt v. Merchants Despatch Transp. Co.,* 270 N.Y. 287, 200 N.E. 824 (1936). *See PJI §§2:25-2:28.*

The violation of an ordinance, regulation, or administrative code is *some evidence of negligence*, where the violation was a proximate cause of the accident. *See Ferrer v. Harris,* 55 N.Y.2d 285, 449 N.Y.S.2d 162 (1982). For example, a violation of the Administrative Code of the City of New York (which encompasses the "NYC Building Code") constitutes some evidence of negligence, regardless of whether the provision is specific. *Elliott v. City of New York*, 95 N.Y.2d. 730, 724 N.Y.S.2d 397 (2001). *See PJI §2:29.*

Practice Tip: There is no requirement that the plaintiff plead or prove violations of statute, code, or ordinance, but they certainly can bolster a case. Sometimes an alleged violation can be the difference in defeating a defendant's motion for summary judgment. Further, the ability to offer proof of such violations at trial can often be dispositive. Employing an expert (e.g., professional engineer) is typically the best way to determine if any such violations exist.

[5] *Res Ipsa Loquitur*

[a] *Res Ipsa Loquitur* – In General

The plaintiff's attorney should always keep the doctrine of *res ipsa loquitur*, Latin for "the thing speaks for itself", in mind – whether conducting depositions, defending a motion for summary judgment, discussing settlement, selecting a jury, or on trial. In a *"res ipsa"* case, negligence can be inferred, simply from the happening of the accident and the defendant's relation to it. This means that, if certain circumstances are present, the plaintiff does not have to offer any evidence of actual or constructive notice of the dangerous or defective condition, as notice may be inferred under *res ipsa loquitur*. *See Dittiger v. Isal Realty Corp.*, 290 N.Y.492, 49 N.E.2d 980 (1942). Examples of cases where *"res ipsa"* may apply include: a collapsing deck, an elevator accident (*see Myron v. Millar Elevator Industries, Inc.*, 182 A.D.2d 558, 582 N.Y.S.2d 201 [1st Dep't 1992]), and a door falling off its hinges (*see Pavon v. Rudin*, 254 A.D.2d 143, 679 N.Y.S.2d 27 [1st Dep't 1998]).

[b] Elements of *Res Ipsa Loquitur*

In order for *res ipsa loquitur* to apply, the following three elements must exist:

- the event, or the accident, was of a kind that ordinarily does not occur in the absence of negligence; and
- the event was caused by an agency or instrumentality within the exclusive control of the defendant (often a question for the jury); and
- the event was not due to any voluntary action or contribution on the part of the plaintiff.

See Raimondi v. New York Racing Association, 213 A.D.2d 708, 709, 624 N.Y.S.2d 273 (2d Dep't 1995) (setting forth elements necessary for submission of case to jury on theory of *res ipsa loquitur*).

With respect to the last element (above), however, a plaintiff can be found comparatively negligent in a *"res ipsa"* case. For example, where the plaintiff had no control over the misleveling of an elevator, s/he can still be held partially at fault for the trip and fall. *Burgess v. Otis Elevator Co.*, 114 A.D.2d 784, 785, 495 N.Y.S.2d 376, 379 (1st Dep't 1985) (*res ipsa loquitur* properly charged and plaintiff held comparatively negligent).

It is not required that only one person / entity be in control for *res ipsa loquitur* to apply. For example, *res ipsa loquitur* can be charged in a case where the owner of a building *and* the elevator maintenance company have exclusive control over the elevator. *Myron v. Millar Elevator Industries, Inc.*, 182 A.D.2d 558, 582 N.Y.S.2d 201 (1st Dep't 1992). Evidence, however, of third-parties having access to the instrumentality negates the inference of negligence on behalf of the one normally in control, namely the defendant.

> **Practice Tip:** There is a great deal of case law involving *res ipsa loquitur*. The plaintiff's attorney should, at a minimum, review the case law to determine the types of cases in which *res ipsa loquitur* was found to apply, and found not to apply. *See PJI §2:65.*

[c] Proving Specific Acts of Negligence as Alternative

Because a *"res ipsa"* jury charge creates only an inference of negligence (which can be rebutted by the defense), the plaintiff must be prepared (at trial or on a summary judgment motion) to also offer evidence of negligence (or otherwise risk losing the case). The jury will decide between conflicting inferences. *See States v. Lourdes Hosp.*, 100 N.Y.2d 208, 762 N.Y.S.2d 1 (2003).

Plaintiff's claims may be based upon specific acts of negligence <u>and</u> *res ipsa loquitur* and, thus, a judge may charge the jury on both. *Rosetti v. Board of Education of Schalmont Central School District*, 277 A.D.2d 668, 671, 716 N.Y.S.2d 460, 462 (3d Dep't 2000) (plaintiff not precluded from relying on *res ipsa loquitur* notwithstanding introducing specific acts of negligence). Evidence of specific acts of negligence may, however, negate the inference of negligence; this will only occur where the showing of precisely how the accident occurred diminishes the likelihood of the defendant's negligence. *See Abbott v. Page Airways, Inc.*, 23 N.Y.2d 502, 513, 297 N.Y.S.2d 713 (1969).

[6] Proximate Cause

For liability to attach, the negligence of the owner or possessor of the premises must be a proximate cause of the injuries sustained. *See Olsen v. Richfield*, 81 N.Y.2d 1024, 599 N.Y.S.2d 912 (1993). Essentially, the plaintiff must show that the defendant's conduct was a substantial causative factor in the sequence of events that led to the plaintiff's injury. *Nallan v. Helmsley-Spear, Inc.*, 50 N.Y.2d 507, 429 N.Y.S.2d 606 (1980). The issue of proximate cause is for the finder(s) of fact to determine once a *prima facie* case has been established. *See Olsen v. Richfield*, 81 N.Y.2d 1024, 599 N.Y.S.2d 912 (1993). There can be more than one proximate cause to an accident. *Kalam v. K-Metal Fabrications, Inc.*, 286 A.D.2d 603, 730 N.Y.S.2d 299 (1st Dep't 2001).

§ 5.03 Comparative Negligence / Assumption of Risk

Comparative negligence applies to most premises liability cases. Pursuant to comparative negligence principles, plaintiff's fault may proportionately diminish his or her recovery, but will not preclude recovery unless plaintiff was solely at fault. *CPLR §1411.* Plaintiff may, however, be precluded from recovery where his or her actions were a serious violation of law and the injuries were sustained as a result of that violation. *Alami v. Volkswagon of America, Inc.*, 97 N.Y.2d 281, 739 N.Y.S.2d 867 (2002). Where it is alleged that the injury-causing defect was an "open and obvious" condition, this presents a question for the jury regarding comparative negligence. *Sewitch v. LaFrese*, 41 A.D.3d 695, 839 N.Y.S.2d 114 (2d Dep't 2007); *see also Imtanios v. Goldman Sachs*, 44 A.D.3d 383, 843 N.Y.S.2d 369 (1st Dep't 2007). "Implied" assumption of risk – where plaintiff voluntarily encounters the risk with a full understanding of the possible harm – also allows for comparative negligence, serving to proportionately diminish plaintiff's recovery.

"Primary" and "express" assumption of risk, however, bar recovery for a plaintiff. Primary assumption of risk applies where the activity in which the plaintiff is voluntarily participating (e.g., playing a sport) is inherently risky and the injury-causing event is a known, apparent, or reasonably foreseeable consequence of such participation. *Turcotte v. Fell*, 68 N.Y.2d 432, 510 N.Y.S.2d 49 (1986). See §5.12. Express assumption of risk involves an agreement between the parties in advance that the defendant need not use reasonable care for the benefit of the plaintiff and will not be liable to the plaintiff as a result of negligent conduct. *Arbegast v. Board of Education*, 65 N.Y.2d 161, 490 N.Y.S.2d 751 (1985).

PART C: PREMISES LIABILITY INTAKE

§ 5.04 Gathering Information at Premises Liability Intake

[1] Liability

At the intake meeting with the prospective client, the attorney needs to gather as much information as possible. In preliminarily assessing liability, the attorney should obtain:

- a description of the incident;
- a description of the dangerous / defective condition that caused the accident;
- the date, time, and precise location of the accident;
- photographs of the accident scene, if any;
- the names of the potentially responsible entities and/or persons;
- accident reports, if any;
- the names, addresses, and phone numbers of any witnesses to the accident;
- the names, addresses, and phone numbers of any people, known as notice witnesses, who have made complaints to the potential defendant(s) about the dangerous or defective condition prior to the accident; and
- additional information related to the accident, including the lighting, type of flooring, type of shoes worn, weather conditions, and whether the injured party was under the influence of any drugs/medications or disability which may have caused dizziness or poor vision at the time of the accident.

[2] Damages

In assessing a prospective client's potential damages, the attorney should inquire regarding the following:

- the extent of the injuries;
- the names and addresses of all hospitals, physicians, and other healthcare providers (such as physical therapists) utilized in connection with the injuries;
- whether any surgery has been performed;
- whether there is any future surgery or treatment scheduled or recommended;
- whether there are any potential economic losses;
- whether the injured party had photographs taken which depict the injuries; and

- whether the injured party ever previously injured the same part(s) of the body claimed to have been injured in the present accident.

Obtaining a copy of all related medical records is essential, for the prospective client may not know the precise nature of the injuries. Further, the medical records (especially the ambulance call report and the emergency room records) often impact liability (for there may be descriptions of the accident). See chapter 10, §10.04[2].

[3] Venue

Venue possibilities should also, preliminarily, be explored at intake. In doing so, the attorney should obtain the address of the potential client, the names and addresses of the potential defendants, and the address of the accident location. See §5.05[4] and §5.17[3] below.

§ 5.05 Deciding to Accept, Reject, or Investigate Premises Liability Case

[1] Factors to be Considered

In deciding whether to accept, reject, or investigate the case, the attorney should conduct an analysis of the following key factors:

- liability;
- potential damages;
- potential insurance coverage;
- venue; and
- the applicable statute of limitations and other conditions precedent to litigation.

Each of these factors is discussed below.

[2] Weighing Liability and Damages

Proving liability in a premises liability case is often a difficult task which can be time-consuming. Several years of work may be involved, including taking numerous depositions of defendants and defending motions for summary judgment. Further, retaining a professional engineer and/or other expert, along with hiring an investigator, make proving liability in a premises liability case costly for the plaintiff's attorney.

Moreover, premises liability cases are often susceptible to a defendant's motion for summary judgment on the issue of liability. This means the plaintiff's attorney may end up spending significant time and money – over the course of several years, with the case ultimately being dismissed.

Thus, the plaintiff's attorney must be selective in deciding which premises liability cases s/he wishes to be retained on. If the damages are not significant (i.e., confirmed sizeable injury such as a fracture, surgery, tear, or significant scarring, or significant economic losses), it is probably not wise to pursue such an action. If the damages are significant (as confirmed by medical records), the plaintiff's attorney must assess the facts to determine whether s/he believes a *prima facie* showing of negligence can be set forth. The plaintiff's attorney should also gather the medical records (including the ambulance call report and the emergency room records) and obtain witness statements to determine potential liability hurdles. See chapter 10, §10.04[2].

> **Practice Tip:** Attempting to prove a premises liability case with only minor damages, such as "soft-tissue" injuries, translates into significant work and disbursements with limited economic upside. Premises liability cases with significant damages, even where liability is questionable, have a far greater upside; these cases are of great concern to insurance companies due to the potential exposure – especially in plaintiff-friendly venues.

[3] Insurance Coverage

Another factor to be considered is potential insurance coverage. In premises liability cases, insurance coverage usually exists, and is generally sufficient (with typical policies being $300,000 or greater) to cover cases with significant damages.

> **Practice Tip:** Where an accident occurs in a residential tenant's dwelling, the tenant will often be uninsured, and thus, the plaintiff's attorney should assess a potential case against the owner.

> **Warning:** The attorney should be cognizant that certain types of cases may pose insurance problems. Intentional torts, for example, will generally be committed by people who do not have any insurance. Moreover, even if there is insurance coverage in place, intentional torts are generally excluded from the insurance policy coverage. Further, there are an increasing number of insurance policies with exclusions for lead-paint poisoning. See §§5.11-5.15 below.

> **Practice Tip:** A negligence cause of action can be brought where intentional torts are committed (e.g., negligent hiring, negligent supervision, or negligent security), thereby circumventing potential insurance coverage deficiencies. See §5.15 below.

[4] Considering Venue

Venue possibilities may be the difference between accepting and rejecting certain premises liability cases. The plaintiff's attorney controls the venue of the case at the outset, choosing where to file the lawsuit. Forum shopping for the most plaintiff-friendly venue can be the most important decision of the case. Venue, in a negligence lawsuit, is generally based upon any residence of the plaintiff or any defendant on the date the lawsuit is commenced. *See CPLR §504.*

There are additional venue considerations with respect to corporations and municipalities, as set forth in *CPLR §§503, 505*. See also chapter 7, §7.07. Information should be obtained regarding the injured party's residence(s), as well as sufficient residence information regarding the potential defendants, in order to be able to determine the venue possibilities. See §5.04[3] above and §5.17[3] below.

Practice Tip: Being able to bring the case in counties such as Erie, Kings, and the Bronx generally provides a great advantage to the plaintiff, whereas counties such as Westchester, Nassau, and Suffolk generally provide a similar edge to the defendant.

[5] Statutes of Limitations and Conditions Precedent to Litigation

The applicable statute of limitations must also be taken into account at the intake. Generally, there is a three-year statute of limitations regarding negligence cases. *CPLR §214.*

Practice Tip: Where the statute of limitations date is approaching, the attorney should be very careful before accepting a premises liability case. There are often responsible parties whose names are not yet known at the time of intake, and do not become known until almost a year later through discovery and depositions. Accepting a premises liability case two or more years after the accident may eventually result in a legal malpractice situation.

The attorney should also be aware that where a municipality is involved, there are stringent notice of claim requirements (generally 90 days from the date of the accident) and a shortened statute of limitations (generally one year and 90 days from the date of accident). See chapter 7, §§7.05, 7.12. Further, the attorney should be mindful of the shortened statute of limitations periods associated with intentional torts (one year) and wrongful death cases (two years from the date of death or the applicable statute of limitations period, whichever is shorter). *See CPLR §§210, 215.* The attorney should also be cognizant that the statute of limitations period (but not notice of claim time limitations) for infants (i.e., under 18 years of age) is automatically tolled during the infancy. *See CPLR §208.* See §5.17[3] below.

§ 5.06 Premises Liability Retainer Agreement

[1] Retainer Agreement in Premises Liability Case – In General

If the attorney decides to accept the premises liability case, the client must sign a retainer agreement. A premises liability retainer agreement should set forth the contingency fee; the standard contingency fee (and maximum allowed contingency fee in a non-medical malpractice personal injury case) is 33 1/3% of the net recovery. The retainer agreement should set forth the fact that all disbursements such as fees for court costs, process servers, medical records, investigators, experts, and other costs are to be reimbursed at the conclusion of the case. The *net* recovery is then used to compute the attorney's contingency fee. Further, the retainer agreement should also make clear that all liens are the sole responsibility of the client, and are to be paid out from the client's share of the proceeds. The premises liability retainer agreement should explicitly list liens, such as workers' compensation, Medicaid, Medicare, Department of Social Services, and medical liens, as the client's responsibility.

[2] Scope of Representation in Premises Liability Retainer Agreement

The premises liability retainer agreement should expressly exclude representation for workers' compensation, New York State Disability claims, and appellate work. It should clearly state that the attorney is being retained to represent the plaintiff regarding a third-party negligence claim only. The retainer agreement should state that the law firm is accepting the case subject to investigation. This will allow the attorney to terminate the agreement at any time prior to litigation, for any reason such as a determination that liability is poor or the injuries are minor.

[3] Executing Authorizations

At the same time the client signs the retainer agreement, s/he should also sign several sets of authorizations to obtain medical records, employment records, and workers' compensation records (if applicable) and/or other collateral source records at the intake. This will allow the attorney to obtain copies of the records, as well as to send authorizations to the tortfeasor's claims representative regarding evaluation and possible settlement of the case.

[4] Filing OCA Retainer Statement

After becoming retained, a retainer statement must be promptly filed with the Office of Court Administration (OCA). A self-addressed stamped postcard should be included for OCA to stamp the retainer number which must then be used on the closing statement at the conclusion of the case. In the event that the retainer statement is not timely filed, an attorney's affirmation setting forth the reason for lateness and a request that the retainer statement be filed *nunc pro tunc* (i.e., as if it were filed timely) should be included.

§ 5.07 Conducting Proper Investigation in Premises Liability Case

Proper investigation and use of experts is crucial in premises liability cases. It is essential to obtain photographs of the accident site and witness statements soon after the accident. Also, the ambulance call report, emergency room records, and medical records typically contain descriptions of the accident and, hence, must be obtained. Further, depending on the type of case and severity of the injuries, retaining an expert, such as a professional engineer, early-on can greatly impact the outcome of the case. Unless the injuries are substantial, however, it usually does not make economic sense to hire an investigator or expert.

Practice Tip: The plaintiff has a sizeable advantage regarding investigation of a premises liability case, for the investigation often takes place before the defendant and its insurance carrier are aware of the accident and/or the potential lawsuit. Once, however, the defendant's insurance carrier becomes aware of the claim, they will have significant resources to conduct a thorough investigation and build a case. Hence, it is essential for the plaintiff's attorney to promptly investigate. Otherwise, a decisive advantage will shift to the defendant once their investigation commences.

PART D: EVALUATING PARTICULAR TYPES OF PREMISES LIABILITY CASES

§ 5.08 Sidewalk Cases

[1] General Rule

The owner, or person in possession, of property abutting a public sidewalk is generally not liable to the plaintiff for an accident occurring on the public sidewalk unless:

- a local ordinance gives the abutting landowner the responsibility to maintain the sidewalk *and* imposes tort liability on the abutting landowner for failure to do so; or
- the abutting landowner *created* the dangerous condition (e.g., patchwork on the sidewalk); or
- the abutting landowner utilized that part of the sidewalk for a "special use" (e.g., a newspaper vending machine, basement trap door, or driveway).

See Bloch v. Potter, 204 A.D.2d 672, 673, 612 N.Y.S.2d 236, 237 (2d Dep't 1994) (setting forth standard). In the event the claim falls into one of the three enumerated categories above, the plaintiff must still set forth all the required elements of a negligence claim. See §5.02 above; see also chapter 7, §§7.21, 7.22.

[2] Sidewalk Claims in City of New York

For all accidents occurring after September 14, 2003, the City of New York has shifted the responsibility (along with tort liability) for sidewalk maintenance onto the abutting landowners, except with regard to one, two, or three-family residential properties that are at least partially owner-occupied and used exclusively for residential purposes. *NYC Admin. Code §7-210.* Further, where the abutting landowner is either uninsured or under-insured, a claimant may qualify for a city disbursement. The City of New York, however, remains responsible for trees and tree wells, as they are not intended for pedestrian use and are, therefore, not considered part of the sidewalk. *Vucetovic v. Epsom Downs, Inc.*, 45 A.D.3d 28, 841 N.Y.S.2d 301 (1st Dep't 2007). See chapter 7, §§7.21, 7.22.

> **Practice Tip:** *New York City Administrative Code §7-210* places the responsibility on "property owners", not possessors or lessees. Hence, even an out-of-possession owner is liable for sidewalks; leasing a premises to a store will not relieve this non-delegable duty imposed on the premises owner.

[3] "Open and Obvious" and "De Minimis Defect" Defenses

In sidewalk cases, the defendants will rely on the "open and obvious" defense, as well as the "de minimis defect" defense, placing plaintiffs in the unenviable position of proving the defect was too small to be "open and obvious", yet too large to be "de minimis". The "open and obvious" doctrine does not preclude a liability finding, but rather presents a question for the jury regarding comparative negligence. *Sewitch v.*

LaFrese, 41 A.D.3d 695, 839 N.Y.S.2d 114 (2d Dep't 2007); *see also Imtanios v. Goldman Sachs*, 44 A.D.3d 383, 843 N.Y.S.2d 369 (1st Dep't 2007).

If the claim is that the accident was caused by an elevation between two sidewalk slabs, the plaintiff must provide evidence quantifying the defect; otherwise, the court will conclude it is immaterial. *See Morales v. Riverbay Corporation*, 226 A.D.2d 271, 641 N.Y.S.2d 276, 277 (1st Dep't 1996) (one inch differential between sidewalk slabs without characteristics of trap or snare held to be nonactionable). *See also Hawkins v. Carter Community Housing Development Fund*, 40 A.D.3d 812, 835 N.Y.S.2d 731 (2d Dep't 2007) (1.25" - 1.5" deep gap between adjacent sidewalk slabs not actionable because defect lacked characteristics of trap or snare and was too trivial). Whether a particular height difference between slabs constitutes a dangerous or defective condition depends on the case-specific facts. Factors to be considered include width, depth, elevation, irregularity, and appearance of the defect, as well as the time, place, and circumstances of the injury. *See McKenzie v. Crossroads Arena, LLC*, 291 A.D.2d 860, 861, 738 N.Y.S.2d 779, 780 (4th Dep't 2002). There is no requirement that a sidewalk defect be a certain minimum size in order for liability to be imposed. *See McKenzie v. Crossroads Arena, LLC*, 291 A.D.2d 860, 861, 738 N.Y.S.2d 779, 780 (4th Dep't 2002) (3/4 inch height differential between concrete slabs held not to be trivial defect, particularly where height differential was not gradual, but abrupt). *See also Zalkin v. City of New York*, 36 A.D.3d 801, 828 N.Y.S.2d 485 (2d Dep't 2007) (3/4 inch height differential held too trivial to be actionable).

§ 5.09 Snow and Ice Cases
[1]Public Sidewalks
[a] General Rule Regarding Public Sidewalks

Public sidewalks are generally the responsibility of the municipality. *See Tremblay v. Harmony Mills*, 171 N.Y. 598, 601 (1902). A landowner of property abutting a public sidewalk generally does not owe a duty to pedestrians to remove natural accumulations of snow and ice from the public sidewalk. *See Roark v. Hunting*, 24 N.Y.2d 470, 477, 301 N.Y.S.2d 59 (1996) (case dismissed as responsibility for maintaining sidewalk rested upon municipality, not abutting landowner). See chapter 7, §7.22 regarding municipal liability in snow and ice cases.

[b] Landowner Responsible for Public Sidewalk Where Liability Shifted Via Statute or Ordinance

A landowner of property abutting a public sidewalk is responsible to clear the snow and ice from the public sidewalk where a local municipal statute or ordinance shifts the responsibility to the abutting landowner and imposes *tort* liability upon the landowner in favor of the injured pedestrian. *See City of Rochester v. Campbell*, 123 N.Y. 405, 414, 25 N.E. 937, 939 (1890). New York City, for example, has shifted the responsibility (along with tort liability) for sidewalk maintenance onto the abutting landowners, except with regard to one, two, or three-family residential properties that are at least partially owner-occupied and used exclusively for residential purposes. *NYC Admin. Code §7-210*. Thus, in the City of New York, an owner of property abutting a sidewalk is liable for a dangerous condition of that sidewalk, including snow and ice. *See Martinez v. City of New York*, 20 A.D.3d 513 (2d Dep't 2005). Once the abutting landowner is placed with the responsibility, the general rules regarding clearance of snow apply in determining whether the landowner was negligent in its snow and ice removal efforts (or lack thereof). See §§5.09[2] and 5.09[3] below.

> **Practice Tip:** As discussed in §5.08[2] above, *New York City Administrative Code §7-210* places the responsibility on "property owners", not possessors or lessees. Hence, even an out-of-possession owner is liable for sidewalks, including snow and ice; leasing a premises to a store will not relieve the non-delegable duty imposed on the premises owner.

[c] Landowner Liable for Negligent Repair or "Special Use" of Public Sidewalk

Where the abutting landowner negligently repairs the public sidewalk or his or her "special use" of the public sidewalk results in a defective condition, and ice forms as a result of the defect created, the abutting landowner may be held liable. *See Blum v. New York*, 267 A.D.2d 341, 342, 700 N.Y.S.2d 65, 66 (2d Dep't 1999) (case dismissed where no proof that defendant created dangerous or defective condition or caused such condition by use of their driveway). Examples of "special use" include driveways, newspaper vending machines, and street vendors. Liability may also be imposed on a landowner whose unreasonable obstruction of a sidewalk causes an injury to a pedestrian while walking on the icy street. *See Fleischer v. White Rose Food Corp.*, 152 A.D.2d 489, 543 N.Y.S.2d 456, 457 (1st Dep't 1989) (plaintiff injured while forced to walk around parked truck blocking sidewalk, slipping on ice patch).

[d] Additional Landowner Liability for Public Sidewalk

A landowner of property abutting a public sidewalk may also be held liable for snow and/or ice on the public sidewalk where:

- snow and ice are transferred by artificial means from the abutting premises to the public sidewalk; or
- water is permitted to flow from the property, by artificial means, to the public sidewalk where it freezes. *See Roark v. Hunting*, 24 N.Y.2d 470, 475, 301 N.Y.S.2d 59, 62 (1969) (no evidence that water flowed from building or any other instrumentality owned or controlled by defendants).

Examples include: (i) melted snow dripping from a sign; (ii) allowing water from a broken well to run out onto the road; and (iii) a drainage leader discharging water from a roof onto the sidewalk.

[2] Liability Where Notice of Snow / Ice Condition
[a] "Storm in Progress" Doctrine

A party in possession or control (i.e., landowner, tenant-in-possession, management company, snow removal contractor, and/or maintenance company) of real property (i.e., private property, or public sidewalk where responsible, as discussed in §5.09[1][b] above) has a reasonable period of time after the cessation of a storm to take protective measures to correct storm-created hazardous ice and snow conditions. *See Whitt v. St. Johns Episcopal Hospital*, 258 A.D.2d 648, 685 N.Y.S.2d 789 (2d Dep't 1999) (defendant entitled to summary judgment where storm ceased only 5 to 6 hours before accident). In the City of New York, property owners are given four hours after a storm ceases within which to clear snow and ice, excluding the hours of 9 p.m. to 7 a.m. from the calculation. *NYC Admin. Code §16-123*. Thus, a landowner has no responsibility for removing snow and ice from his or her property while a storm is in progress. *See Baum v. Knoll Farm*, 259 A.D.2d 456, 686 N.Y.S.2d 83 (2d Dep't 1999) (defendant entitled to summary judgment where plaintiff testified it was snowing at time of accident). See chapter 7, §7.22 regarding municipal liability in snow and ice cases.

[b] Cessation of Storm

A party in possession or control (e.g., landowner and/or tenant-in-possession) may be held liable under a notice theory where the storm ceased in enough time to clear the snow and ice from the premises. *See Gonzalez v. American Oil Co.*, 836 N.Y.S.2d 611 (1st Dep't 2007) (question of fact as to whether defendant had constructive notice of ice condition created by snowfall day prior). However, where the property owner is a municipality, even where the municipality is responsible to clear snow and ice, the municipality will be afforded more leeway. *See Garricks v. City of New York*, 1 N.Y.3d 22, 769 N.Y.S.2d 152 (2003); *see also Martinez v. Columbia Presbyterian Med. Ctr.*, 238 A.D.2d 286, 656 N.Y.S.2d 271 (1st Dep't 1997) (city not obligated to clear snow within 48 hours where two large snow storms struck in a row).

Practice Tip: In a snow and ice case, the plaintiff's attorney should order the weather records from the National Oceanic and Atmospheric Administration (NOAA) of the National Climatic Data Center (NCDC) showing daily precipitation totals and surface weather observations on the date of the accident and the few weeks prior. For example, being able to show that the snow and ice was from 7 days prior to the date of accident helps to prove notice. These records can be ordered at www.noaa.com or by calling (828) 271-4800. A meteorologist can also be retained to interpret the weather records and provide an expert opinion for opposing a motion for summary judgment (and, ultimately, trial).

[3] Liability Where Natural Hazard is Increased

A party in possession or control of a sidewalk may also be held liable where the snow and ice removal actually *creates* a dangerous condition, increasing the natural hazard. *See Zahn v. New York*, 299 N.Y. 581, 86 N.E.2d 105 (1949) (owner responsible where he caused snow to be piled on sidewalk); *see also Joseph v. Pitkin Carpet, Inc.*, 44 A.D.3d 462, 843 N.Y.S.2d 586 (1st Dep't 2007) (plaintiff failed to show that defendant's snow removal efforts actually made the sidewalk more dangerous, resulting in dismissal of the action). Where a landowner (or tenant-in-possession, snow removal contractor, and/or building maintenance contractor) *does* clear snow and ice while a storm is in progress, s/he can be held liable for creating or exacerbating a dangerous condition. *See Rugova v. 2199 Holland Avenue Apartment Corp.*, 272 A.D.2d 261, 262, 708 N.Y.S.2d 390, 391 (1st Dep't 2000) (summary judgment improperly granted where issue of fact existed as to whether defendant made sidewalk more dangerous by clearing away snow and revealing patches of ice that were not properly removed).

§ 5.10 Transient Substance Cases

[1] Proving Actual or Constructive Notice, as Opposed to General Awareness

Transient substance cases involve accidents which result from a dangerous condition that only temporarily exists. Examples include slip and fall accidents on water, debris, fruit, wax, oil, etc. These cases are very difficult for a plaintiff to prove, as a general awareness by the defendant regarding transient conditions is not sufficient to hold the defendant liable. Rather, the plaintiff must prove that the defendant created, or had actual or constructive notice of, the condition. *See Gordon v. American Museum of Natural History*, 67 N.Y.2d 836, 837, 501 N.Y.S.2d 646, 647 (1986) (case dismissed where accident occurred on litter in crowded outdoor area, on front steps of popular museum). To establish constructive notice in transient substance cases, the condition must be visible and apparent and must have existed for a sufficient length of time prior to the accident so that the defendant's employees had an opportunity to discover and remedy it. *Id.*

[2] Distinguishing Between General Awareness and Recurring Condition

Courts have distinguished between a "general awareness" and a "recurring condition" in transient substance cases. They have reasoned that actual notice of a "recurring condition" is qualitatively different from a mere "general awareness" that a dangerous condition may be present. *See Weisenthal v. Pickman*, 153 A.D.2d 849, 851, 545 N.Y.S.2d 369, 371 (2d Dep't 1989) (slip and fall on litter in stairwell, which court found could have been cleaned on a daily basis, was held to be "recurring condition"). *See also Bido v. 876-882 Realty, LLC*, 41 A.D.3d 311, 839 N.Y.S.2d 54 (1st Dep't 2007) (oily substance a recurring condition and, therefore, actionable). The defendant can be held liable where it had notice of a "recurring condition", as opposed to a "general awareness". *Sewitch v. LaFrese*, 41 A.D.3d 695, 839 N.Y.S.2d 114 (1st Dep't 2007) (ice, within missing portions of brick and mortar on steps, as recurring condition).

[3] Proving Defendant Created Condition

In transient substance cases, proof that the defendant created the condition, such as the negligent application of wax or polish, can establish actual notice. *See Lewis v. Metropolitan Transit Authority*, 99 A.D.2d 246, 251, 472 N.Y.S.2d 368, 372 (1st Dep't 1984) (complaint dismissed where no evidence defendant created, or had actual or constructive notice of, the slippery substance on train).

§ 5.11 Lead Paint Poisoning Cases

[1] New York City's Local Law 1

When claiming injury due to lead-based paint (e.g., where a child ingested paint chips from the wall or inhaled lead through dust), there are different levels of proof required depending on whether New York City's Local Law 1 applies. See Local Law, 1982, of the City of New York, Sec. 1 (codified at *NYC Admin. Code §27-2013[h][2]*). The Court of Appeals recognized Local Law 1 (which presumes the existence of lead in New York City multiple dwellings built prior to 1960 in which a child less than seven years of age resides) and noted that no legislation exists requiring the landowner to test for, or abate, lead-based paint hazards absent official notification of a problem. *See Chapman v. Silber* and *Stover v. Robilotto*, 97 N.Y.2d 9, 15, 734 N.Y.S.2d 541, 543 (2001) (consolidated decision).

The court held that, absent controlling legislation, a triable issue of fact is raised (i.e., the case cannot be dismissed on defendant's motion for summary judgment) when the defendant:

- retained a right of entry and assumed a duty to make repairs;
- knew the apartment was constructed before lead-based paint was banned (i.e., pre-1960);
- was aware the paint was peeling in the premises;
- knew of the hazards of lead to young children; and
- knew a young child lived in the apartment.

Id. See also Matter of New York City Coalition to End Lead Poisoning Inc. v. Vallone, 100 N.Y.2d 337, 350, 736 N.Y.S. 530, 536 (2003) (Local Law 38 [1999] of the City of New York rendered null and void, reviving Local Law 1 [1982]). The Court of Appeals' holding in *Chapman* also applies to non-multiple dwellings in the City of New York. *See Bellony v. Siegel*, 288 A.D.2d 411, 732 N.Y.S.2d 647 (2d Dep't 2001) (applying *Chapman* holding to two-family house).

> **Practice Tip:** The plaintiff must (at a minimum) establish issues of fact that the landlord had actual notice of all the factors above as a prerequisite to finding constructive notice of a lead hazard, hence defeating a defendant's motion for summary judgment.

In addition, the City of New York enacted a bill in 2004, known as the *Childhood Lead Prevention Act.* See Local Law 1 (2004) of the City of New York. This law requires *corrections* of all lead paint hazards, including but not limited to lead dust-generating friction surfaces and protruding window sills that could be a teething hazard for young children in their apartments and in common areas of the building. Landlords are held accountable for using reasonable care. As such, corrections of lead paint hazards need to be performed by trained workers and followed up with proper testing for dust-clearing. Landlords may leave toxic lead paint on inside surfaces of dwellings as long as reasonable measures (e.g., permanent covering of lead paint) are taken to protect young children.

[2] Cases Where New York City's Local Law 1 Not Applicable

In premises liability cases where New York City's Local Law 1 does not apply, the plaintiff cannot rely on the statutory presumption that paint in older buildings in New York City contains lead, but rather must establish the necessary elements under common-law negligence:

- that the premises were not reasonably safe;
- that the defendant had actual or constructive notice of the defective lead-based condition; and
- that the defendant's negligence was a substantial factor in causing the plaintiff's injuries.

See Perry v. Walter Uccelini Enterprises Inc., 275 A.D.2d 495, 711 N.Y.S.2d 631 (3d Dep't 2000).

The courts have been generous to plaintiffs in terms of establishing notice in lead-paint cases. Evidence of unsatisfactory levels of lead leading to earlier violations in other units in the same building is admissible to establish notice. *See Rodriguez v. Amigo*, 244 A.D.2d 323, 325, 663 N.Y.S.2d 873, 875 (2d Dep't 1997) (actual notice of prior lead condition in another apartment in same building as plaintiff created issue of fact as to constructive notice of lead in plaintiff's apartment).

[3] Evaluating Extent of Injuries

Also of great significance in lead-paint poisoning cases is the level of lead in the blood. *New York Public Health Law §1370(6)* defines elevated lead level as "a blood level greater than or equal to 10 micrograms per deciliter of whole blood." Levels below 10 mcg/dcl are thus non-actionable. *See Pub. Health Law §1370(6); see also 10 NYCRR §67-1.1(d), New York City Health Code, 24 R CNY §11.03.*

> **Practice Tip:** From a plaintiff's perspective, levels greater than 10 mcg/dcl are toxic and cause brain damage and other irreversible injuries. Examples include nervous and reproductive system developmental disorders, delays in neuropsychological and physical development, cognitive and behavioral changes, hypertension, and hyperactivity. Young children are particularly susceptible to lead exposure. Levels as low as 2 mcg/dcl in children less than seven years old lowers IQ, stunts growth, and causes behavioral disorders. *See Williamsburgh Around the Block Association v. Giuliani*, 223 A.D.2d 64, 66, 644 N.Y.S.2d 252, 254 (1st Dep't 1996). The injuries need to be identified and confirmed by a neuropsychological evaluation.

[4] Insurance Issues

When handling lead-paint cases, the plaintiff's attorney should also be aware that many insurance policies do not include coverage for lead-based paint cases.

Practice Tip: The plaintiff's attorney must attempt to have all insurance carriers (i.e., for each year child lived at residence and was thus exposed to the lead) placed on notice of a claim. Thus, although one or more insurers may disclaim based upon a lead paint exclusion in the insurance policy, at least one year's policy may provide coverage.

§ 5.12 Sports-Related Injury Cases

With respect to sports, the plaintiff assumes all risks known, apparent, or foreseeable. *See Capello v. Village of Suffern*, 232 A.D.2d 599, 600, 648 N.Y.S.2d 699, 700 (2d Dep't 1996) (plaintiff assumed risk of injury inherent in playing basketball on court he knew to be slippery). This doctrine of primary assumption of risk relieves a defendant of its duty of reasonable care and is a complete bar to recovery. *See Schneider v. Levittown Union Free School Dist.*, 303 A.D.2d 394, 756 N.Y.S.2d 276 (2d Dep't 2003) (chance of getting hit in eye with ball during game of "war" was inherent risk in game). The doctrine of "assumption of risk", however, should not be applied with the same force against a "neophyte", as opposed to that of an experienced athlete in the sport. *Calouri v. County of Suffolk*, 43 A.D.3d 456, 841 N.Y.S.2d 598 (2d Dep't 2007); *see also Morales v. Beacon City School District*, 843 N.Y.S.2s 646 (2d Dep't 2007) (question of fact as to whether defendant "unreasonably increased risk of injury because it negligently supervised and trained plaintiff," a novice hurdler).

However, the plaintiff assumes only the risks inherent in the game and not those beyond the game. *See Royal v. City of Syracuse*, 765 N.Y.S.2d 560, 561 (4th Dep't 2003) (failure of cheerleading coach to provide spotter for cheerleader unreasonably increased risk of injury). Thus, in order for a plaintiff to succeed in a sports-related injury case, a risk beyond the sport must be demonstrated, such as a defective court, field, or equipment. *See Clark v. State of New York*, 245 A.D.2d 413, 666 N.Y.S.2d 209 (1997) (basketball player did not assume risk of injury caused by steep drop-off of several inches from edge of playing area's asphalt surface); *see also Cole v. New York Racing Association*, 241 A.D.2d 993, 266 N.Y.S.2d 267, 269 (2d Dep't 1965) (defendant race track was negligent in erecting and maintaining raised concrete footing under track's railing which was proximate cause of jockey's death). *See PJI §2:55.*

Exception: Express assumption of risk is inapplicable to a child under four years of age who, as a matter of law, is incapable of being responsible for his or her actions. *See Smith v. Sapienza*, 115 A.D.2d 723, 724, 496 N.Y.S.2d 538, 540 (2d Dep't 1985).

§ 5.13 Cases Involving Service of Alcohol

[1] *General Obligations Law §§ 11-101* and *11-100*

When the individual tortfeasor (who generally has few assets and no insurance coverage) was intoxicated at the time of the incident, the plaintiff's attorney should explore the possibility of liability against the "dram shop" (i.e., the bar, restaurant, convenience store, etc.). The Dram Shop Act states that for liability to exist, the claimant must establish that the "dram shop" furnished an alcoholic beverage to a "visibly intoxicated person". *See GOL §11-101.* To recover under *GOL §11-101*, a plaintiff must prove the following four elements:

- an unlawful sale
- of liquor
- to an intoxicated person
- which caused injury.

See Catania v. 124 In-To-Go Corp., 287 A.D.2d 476, 477, 731 N.Y.S.2d 207, 208 (2d Dep't 2001) (rule as stated in case where intoxicated nightclub patron assaulted plaintiff after being served alcohol while visibly intoxicated). Notwithstanding the potential liability of the owner of the premises under *GOL §11-101*, the owner has no duty to determine whether or not each departing patron is fit to drive safely, or to take steps to prevent intoxicated patrons from driving. *See Vale v. Yawarski*, 78 Misc.2d 522, 357 N.Y.S.2d 791 (Sup. Ct. Herkimer County 1974).

Another section of the General Obligations Law, *GOL §11-100*, does not require a sale to take place, but rather covers liability where the following three elements are met:

- furnishing alcohol
- to any person under 21 years of age
- who, by reason of the intoxication or impairment, caused injury.

GOL §11-100.

[2] Evidence Required in "Dram Shop" Cases

An expert's affidavit offered as the sole evidence to defeat a motion for summary judgment must contain sufficient allegations to demonstrate that its conclusions are more than mere speculation and would, if offered alone at trial, support a verdict in the proponent's favor. *See Romano v. Stanley*, 90 N.Y.2d 444, 451, 661 N.Y.S.2d 589, 592 (1997) (expert's affidavit insufficient to raise triable issue of fact where expert's conclusions not based on laboratory tests, but rather were found to be speculative and conclusory). The plaintiff will generally need evidence of the alcohol level in the blood or urine and/or evidence of how much the tortfeasor was drinking, in addition to expert testimony. The plaintiff's claim should be brought under both the Dram Shop Act and common-law negligence (i.e., notice of dangerous condition).

§ 5.14 Dog Bite Cases
[1] Strict Liability – In General

Dog bite cases should be brought under both strict liability and common-law negligence theories. To recover under strict liability for an injury inflicted by a domestic animal, the plaintiff must establish that:

- the animal had vicious propensities; and
- the defendant (i.e., the dog owner and/or keeper and/or landlord) knew or should have known of the animal's vicious propensities.

See Bard v. Jahnke, 6 N.Y.3d 592, 597, 815 N.Y.S.2d 16, 848 N.E.2d 463 (2006); *see also Collier v. Zambito*, 1 N.Y.3d 444, 446, 775 N.Y.S.2d 205, 807 N.E.2d 254 (2004).

[a] Strict Liability Against Landlord

Landlords may be subject to strict liability where they have control of the premises and knowledge of the vicious propensities. S*ee Baisi v. Gonzalez*, 97 N.Y.2d 694, 739 N.Y.S.2d 92 (2002) (issues of fact present as to landlord's knowledge of presence of dog with vicious propensities and landlord's control of premises, so as to allow him to remove or confine dog).

[b] "Vicious Propensity"

Courts refuse to take judicial notice of vicious propensities, such as a finding that a pit bull is inherently dangerous. S*ee Carter v. Metro North Associates*, 255 A.D.2d 251, 680 N.Y.S.2d 239, 240 (1st Dep't 1998) (alternative opinions on subject of propensities of pit bull terriers as a breed precludes judicial notice). Thus, evidence of inherently vicious propensities of a particular breed is inadmissible.

The courts have defined vicious propensity as any act which might endanger another, *see Lagoda v. Dorr*, 28 A.D.2d 208, 209, 284 N.Y.S.2d 130, 132 (3d Dep't 1967) (dog chained to garage, trained and used as watchdog, jumped on and chased people in past was sufficient to raise issue of fact for jury), and therefore even playful behavior may constitute vicious propensity. *See Provorse v. Curtis*, 288 A.D.2d 832, 732 N.Y.S.2d 310, 311 (4th Dep't 2001) ("muzzle greet" may be playful behavior, but may nonetheless endanger safety of another). A "Beware of Dog" sign, absent other evidence of vicious propensity, is insufficient to raise an issue of fact regarding vicious propensity. *See Lugo v. Angle of Green, Inc.*, 268 A.D.2d 567, 702 N.Y.S.2d 608, 609 (2d Dep't 2000).

[c] Proving "Vicious Propensity"

In proving vicious propensity, the plaintiff's attorney should research the animal's history. The local Society for the Prevention of Cruelty to Animals (SPCA) generally has a database of all dogs and any prior incidents, since police, healthcare facilities, ambulances, and local Departments of Health are required to report incidents to them. The NYC Department of Health also maintains records of prior reported dog bites. The *New York State Dangerous Dog Law*, encompassed in *New York State Agriculture and*

Markets Law §121, and also incorporated into local laws, requires a detailed database on adjudicated "dangerous dogs". *See Agric. & Mkts. L. §121.*

At the deposition, the plaintiff's attorney should inquire about:

- a history of prior bites or similar incidents, if any;
- the breed and size of the dog;
- whether the dog was trained, and to what extent;
- where and how the dog is normally kept (and the dog's normal behavior there), as well as the number of doors or gates, if any, that were secured;
- whether the dog has a history of barking, growling, and/or displaying its teeth, and with what frequency;
- whether the owner uses a leash, chain, or muzzle for the dog, and whether the dog pulls on the chain or leash, tends to break away from the chain or leash, or has otherwise escaped the premises;
- the dog's disposition towards people, whether the dog tends to jump up onto people, and how often;
- whether the owner displays any "Beware of Dog" signs; and
- whether veterinary care and shots have been provided for the dog, and what medication, if any, the dog was taking.

[2] Common-Law Negligence Cause of Action

A cause of action under common-law negligence should also be brought, although unlikely to prove successful; the courts have, in very limited situations, held that a defendant's breach of a duty of care may result in the imposition of liability. Under common-law negligence, the plaintiff only has to prove negligence in harboring the dog and that the injuries were foreseeable; proving vicious propensity is not required. *See Colarusso v. Dunne*, 286 A.D.2d 37, 39, 732 N.Y.S.2d 424, 426 (2d Dep't 2001). A cause of action for common-law negligence may be essential where the history of known vicious propensities is weak. *Id. See also Goldberg v. Lorusso*, 288 A.D.2d 257, 259, 733 N.Y.S.2d 117, 119 (2d Dep't 2001) (defendant's motion for summary judgment denied notwithstanding lack of evidence of vicious propensity). A violation of a local leash law, in and of itself, is generally not dispositive of finding a breach of a duty on the part of the dog owner, *see Vavosa v. Stiles*, 220 A.D.2d 363, 365, 632 N.Y.S.2d 791, 793 (1st Dep't 1995) (leash law violation by itself not necessarily dispositive of negligence, but rather only some evidence of negligence), although it could constitute some evidence of negligence. *See Clo v. McDermott*, 239 A.D.2d 4, 608 N.Y.S.2d 743 (3d Dep't 1998) (where jury finds violation of town's animal control ordinance, it may consider such violation as some evidence of negligence). A common-law negligence cause of action is permissible only in limited circumstances when the court's adopt an enhanced duty rule. *See Bard v. Jahnke*, 6 N.Y.3d 592, 597, 815 N.Y.S.2d 16, 848 N.E.2d 463 (2006) (court essentially bars negligence claims against owners of domestic animals which, according to dissent, will likely be eroded by future *ad hoc* exceptions).

§ 5.15 Negligent Security / Intentional Tort Cases

Where a negligent landlord has breached security measures and a crime is committed on the premises, the plaintiff can bring a claim against the (deep pocket) landlord for negligent security (as opposed to bringing a claim against the generally indigent, uninsured intentional tortfeasor). Even murder has been held to be an "accident" from the standpoint of the insured landlord – hence, affording insurance coverage. *See Agoado v. United International Ins. Co.*, 95 N.Y.2d 141, 711 N.Y.S.2d 141 (2000) (murder constituted accident for purposes of determining defendant's obligations to plaintiff insured); *RJC Holding Corp. v. Republic Franklin Insurance Company*, 2 N.Y.3d 158, 777 N.Y.S.2d 4 (2004) (insurer obligated to defend and indemnify its insured in action brought against insured based on intentional assault by insured's employee, as court held alleged assault to be "accident" within meaning of policy).

Under *CPLR §1601*, however, liability may be apportioned between the negligent landlord and the non-party assailant in order to limit the landlord's liability. *See Chianese v. Meier*, 98 N.Y.2d 270, 277, 746 N.Y.S.2d 657, 661 (2002). Since the plaintiff's claim of negligence is <u>not</u> an "action requiring proof of intent", *CPLR §1602(5)* (which states that joint and several liability applies to actions requiring proof of intent) does not apply to apportionment (i.e., joint and several liability does not apply to non-economic damages). See also §5.17[4] below.

> **Warning:** As a result of *Chianese*, it is more risky for a plaintiff's attorney to pursue a negligent security / intentional tort case against a landlord, for the landlord's liability, if any, may be significantly reduced once apportionment takes place. For example, if there is a verdict of $150,000 for pain and suffering, but the jury finds the non-party (uninsured, judgment-proof) intentional tortfeasor 95% at fault and the (insured) negligent landlord 5% at fault, the result will be a measly $7,500 payday.

PART E: LITIGATING PREMISES LIABILITY CASE

§ 5.16 Identifying Proper Defendants in Premises Liability Case

[1] Determining Ownership

In determining the proper defendant(s) in a premises liability case, the plaintiff's attorney should first determine who owned the premises on the date of the accident. This information can be easily ascertained by obtaining a copy of the deed to the premises (either by accessing a copy online or by ordering an "owner search" from a title insurance company). The owner of the premises on the date of the accident should invariably be named as a defendant in the lawsuit.

> **Practice Tip:** The "owner search" should even be conducted when taking over an existing case from another attorney, for the outgoing attorney may not have sued the proper parties.

[2] Identifying Additional Defendants

In addition to ownership, liability may attach to parties who occupied, controlled, maintained, or made special use of the premises on the date of the accident. *Portaro v. Tillis Inv. Co.*, 304 A.D.2d 635, 757 N.Y.S.2d 606, 607 (2d Dep't 2003). Additional defendants may include, where applicable, the managing agent, cooperative corporation, lessor, lessee, tenant, contractor, maintenance company, engineering company, etc.

> **Practice Tip:** It is often wise for the plaintiff's attorney, or an investigator, to visit the accident site to see what is there (e.g., a sign with the managing agent's name and telephone number) and to ask questions of the residents and/or neighbors (i.e., "Who is responsible for maintenance?"). If unsure as to who to name as defendants, it is generally wiser to be cautious; all who may be legally responsible should be named in the lawsuit. Appropriate searches should be made to identify the names and addresses – for venue purposes – of all the potential defendants. Regarding corporations and limited liability companies, the Department of State's website, www.dos.state.ny.us, should be utilized.

> **Practice Tip:** Targeted defendants should be those likely to have insurance coverage, or substantial assets. Suing an indigent residential tenant, for example, will not lead to a monetary recovery for the plaintiff.

§ 5.17 Preparing Premises Liability Complaint

[1] Required Elements of Premises Liability Complaint

A premises liability complaint should, at a bare minimum, allege facts showing that:

- the defendant(s), on the date of the accident, owned, possessed, maintained, controlled, and/or made "special use" of the premises;
- the defendant(s) failed to exercise reasonable care in maintaining the premises; and
- the lack of due care of the defendant(s) was a proximate cause of the plaintiff's injuries and economic damages.

See Quinlan v. Cecchini, 41 N.Y.2d 686, 394 N.Y.S.2d 872 (1977). *See also GOL §5-321* (invalidating any agreement under which lessor is exempted from liability due to negligence). The complaint should also allege that the defendant(s), its agent(s), or its employee(s) caused / created the dangerous condition or had actual or constructive notice of the dangerous condition. *See Madred v. City of New York*, 42 N.Y.2d 1039, 399 N.Y.S.2d 205 (1977) (involving slip and fall accident).

[2] Suing Proper Defendants

When preparing the complaint, each defendant should be identified individually, in a separate allegation, so that the correct defendants admit or deny ownership and control of the premises. Plaintiff's counsel should seek to obtain an admission regarding ownership – via the defendant's answer, a response to a notice to admit, or at an examination before trial – prior to the expiration of the statute of limitations; otherwise, the plaintiff may end up pursuing a claim against the wrong party, and may ultimately be barred from pursuing a claim against the proper party.

> **Practice Tip:** For each defendant, it should be alleged, in separate paragraphs in the complaint, that the defendant owned, was lessor, was lessee, occupied, operated, maintained, controlled, managed, and made "special use" of the premises on the date of the accident. If lumped together in one paragraph, the defendant can properly deny the entire paragraph as a result of a denial of any one allegation.

> **Practice Tip:** Where ownership is denied in a defendant's answer, plaintiff's counsel should immediately serve a notice to admit on defense counsel. *See CPLR §3123.* The notice to admit should seek admissions regarding ownership and the accuracy of a copy of the deed to the premises. Defense attorneys will often deny allegations in their answers, yet admit them when served with a notice to admit.

[3] Pleading Applicable *CPLR §1602* Exceptions

The rule of "joint and several" liability in tort cases means that each tortfeasor is responsible for not only the share of plaintiff's damages that s/he caused, but for the shares attributable to all other tortfeasors, as well. Article 16 of the *CPLR* was enacted to limit joint and several liability with respect to the non-economic damages of a personal injury claim (i.e., pain and suffering); joint and several liability continues to exist with respect to economic damages – such as loss of earnings and out-of-pocket expenses – as well as non-personal injury claims, such as claims for property damage and wrongful death.

Pursuant to *CPLR §1601*, a tortfeasor is *not* jointly and severally liable for the plaintiff's non-economic damages if his or her fault is fifty percent or less of the total liability assigned to all parties liable; the culpable conduct of any person not a party to the action is not to be considered. There are, however, specific exceptions to *CPLR §1601* (enumerated in *CPLR §1602*) which allow for complete joint and several liability (i.e., even for non-economic damages). In a premises liability case, case-specific *CPLR §1602* exceptions must be plead in the complaint. It is not sufficient to state that "this action falls into one of the exceptions set forth in *CPLR §1602.*" Rather, the specific section(s) must be cited.

Any premises liability complaint with multiple defendants should specify all *CPLR §1602* exceptions that could possibly allow for complete joint and several liability in the particular case. Examples include actions involving:

- proof of intent (*CPLR §1602[5]*);

- persons causing injury to the plaintiff by acting with reckless disregard for the safety of others (*CPLR §1602[7]*);
- unlawful release of a hazardous substance into the environment (*CPLR §1602[9]*); and
- parties found to have acted intentionally and in concert (*CPLR §1602[11]*).

[4] Choosing Best Venue

The plaintiff's attorney controls the venue of the case at the outset, choosing where to file the lawsuit. Forum shopping for the most plaintiff-friendly venue can be the most important decision of the case. The plaintiff may bring the action in any county in which any one of the parties maintains a residence on the date the lawsuit is commenced. Further, a party may have more than one residence; any one of them is a proper venue, increasing plaintiff's venue options. *See CPLR §§503, 504, 505.* See also §5.04[3] above.

Practice Tip: Sometimes the deed will list several owners. The plaintiff's attorney should utilize this to his or her advantage in choosing the most plaintiff-friendly venue for the case.

Practice Tip: The plaintiff's attorney must be careful not to miss an opportunity. For example, if the plaintiff and target defendant both reside in Nassau County, but the target defendant's negligent employee resides in Queens County, the plaintiff's attorney should add the employee as a defendant and bring the lawsuit in Queens County.

Practice Tip: Where the liability is questionable and the damages are significant, the plaintiff may find it advantageous to bring the action in a county that has unified, as opposed to bifurcated, trials. A typical example is choosing New York County (a First Department / unified trial venue) over Queens County (a Second Department / bifurcated venue). If a trial is bifurcated, only in the event the plaintiff succeeds at the liability trial will there be a damages trial. In such instances, the insurance carrier has the luxury of forcing a trial on the issue of liability before offering a reasonable, or *any*, amount of money. The insurance carrier can essentially make the plaintiff prove liability to a jury before reasonably discussing settlement. In a unified trial venue, however, the insurance company knows that the jury will hear about the significant damages before deciding liability; the jury will determine liability and damages at the same time. The uncertainty of a jury and the possibility of a large verdict are conducive to a fair settlement.

§ 5.18 Seeking Disclosure of Particular Items in Premises Liability Case

[1] General Demands for Disclosure

In every case, the plaintiff should serve general disclosure demands on the defendant, pursuant to *CPLR §3101*, seeking the following:

- insurance information (including primary, excess, and umbrella policies);
- surveillance films (of not only the plaintiff, but also of the actual accident, if any);
- photographs;
- accident reports;
- statements attributable to the plaintiff (written or recorded);
- expert witness information; and
- names and addresses of witnesses (to the accident, the conditions existing at the time of the accident, to notice of the dangerous / defective conditions or lack thereof, and the physical condition of the plaintiff);

These demands should be served on the defendant(s) as soon as the answer is received. The plaintiff is entitled to all of the aforementioned information, other than expert witness disclosure, prior to the commencement of depositions. *See Tai Tran v. New Rochelle Hospital*, 99 N.Y.2d 383, 389, 756 N.Y.S.2d 509, 513 (2003) (*CPLR §3101*'s full disclosure requirement gave plaintiff right to obtain any surveillance material on demand, prior to depositions).

[2] Disclosure Re: Maintenance and Control of Premises

To demonstrate that the defendant maintained or controlled the premises, the plaintiff's attorney should seek all contracts (including leases and maintenance contracts) affecting the area of the premises where the accident occurred (e.g., managing agent contract, snow removal contract). The contracts can be used to establish maintenance and control, as well as to discover additional potentially responsible parties.

[3] Disclosure Re: Creation of Dangerous or Defective Condition(s)

Items which help prove that the defendant created the dangerous / defective condition(s) should be sought. Examples include items such as:

- specifications, plans, blue prints, and drawings;
- applications for permits, permits, certificates of occupancy, etc.;
- construction records; and
- alteration / repair records.

[4] Disclosure Re: Actual Notice of Dangerous or Defective Condition(s)

The plaintiff's attorney should seek to obtain records to help prove actual notice of the dangerous / defective condition(s), such as:

- accident reports regarding prior similar accidents;
- information regarding prior lawsuits;

- prior complaints;
- prior repair requests and repair records;
- inspection records; and
- minutes from meetings (e.g., job meetings, board meetings, etc.).

The plaintiff is entitled to records concerning prior similar incidents and/or complaints that would show notice and the existence of a dangerous condition. *See Klatz v. Armor Elevator Co., Inc.*, 93 A.D.2d 633, 634, 462 N.Y.S.2d 677, 680 (2d Dep't 1983) (defendant required to produce records of prior similar accidents involving elevator); *Coan v. Long Island Railroad*, 246 A.D.2d 569, 668 N.Y.S.2d 44, 45 (2d Dep't 1998) (defendant required to produce accident reports of prior similar accidents pursuant to *CPLR §3101[a]*). Further, with respect to prior lawsuits, the courts have allowed disclosure of the captions, index numbers, names of attorneys, depositions and trial transcripts. *Ielovich v. Taylor Mach. Works, Inc.*, 128 A.D.2d 676, 513 N.Y.S.2d 175 (2d Dep't 1987).

[5] Disclosure Re: Constructive Notice of Dangerous or Defective Condition(s)

The plaintiff's attorney should seek to obtain records to help prove constructive notice of the dangerous / defective condition(s), such as:
- repair records;
- maintenance records; and
- inspection records.

See Klatz v. Armor Elevator Co., Inc., supra; Coan v. Long Island Railroad, supra.

[6] Inspection of Premises

Pursuant to *CPLR §3120*, the plaintiff is entitled to enter and conduct tests on land with proper notice. While the courts may preclude expert proof resting on unauthorized access to private property, a party need not notify an adverse party when inspecting real property open to the public. *Dorsa v. National Amusements, Inc.*, 6 A.D.3d 654, 775 N.Y.S.2d 556 (2d Dep't 2004) (party not required to serve adverse party with notice to inspect real property that is open to general public). A request to enter and inspect land may be denied by the court, as supervision of disclosure is generally left to the sound discretion of the trial court. *See Silcox v. City of New York*, 233 A.D.2d 494, 650 N.Y.S.2d 305 (2d Dep't 1996) (where defendant raised legitimate security concerns, significant amount of time passed since the date of accident, and where plaintiff failed to properly notice inspection, plaintiff was denied access to premises).

Practice Tip: Where the plaintiff's attorney needs access to the premises for expert inspection, it is important that the preliminary conference order specifies that such access be given *prior* to depositions.

[7] Preliminary Conference and Compliance Conference in Premises Liability Case

If, at the time of the preliminary conference, the plaintiff's demands have not yet been complied with (which will generally be the case) or have not yet been made, the demands should be explicitly set forth in the preliminary conference order. Thus, they will become court-ordered, requiring the defendant(s) to comply. The same is true with respect to a compliance conference order.

> **Practice Tip:** It is preferable to have each disclosure demand specifically enumerated in the preliminary, or compliance, conference order (as opposed to simply stating that the defendant shall provide a response to prior disclosure demands). This will limit the defendant's ability to set forth an objection to a demand since the precise demand has been court-ordered.

In arguing for the disclosure of certain information at a preliminary or compliance conference, the fact that the defendant may have to produce or look for a number of documents is irrelevant. *Shapiro v. Fine*, 95 A.D.2d 714, 464 N.Y.S.2d 126 (1st Dep't 1983) (production of 53 of 55 requested documents required). Moreover, in premises liability cases, disclosure of all records for a five-year period has been held to be proper, *see Boone v. Supermarket General Corp.*, 109 A.D.2d 771, 486 N.Y.S.2d 284 (2d Dep't 1985) (disclosure of all slip and fall accidents that occurred in defendant's supermarket five years prior to date of accident allowed), and courts have held that records spanning even longer are discoverable. *See Taylor v. John Doe*, 167 A.D.2d 984 (4th Dep't 1984) (requests for prior similar accidents from date of construction through date of accident held proper). Further, there is no restrictive rule limiting disclosure to the specific building or precise location where the accident occurred. *Petty v. Riverbay Corp.*, 92 A.D.2d 525, 459 N.Y.S.2d 441, 442 (1st Dep't 1983) (production of documents required for building where assault took place, as well as two adjacent buildings); *Dukes v. 800 Grand Concourse Owners, Inc.*, 198 A.D.2d 13, 14, 603 N.Y.S.2d 138, 139 (1st Dep't 1993) (proof of prior leakage in other units in building admissible). See chapter 11, §11.03 for a preliminary conference checklist in a premises liability case.

§ 5.19 Examinations Before Trial in Premises Liability Case

[1] Preparing Plaintiff for Examination Before Trial

[a] Liability

[1] Establishing Liability

In a premises liability case, the plaintiff should be prepared to properly describe the defect alleged. Further, the plaintiff must ultimately be able to prove that the defendant either had actual or constructive notice of, or created, the dangerous condition. *See Peralta v. Henriquez*, 100 N.Y.2d 139, 145, 760 N.Y.S.2d 741, 745 (2003) (defendant's creation of dangerous condition may relieve plaintiff's obligation of proving notice of that condition). Plaintiff's testimony can help prove this, or at least create an issue of fact.

Defense attorneys will often attempt to ask how the accident occurred in several different ways (i.e., asking the plaintiff about various conversations s/he had with others regarding how the accident occurred). Medical records, ambulance call reports, emergency room records, and the records of subsequent healthcare providers (which often include the plaintiff's description of how the accident occurred) should be consulted and reviewed.

> **Practice Tip:** In *advance* of the deposition, the plaintiff should be prepared to describe how the accident occurred in one or two concise sentences. This way the plaintiff will not be flustered attempting to answer the most important question of the deposition.

> **Practice Tip:** It is vital that the plaintiff be consistent with respect to each conversation s/he may have had regarding the accident. To the extent the plaintiff does not recall the specific conversation(s), s/he should not guess. The more conversations s/he attempts to recount regarding the accident, the more likely inconsistencies will result. Further, recounting details of such conversations can generally only help the defense (i.e., admissions), for they are generally inadmissible if offered by the plaintiff (i.e., bolstering).

The plaintiff should also be familiarized with the relevant photographs, witness' statements, and the relevant portions of the bill(s) of particulars.

[2] Combating Claim of Comparative Negligence

The plaintiff's attorney must also be sure that the plaintiff is cognizant of the applicable affirmative defenses, most notably the comparative negligence defense, in a premises liability case. The defense attorney(s) may attempt to establish any number of the following:

- that the plaintiff traversed the area of the accident previously and therefore should have known to avoid the dangerous or defective condition;
- that the plaintiff failed to wear his or her prescription eyeglasses;
- that the plaintiff failed to look where s/he was walking, or was otherwise distracted;
- that the plaintiff has had prior falls;
- that the plaintiff consumed prescription medication with the side effect of dizziness;
- that the plaintiff consumed alcohol or ingested drugs / medication (or failed to take required prescription medication) within the 24 hours prior to the accident; and/or
- that the plaintiff was in a rush to arrive somewhere.

[b] Damages

[1] Pain and Suffering

The plaintiff should be prepared to answer questions regarding pain, medical treatment, objective testing, surgeries undergone and future surgeries, scarring, hospital stays, prescription and non-prescription pain medications, casts, and assistive devices prescribed (e.g., wheelchairs, walkers, crutches, and canes).

[2] Prior and Subsequent Accidents and Injuries

The plaintiff should be prepared to answer questions regarding prior and subsequent accidents and injuries. The insurance companies have access to a system whereby they can obtain information regarding prior claims the plaintiff has made.[6]

> **Practice Tip:** It is important that the plaintiff testify truthfully about the existence of documented priors. However, where applicable, it is also important to relate the fact that the prior condition was not as significant as the defense may believe, and it had not been a problem for a long period of time prior to the accident.

The plaintiff should also be prepared for questions regarding whether the plaintiff re-injured himself / herself after the accident.

[3] Economic Losses / Out-of-Pocket Expenses

The plaintiff should be well-prepared to testify about loss of earnings (including loss of pension, annuities, health insurance, etc.), non-reimbursed medical bills, and any other monies the plaintiff had to expend as a result of the accident (e.g., co-payments, cleaning service, etc.). The plaintiff should also anticipate questions regarding why s/he is unable to work, attempts to work, attempts to seek alternative employment, job applications, whether the assistance of a vocational rehabilitation professional (i.e., job counselor) was sought, educational background, other skills, whether s/he applied for disability, and how s/he is presently supporting him or herself.

> **Practice Tip:** The largest cases are often derived from a plaintiff who is never able to return to work, making for a potentially huge loss of earnings claim. These cases scare insurance carriers because even a large verdict for economic losses will be affirmed on appeal.

[c] Derivative Plaintiff

[1] Derivative Claims

When the injured party's spouse is also named as a plaintiff in the action for loss of services, society, consortium, and expenses incurred, that derivative plaintiff will generally also be required to testify at a deposition. Both spouses should be prepared to testify as to how the accident has affected the marriage. Testimony may include the

---

6   The plaintiff's attorney may want to run his or her own search on the client, so as not to be caught "off guard" later on. For a nominal fee, a search can be made through Insurance Services Offices, 545 Washington Boulevard, Jersey City, NJ, (800) 888-4476, www.iso.com.

plaintiff's inability to perform housework (e.g., cooking, cleaning, gardening, and food shopping), problems with sex life, difficulties caring for children, and other marital discord. Further, the plaintiff should be prepared to testify as to how the derivative plaintiff has had to perform many of the plaintiff's household duties. *See PJI §§2:315, 2:316.*

[2] Questions About Underlying Claim

Most importantly, the derivative plaintiff must be prepared to answer questions posed regarding liability and damages in the underlying claim. The derivative plaintiff should be prepared to answer questions about the accident and the accident scene (if s/he has personal knowledge), prior notice, whether s/he is aware of any photographs, discussions / conversations with the plaintiff about how the accident occurred (which are admissions and, therefore, not hearsay), photographs, the status of the plaintiff's injuries, etc. The derivative plaintiff must be properly prepared, particularly with respect to conversations with his or her spouse about how the accident occurred. Inconsistencies can be extremely detrimental to the case.

Practice Tip: Derivative claims generally add little, if any, settlement value to the lawsuit. Further, derivative claims generally do more harm than good for the plaintiff, particularly where liability is at issue. Generally, premises liability cases are not clear-cut on the issue of liability. As such, derivative claims should be avoided where possible. Such claim should be discussed with the plaintiff and, to the extent s/he agrees to not proceed with a derivative cause of action, s/he should sign-off on it via a waiver. *See Wingate, Russotti & Shapiro, LLP v. Friedman, Khafif & Associates*, 41 A.D.3d 367 (1st Dep't 2007) (failure to bring derivative action on behalf of spouse can result in discharge for cause).

[2] Conducting Examinations Before Trial in Premises Liability Case

[a] Establishing Ownership, Possession, Maintenance, and Control

In conducting a deposition of the defendant in a premises liability case, the plaintiff's attorney should first decipher the relationship between all the parties involved at the premises, attempting to determine who may be liable – including parties who have not yet been sued. Questions should be asked regarding ownership, landlord-tenant relationships, and the existence of leases and contracts (e.g., maintenance contracts, snow removal contracts, etc.) affecting the premises at the time of the accident. Questions regarding control, possession, "special use", maintenance, repair, and the associated procedures should be asked, as well.

[b] Establishing Negligence

In a premises liability case, the plaintiff is generally seeking to prove one or more of the following (as well as proximate cause):

- that the defendant created the dangerous / defective condition;

- that the defendant had actual notice of the dangerous / defective condition;
- that the defendant had constructive notice of the dangerous / defective condition;
- that the defendant violated an applicable statute, code, or ordinance; and/ or
- that *res ipsa loquitur* applies.

See §5.02 above. Thus, the plaintiff's attorney should always have these goals in mind when questioning the defendant(s).

[1] Establishing Defendant Created Dangerous / Defective Condition(s)

The plaintiff's attorney should explore, and try to obtain admissions regarding the fact that the defendant created the dangerous / defective condition(s). Questions regarding construction, design, and repair should be asked, including the existence of records (e.g., plans, blueprints, change orders, daily logs of work performed, bills, invoices, inspections, etc.) maintained in the ordinary course of business.

[2] Establishing Actual / Constructive Notice

The plaintiff's attorney should further inquire regarding actual and constructive notice of the dangerous / defective condition(s) that caused the accident. Questions regarding prior claims and lawsuits, prior accident reports, prior complaints, records of defects, repair requests, summonses and citations, maintenance records, and maintenance procedures should be asked on the issue of actual notice. Questions, including those regarding maintenance procedures and inspections of the premises, should also be asked on the issue of constructive notice of the dangerous or defective condition(s).

Practice Tip: To help avoid dismissal of the case on summary judgment, the plaintiff's attorney should ask several questions in a row (regarding whether the defendant's specific maintenance procedures were followed the days prior to the accident) which will elicit "I don't know" responses. This will help prove constructive notice (i.e., defendant should have known). For example, "Did you check…? Did you look at…? Did you…?"

[3] *Res Ipsa Loquitur*, Violations of Statutes / Ordinances, and Specific Law

Where applicable, questions should also be asked regarding exclusive control (with the idea of a *res ipsa loquitur* charge to the jury in mind). Also, if the plaintiff believes a particular violation of a statute or ordinance occurred, the proper questions should be asked to help prove that the statute or ordinance was violated. Further, questions should be asked regarding case-specific law. For example, the law requires that specific elements need to be proven in lead-paint cases, dog bite cases, dram shop cases, and sidewalk cases.

See chapter 11, §11.06 for an outline of topics for conducting a premises liability deposition.

CHAPTER 6

CONSTRUCTION ACCIDENTS

PART A: OVERVIEW

§ 6.01 Overview – Construction Accidents

Construction (or Labor Law) accident cases involve on-the-job injuries of contractors in various trades in the construction industry including, but not limited to, the following:

- scaffolding erection-dismantling;
- plastering-drywall;
- roofing-siding;
- window washing;
- carpentry;
- masonry-stone setting;
- wrecking-demolition;
- painting / paper-hanging;
- welding / sheet metal work;
- floor-wall-ceiling tiling;
- floor laying and other floor work;
- concrete work;
- glass and glazing work;
- installation of building equipment;
- water-well drilling;
- steam fitting;
- structural steel erection; and
- other specialized trades.

Workers' Compensation Law bars most work-related lawsuits against the injured party's employer or co-employee. Hence, most claims regarding work-related accidents must be brought against third-parties, typically the property owner and/or the general contractor. There are, however, certain rare situations where the employer (or co-employee) may be directly sued or brought in as a third-party defendant for contribution. See §6.02 below.

The plaintiff's goal in a Labor Law accident case is to establish that the claim is covered by an absolute liability provision (i.e., *Labor Law §§240(1),(2), or (3); 241(1),(2),(3),(4), or (5); or 241-a*), and to eventually prevail on a motion for summary judgment on the issue of liability. The defendant's initial goal in a Labor Law accident case, on the other hand, is to bring the case outside of the aforementioned absolute liability provisions, and into the confines of *Labor Law §200 or §241(6)*, or the common-law. When outside the scope of the absolute liability provisions of the Labor Law, the plaintiff's comparative negligence and assumption of risk will proportionately reduce his or her award.

PART B: DETERMINING WHETHER WORKERS' COMPENSATION LAW BARS CLAIM

§ 6.02 Workers' Compensation Law as Bar

Where an employee is covered by workers' compensation insurance, workers' compensation insurance benefits (i.e., first-party benefits paid for on-the-job injuries, regardless of fault, for medical expenses and loss of earnings) are the employee's exclusive remedy against an employer or co-employee for injuries or death arising in the course of employment; third-party negligence actions against the employer and co-employees are barred. *See WC Law §§11 and 29(6).*

By covering the employee under a workers' compensation insurance policy, the employer is insulated from a lawsuit brought by the injured employee. The injured employee is then only able to bring a lawsuit against someone other than his or her employer or co-employee. Thus, in a work-related accident, the injured employee may have two separate claims: a workers' compensation claim (which is similar to a no-fault claim in the motor vehicle accident setting) and a third-party negligence / statutory liability claim.

Workers' Compensation Law similarly bars such actions against an employer or co-employee in another capacity that bears a direct relationship to the employment, such as an owner of a building or the manufacturer of a product that causes injury. *See Molinari v. Kar-San Development, Ltd.,* 69 N.Y.2d 910, 516 N.Y.S.2d 457 (employer, owner of airplane that crashed while employee returned from business trip, successfully relied on exclusive remedy of workers' compensation to bar wrongful death claim).

Practice Tip: Even where the employer is the premises owner, an injured worker can bring a successful claim against the *managing agent. See Tushaj v. Elm Management Associates, Inc.,* 293 A.D.2d 44, 740 N.Y.S.2d 40 (1st Dep't 2002) (superintendent of cooperative apartment building successfully maintained action against managing agent of building for injuries sustained inside building in course of employment).

§ 6.03 Situations Where Employer Responsible for Contribution and Indemnification

[1] "Grave Injury"

A defendant (e.g., the owner or general contractor) may *implead* the plaintiff's employer into the negligence / statutory liability action as a third-party defendant, seeking contribution and indemnification from the employer. An employer is exempt from contribution and indemnification (i.e., as a third-party defendant in a negligence / statutory liability action), however, except in cases of "grave injury". *See Dole v. Dow Chemical*, 30 N.Y.2d 143, 331 N.Y.S.2d 382 (1972). *See also CPLR Article 14.* Pursuant to *Workers' Compensation Law §11*, "grave injury" is limited to:

- death;
- permanent and total loss or amputation of an arm, leg, hand, or foot;
- permanent and total loss of multiple fingers;
- permanent and total loss of multiple toes;
- paraplegia or quadriplegia;
- total and permanent blindness;
- total and permanent deafness;
- loss of nose;
- loss of an ear;
- permanent and severe facial disfigurement;
- loss of index finger; or
- acquired injury to the brain caused by an external force resulting in permanent total disability.

See WC Law §11. Thus, in a case involving a "grave injury", the plaintiff's *employer* may ultimately be responsible for the damages.

> **Warning:** The existence of "grave injury" does not give the plaintiff the right to bring a lawsuit directly against his or her employer. Rather, the plaintiff must rely upon one of the defendants to implead the plaintiff's employer as a third-party defendant.

> **Practice Tip:** The attorneys for the defendants (i.e., typically the owner and general contractor) will generally want to inflate the plaintiff's claim to the point of "grave injury", allowing them to sustain a third-party action against the employer for contribution and indemnification.

[2] Contractual Indemnification

In addition to "grave injury" cases, the defendants (i.e., typically the owner and general contractor) may also implead the plaintiff's employer as a third-party defendant via a claim for contractual indemnification. The right to contractual indemnification exists where the plaintiff's employer, via a contract with the owner and/or general contractor, agrees to indemnify and hold the employer and/or general contractor harmless with respect to injury claims brought by an injured employee.

> **Practice Tip:** Where there is contractual indemnity, the employer is responsible regardless of the severity of the injuries (as opposed to only being exposed to liability where the employee sustained a "grave injury").

§ 6.04 Exceptions to Workers' Compensation Law as Bar

[1] Employer's Failure to Procure Workers' Compensation Insurance

Where the employer fails to procure workers' compensation coverage it is required to obtain by law, the employee may elect to sue his or her employer in lieu of filing a workers' compensation claim. *See WC Law §11.* Workers' compensation coverage is not required for certain specific employment. *See WC Law §3(1).*

> **Practice Tip:** The injured party must be aware that s/he cannot bring both a workers' compensation claim *and* a lawsuit against the employer and/or co-employee. Acceptance of workers' compensation benefits will bar the injured employee from a negligence claim against the employer and co-employees. *See Werner v. State of New York,* 53 N.Y.2d 346, 441 N.Y.S.2d 654 (1981).

> **Practice Tip:** There is usually substantially more money to be made via a negligence claim than with a workers' compensation claim.

In suing the employer where s/he failed to procure the required workers' compensation insurance, the employee is not required to plead or prove that s/he was not comparatively negligent, and the employer is barred from pleading the affirmative defenses of workers' compensation, assumption of risk, or comparative negligence. *See WC Law §11.* Where workers' compensation coverage is not required and has not been voluntarily obtained, an injured employee may sue his or her employer. In such a case, the employer may utilize the comparative negligence defense. *See CPLR §1411.*

[2] Intentional Tort

Where an intentional tort is committed *by, or at the direction of, the employer,* workers' compensation coverage is not a bar to an action against the employer. *See Jones v. State of New York,* 33 N.Y.2d 275, 352 N.Y.S.2d 169 (1973). The employee has the choice of either collecting workers' compensation benefits or bringing a lawsuit against the employer, but cannot do both. *See Werner v. State of New York,* 53 N.Y.2d 346, 441 N.Y.S.2d 654 (1981).

An intentional tort in the course of employment, not committed by or at the direction of the employer, is presumed to arise out of the employment, unless motivated purely by personal animus. *See Rosen v. First Manhattan Bank,* 84 N.Y.2d 856, 617 N.Y.S.2d

455 (1994) (claim that assault by co-employee was motivated by robbery insufficient to overcome statutory presumption that dispute was work-related). Thus, pursuant to *Workers' Compensation Law §21*, it is presumed, in the absence of substantial evidence to the contrary, that the intentional tort is covered under Workers' Compensation Law and a claim against the employer or co-employee is barred. This helps the employer establish that an assault by a co-employee was committed in the scope and course of employment.

[3] Employer's Impairment of Employee's Right to Sue Third-Party

Where the employer willfully or negligently destroys evidence which the employee needs to prosecute an action against a third-party (i.e., resulting in the inability to successfully sue the third-party), workers' compensation insurance coverage does not bar the employee from maintaining a lawsuit against the employer. *See DiDomenico v. C&S Aeromatik Supplies, Inc.*, 252 A.D.2d 41, 682 N.Y.S.2d 452 (2d Dep't 1998) (plaintiff permitted to proceed against employer where employer intentionally destroyed evidence).

[4] Claims Regarding Injured Firefighter or Police Officer

Under *General Municipal Law §205(a)* and *§205(e)*, firefighters and police officers are authorized to sue their employers where a violation of a statute, ordinance, rule, or order of the federal, state, or local government, or any of their departments, divisions, or bureaus is a proximate cause of the injuries sustained. The specific violation must be plead in the complaint. *Maisch v. New York*, 181 A.D.2d 467, 581 N.Y.S.2d 181 (1st Dep't 1992). In actions based on *General Municipal Law §205(a)* and *§205(e)*, neither comparative negligence nor assumption of risk may be raised as an affirmative defense. *See Mullen v. Zoebe, Inc.*, 86 N.Y.2d 135, 630 N.Y.S.2d 269 (1995) (firefighter's culpability in contributing to accident could not be invoked).

Unless the claim is brought under *General Municipal Law §205(a)* or *§205(e)*, the "firefighter's rule" bars a firefighter or police officer from bringing a common-law negligence cause of action against his or her employer or co-employee "when the performance of the police officer's or firefighter's duties increased the risk of the injury happening, and did not merely furnish the occasion for the injury." *Schembri v. City of New York*, 240 A.D.2d 722, 659 N.Y.S.2d 324 (2d Dep't 1997) (police officer's claim against city not barred by firefighter's rule because he was not exposed to heightened risk of injury from falling on defective step while leading a television camera across park). The "firefighter's rule" is based on the principle that they are specially trained and compensated to confront hazards. *See General Obligations Law §11-106.*

Practice Tip: The "firefighter's rule" does not bar claims by police officers and firefighters against negligent third-parties (i.e., parties other than their employers and/or co-employees). *See General Obligations Law §11-106.*

PART C: VARIOUS TYPES OF LABOR LAW CLAIMS AVAILABLE

§ 6.05 Overview of Various Types of Labor Law Claims Available

[1] Overview of *Labor Law §200* Claims

Labor Law §200 is a codification of New York State common-law. *Labor Law §200* simply imposes the duty to provide a safe work site on those who direct or control the work. Under *§200*, a plaintiff generally needs to prove that the defendant had notice of, or created, the dangerous condition that caused plaintiff's injuries, or that *res ipsa loquitur* applies. See §§6.10, 6.11 below.

[2] Overview of *Labor Law §240* Claims

Labor Law §240 is a statutory cause of action for workers who sustain "gravity-related" injuries as a result of falls from elevated heights or due to objects falling from elevated heights. This section imposes specific duties upon premises owners and general contractors, and holds them responsible for compliance with the statute, regardless of whether or not they direct or control the work. A violation of *Labor Law §240* results in absolute liability, rendering plaintiff's comparative negligence irrelevant. Where the plaintiff's conduct was the *sole* proximate cause of the accident, however, s/he cannot prevail. See §§6.12, 6.13, 6.14, 6.15 below.

[3] Overview of *Labor Law §241(1) - (5)* Claims

Labor Law §241 (subsections 1 through 5) is a statutory cause of action, for workers injured as a result of the failure to provide proper flooring and enclosures during construction, demolition, and excavation. The premises owners and general contractors are responsible for complying with this statute regardless of whether or not they direct or control the work. A violation of any of these subsections results in absolute liability, rendering the plaintiff's comparative negligence irrelevant. Where the plaintiff's conduct was the *sole* proximate cause of the accident, however, s/he cannot prevail. See §§6.16, 6.17, 6.18, 6.19 below.

[4] Overview of *Labor Law §241(6)* Claims

Labor Law §241(6), like *§200*, requires workers to be provided with a safe work site. However, under *§241(6)*, the plaintiff must establish a *specific* – as opposed to general – safety violation of the *New York State Industrial Code (see 12 NYCRR §23)*. *Labor Law §241(6)* imposes the duty upon all owners and general contractors, regardless of whether or not they direct or control the work. A violation of this statute merely results in some evidence of negligence, not absolute liability; the plaintiff's comparative negligence may thus proportionately diminish the award. See §§6.20, 6.21, 6.22, 6.23.

[5] Overview of *Labor Law §241-a* Claims

Labor Law §241-a is a statutory cause of action for injuries caused by open stairwells, hatchways, and elevator shafts within buildings which are being constructed or demolished. *Labor Law §241-a* imposes the duty upon owners and general contractors, regardless of whether or not they direct or control the work. A violation of this statute results in absolute liability, rendering plaintiff's comparative negligence irrelevant (except where plaintiff's conduct was the sole proximate cause of the accident).

[6] Overview of *Labor Law §202* Claims – Window Washers

Labor Law §202 protects window washers from hazards associated with cleaning the outside of commercial / public buildings, by requiring that they are provided with adequate safety devices. *Labor Law §202*, however, is not an absolute liability provision; an owner's violation of this statute is merely some evidence of negligence. The plaintiff's comparative negligence is an available defense which may proportionately reduce the award. A plaintiff may, however, maintain causes of action under both *§202* and *§240* (which is an absolute liability provision).

§ 6.06 Role of OSHA and NYS Industrial Code in Labor Law Accident Case

The Occupational Safety & Health Act (OSHA) was enacted to provide safe work sites. Where an employer violates OSHA rules and regulations, the violation(s) simply provide some evidence that the employer was not providing a safe work site. *Landry v. General Motors Corp.*, 210 A.D.2d 898, 621 N.Y.S.2d 255 (4th Dep't 1995) (alleged violations of OSHA regulations could be used to support causes of action under *Labor Law §200* and common-law negligence, and can be used as some evidence of negligence if violation was substantial factor in causing occurrence). OSHA rules and regulations have been mandated as the federal minimum standards at the work site. The New York State Industrial Code Rule*s* were enacted by the State Commissioner of Labor, giving effect to *Labor Law §241(6)*'s requirement that all areas in which construction, excavation, or demolition work is performed be provided with adequate safety protection for the workers.

For claims brought under the absolute liability provisions of *Labor Law §§240, 241(1) - (5)* or *§241-a*, there is generally no need to cite any OSHA standards or *NYS Industrial Code Rule 23 (12 NYCRR §23)* provision – although failure to comply can be used to further buttress a claim. See §6.15[3] below. Under the non-absolute liability provisions (i.e., *Labor Law §200, §241(6)*, or *§202*), however, the jury must determine whether or not the defendant has provided a safe place to work, and OSHA and/or the NYS Industrial Code may be referred to regarding what is safe and/or unsafe. Any such violation(s) can be cited as some evidence of the defendant's failure to provide a safe place to work, but an OSHA violation cannot provide the *basis* (i.e., a NYS Industrial Code violation is necessary) for liability under *§241(6)*. *See Pellescki v. Rochester*, 198 A.D.2d 762, 605 N.Y.S.2d 692 (4th Dep't 1993). See §6.18[1][c] below.

PART D: LABOR LAW ACCIDENT INTAKE

§ 6.07 Gathering Information at Labor Law Accident Intake

The Labor Law accident intake is quite similar to that of the premises liability case. The same information is required, as well as information about workers' compensation coverage (and whether a claim has been made), and the identity and addresses of:

- the general contractor;
- the plaintiff's employer; and
- the property owner.

See chapter 5, §§5.04-5.06.

§ 6.08 Deciding to Accept, Reject, or Investigate Labor Law Accident Case

[1] Liability

A determination must be made as to whether there are any potential defendants against whom a claim is likely *not* barred by Workers' Compensation Law; the identity of the real property owner and general contractor should be ascertained, as well as the name of the injured party's employer (against whom a claim will likely be barred, unless the plaintiff was an independent contractor). The attorney must further determine whether the potential case may fall within the purview of *Labor Law §§240, 241, or 241-a* (discussed fully later in this chapter); elevation-related accidents often have the potential for absolute liability (which can be established via a successful motion for summary judgment). Claims that fall outside the scope of the absolute liability provisions will generally be evaluated in much the same way as premises liability cases.

[2] Damages

While the potential to prevail on a motion for summary judgment on the issue of liability exists in many Labor Law accident cases, there are generally multiple defendants, third-party actions, and extensive litigation involved in these types of cases. As such, the injuries and economic losses, which comprise "damages", should be significant before the attorney decides to become retained on such a matter.

> **Practice Tip:** Labor Law accident cases are often some of the largest damages cases. As a result of a fall from a height, injuries are often significant. Further, since, by definition, the injured party was employed, there is potential for a huge loss of earnings claim. Additionally, 100% liability is often established via a successful motion for summary judgment, thereby allowing for an award or settlement for the full amount of damages.

[3] Insurance Coverage

In Labor Law accident cases, both the property owner and the general contractor typically have substantial insurance coverage. There are often insurance coverage disputes (such as contractual indemnification) amongst the various defendants and third-party defendants, but this is not the problem of the plaintiff.

[4] Venue

Venue options should be considered in seeking to file the lawsuit in the most plaintiff-friendly venue. *See CPLR §§503, 504, 505.* See also chapter 5, §§5.04[3], 5.17[3]; see also chapter 7, §7.07.

> **Practice Tip:** In the area of Labor Law accident cases, the Appellate Division decisions are varied on many legal issues related to liability, depending on the Department. The plaintiff's attorney should research the issues relevant to the particular case before commencing an action, as forum shopping is important in this area. In general, the First Department is the most plaintiff-friendly. Choosing the best Department for the specific case can be dispositive.

[5] Statutes of Limitations and Conditions Precedent to Litigation

The applicable statute of limitations must also be taken into account at the intake. Generally, there is a three-year statute of limitations on Labor Law accident cases. *CPLR §214.*

> **Warning:** Where the statute of limitations date is approaching, the attorney should be very careful before accepting a Labor Law accident case. There are often responsible entities whose names are not yet known at the time of intake, and do not become known until almost a year later through discovery.

The attorney should also be aware that where a municipality is involved, there are stringent notice of claim requirements (generally 90 days from the date of the accident) and a shortened statute of limitations (generally one year and 90 days from the date of accident). See chapter 7, §§7.03, 7.05, 7.10, 7.11, 7.12. The attorney should further be aware of the shortened statute of limitations periods associated with intentional torts (one year) and wrongful death causes of action (two years from the date of death or the applicable statute of limitations period, whichever is shorter). *See CPLR §§210, 215.* The attorney should also be aware that the statute of limitations (but not notice of claim time limitations) for infants (i.e., under 18 years of age) is automatically tolled during the infancy. *See CPLR §208.*

§ 6.09 Labor Law Accident Retainer Agreement

[1] Retainer Agreement in Labor Law Accident Case – In General

If the attorney decides to accept the Labor Law accident case, the client must sign a retainer agreement. A Labor Law accident case retainer agreement should set forth the contingency fee; the standard contingency fee (and maximum allowed contingency fee in a non-medical malpractice personal injury case) is 33 1/3% of the net recovery. The retainer agreement should set forth the fact that disbursements such as fees for court costs, process servers, medical records, investigators, experts, and other related costs are to be reimbursed at the conclusion of the case. The net recovery is then used to compute the attorney's contingency fee. The retainer agreement should also make clear that all liens are the sole responsibility of the client, and are to be paid from the client's share of the proceeds. It should explicitly list liens such as workers' compensation, Medicaid, Medicare, Department of Social Services, and medical liens.

Construction accident victims are often undocumented immigrants who are somewhat hesitant to retain an attorney due to a fear of: (i) being deported and (ii) retaliation by their employers. New York State law, however, allows *all* accident victims – regardless of immigration status – to bring lawsuits for compensation. Filing a lawsuit will not result in deportation, nor will it negatively affect any pending applications for residency or citizenship. Further, injured workers will generally *not* be suing their employers, as the law bars most such claims (see §§5.04-5.06 above). Hence, there is generally nothing for them to be worried about.

[2] Scope of Representation in Labor Law Accident Retainer Agreement

The Labor Law accident retainer agreement should clearly state that the attorney is being retained to represent the plaintiff for a third-party negligence / statutory liability claim only. As such, representation for workers' compensation claims, New York State Disability claims, and appellate work should be expressly excluded.

> **Practice Tip:** The plaintiff's attorney should refer the client to a workers' compensation attorney (preferably one who handles only workers' compensation claims and does not handle third-party negligence / statutory liability claims) for such representation. An accident report (C-2 form) must be filed by the employer within ten days of the date of accident.

[3] Executing Authorizations

At the same time the client signs the retainer agreement, s/he should also sign several sets of authorizations to obtain medical records, workers' compensation records, employment records, union records, and tax returns at the intake.

[4] Filing OCA Retainer Statement

After becoming retained, a retainer statement must be filed with the Office of Court Administration (OCA). A self-addressed stamped postcard should be included for OCA to stamp the retainer number which must then be used on the closing statement at the conclusion of the case. In the event the retainer statement is not timely filed, an attorney's affirmation setting forth the reason for lateness and a request that the retainer statement be filed *nunc pro tunc* should be included.

PART E: *LABOR LAW §200* CLAIM

§ 6.10 Determining Parties Responsible Under *Labor Law §200*

Labor Law §200 is merely a codification of the common-law, as the duty to provide a safe workplace is owed only by those who actually control the work or have the authority to do so.

> **Practice Tip:** The main difference between *Labor Law §200* and *§241(6)* (discussed later in this chapter) is that *§241(6)* imposes the duty upon contractors and owners, and their agents, *regardless* of whether they control the work (i.e., liability can be vicarious).

§ 6.11 Establishing Liability Under *Labor Law §200*

[1] Establishing Plaintiff as Employee at Work Site

Labor Law §200's duty to provide a safe place to work does not apply to non-employees or people not employed at the work site. *Widera v. Ettco Wire and Cable Corp.*, 204 A.D.2d 306, 611 N.Y.S.2d 569 (2d Dep't 1994) (infant born with brain damage sustained in utero was not "employee at work site" and thus defendant's duty did not extend to infant).

[2] Establishing Elements of Common-Law Negligence

Labor Law §200 imposes a general duty to provide a safe place to work. *See Juck v. Fein,* 80 N.Y.2d 965, 590 N.Y.S.2d 878 (1992). A claim alleging a *Labor Law §200* violation is the same as one based on common-law negligence. See chapter 5, §5.02. *Labor Law §200* simply codifies the common-law duty to provide a safe workplace for all those employed at the work site. *See Rusin v. Jackson Heights Shopping Center*, 27 N.Y.2d 103, 313 N.Y.S.2d 715 (1970). Unlike *Labor Law §§240, 241(1) - (5), and Labor Law §241-a, Labor Law §200* does not provide any special benefits to a plaintiff (i.e., over a common-law negligence claim). *See Allen v. Cloutier*, 44 N.Y.2d 290, 405 N.Y.S.2d 630 (1978). Further, unlike Labor Law *§241(6)*, liability can be imposed under *Labor Law §200* only if the party charged with violating it was negligent.

[3] Establishing Element of Control

The critical element analyzed by the courts in *Labor Law §200* claims is that of "control". *See Comes v. New York State Elec. and Gas*, 82 N.Y.2d 876, 609 N.Y.S.2d 168 (1993) (*Labor Law §200* held not to impose liability on owner of construction site premises, even where owner allegedly had notice of an unsafe work practice, where no evidence existed that owner exercised supervisory control). *See also Durfee v. Eastman Kodak Co.*, 212 A.D.2d 971, 624 N.Y.S.2d 704 (4th Dep't 1995) (*Labor Law §200* and common-law negligence causes of action dismissed against owner where dangerous condition arose from contractor's methods, and owner did not exercise supervisory control over work). *See also Palmer v. Center for Nursing and Rehabilitation*, 18 A.D.3d 364, 795 N.Y.S.2d 667 (2d Dep't 2005). Owners and general contractors are able to insulate themselves from liability under *Labor Law §200* by delegating the duty to provide a safe workplace to others. *See Comes v. New York State Elec. and Gas*, 82 N.Y.2d 876, 609 N.Y.S.2d 168 (1993).

[4] Exceptions to Establishing Element of Control

Liability can be imposed despite a defendant's lack of supervisory control over the plaintiff's work where the defendant *created* the dangerous condition which caused the accident. *Verel v. Ferguson Electric Construction Company*, 41 A.D.3d 1154, 838 N.Y.S.2d 280 (4th Dep't 2007). Further, where a dangerous condition exists at the *worksite itself* (i.e., pre-existing the project), the owner will be held liable under *Labor Law §200* so long as it had actual or constructive notice of (or created) the condition, regardless of whether it had supervision or control over the work. *Johnson v. Packaging Corporation of America,* 274 A.D.2d 627, 710 N.Y.S.2d 699 (3d Dep't 2000) (owner's motion for summary judgment under *Labor Law §200* denied where electrical wires were exposed at work site prior to project). *See also Piazza v. Shaw Contract Flooring Services, Inc.*, 39 A.D.3d 1218, 834 N.Y.S.2d 776 (4th Dep't 2007).

[5] Comparative Negligence / Assumption of Risk Defenses

Comparative negligence and assumption of risk are viable defenses to a *Labor Law §200* claim. The plaintiff's negligence will proportionately diminish any award. *See CPLR §1411. See Acevedo v. Camac*, 293 A.D.2d 430, 740 N.Y.S.2d 380 (2d Dep't 2002) (plaintiff's comparative negligence relevant in *§200* claim). The consequences of the plaintiff's comparative negligence and/or assumption of risk may be mitigated if it can be shown that the plaintiff was carrying out responsibilities pursuant his or her superior's instructions. *Broderick v. Cauldwell Wingate Co.*, 301 N.Y. 182 (1950) (subordinate worker is seen as having little, if any, choice but to obey superior's orders). Where the plaintiff is found to be the "sole proximate cause" of the accident, a *Labor Law §200* claim will be barred. *Azad v. 270 5th Realty Corp.*, 46 A.D.3d 728, 848 N.Y.S.2d 688 (2d Dep't 2007). See §6.15[3] below.

PART F: *LABOR LAW §240* CLAIM

§ 6.12 Determining Whether Injured Party Protected By *Labor Law §240*

Labor Law §240 applies to any "person so employed" on a construction project. The injured plaintiff is not required to have been working in the capacity for which s/he was hired in order to be afforded the protection of *Labor Law §240. Reeves v. Red Wing Company, Inc.*, 139 A.D.2d 935, 527 N.Y.S.2d 916 (4th Dep't 1988) (unnecessary for employee to be actually working on his assigned duties at time of injury). All that is required to be shown is that the plaintiff was at the work site because s/he was hired to work on the construction project. *Reinhart v. Long Island Lighting Co., Inc.*, 91 A.D.2d 571, 457 N.Y.S.2d 57 (1st Dep't 1982). An owner or general contractor will still be subject to absolute liability where the injured worker was a foreman or supervisor on the job, even if such worker voluntarily assumed a dangerous position without being ordered to do so. *Colern v. State of New York*, 170 A.D.2d 1000, 566 N.Y.S.2d 154 (4th Dep't 1991).

Warning: Volunteers are not within the class of people protected by *Labor Law §240. Whelen v. Warwick Valley Civic and Social Club*, 47 N.Y.2d 970, 419 N.Y.S.2d 959 (1979).

§ 6.13 Parties Absolutely Liable Under *Labor Law §240*

[1] Owners Absolutely Liable

Labor Law §240 places liability upon "all contractors and owners and their agents." Owners of the work site are absolutely liable for any violation of *§240*, even if they do not control or supervise the work. *See Gordon v. Eastern Ry. Supply, Inc.*, 82 N.Y.2d 555, 606 N.Y.S.2d 127, 626 N.E.2d 912 (1993). A fee owner is not a "statutory" owner if it is "wholly unaware" of the worker's presence and it is "powerless" to insist that a different contractor be hired. *Abbatiello v. Lancaster Studio Associates*, 3 N.Y.3d 46, 781 N.Y.S.2d 477 (2004). A tenant-in-possession may be deemed an owner for *§240* purposes. *Guerra v. Port Authority of New York and New Jersey*, 35 A.D.3d 810, 828 N.Y.S.2d 440 (2d Dep't 2006) (where lessee initiated project and hired general contractor, it should be treated as an owner); *see also Bush v. The Goodyear Tire & Rubber Company*, 9 A.D.3d 252, 779 N.Y.S.2d 206 (1st Dep't 2004).

[2] Exemption for Owners of One and Two-Family Dwellings

Owners of one and two-family dwellings, who contract for but do not control the work, are exempt from the absolute liability provisions under *Labor Law §§240, 241, and 241-a*. However, where the homeowner is substantially involved in the project above that of an owner's typical involvement (e.g., acting as general contractor and/or performing much of the construction), s/he will not be provided the statutory exemption from absolute liability. *See Bartoo v. Buell*, 87 N.Y.2d 362, 639 N.Y.S.2d 778 (1996). *See also McAdam v. Sadler*, 170 A.D.2d 960, 566 N.Y.S.2d 130 (4th Dep't 1991), *app. den.*, 77 N.Y.2d 810, 571 N.Y.S.2d 913 (1991) (statutory exception applied where owner of one-family home did not direct or control work).

> **Practice Tip:** An owner of a one or two-family dwelling is not exempt from *Labor Law §241(6)* liability (i.e., they are responsible for complying with the Industrial Code rules). Hence, as long as there was a specific NYS Industrial Code violation which was a cause of the accident, this exemption will not bar the plaintiff's entire claim against an owner. *See Ferrero v. Best Modular Homes, Inc.*, 33 A.D.3d 847, 823 N.Y.S.2d 477 (2d Dep't 2006).

> **Practice Tip:** The exemption does not apply where the premises are being renovated to prepare the building for *commercial* rental. *Lombardi v. Stout*, 80 N.Y.2d 290, 590 N.Y.S.2d 55 (1992).

[3] General Contractors Absolutely Liable

Labor Law §240 places liability upon "all contractors . . .". Essentially, like the property owner, the general contractor of the construction project is also absolutely liable. The determining factor in holding a contractor absolutely liable under *Labor Law §240* is whether or not it had the right to control the work. A contractor need not be referred to as a "general contractor" or "prime contractor" to be held liable under the statute. *Walls v. Turner Construction Company*, 4 N.Y.3d 861, 798 N.Y.S.2d 351 (2005) (label of "construction manager" versus "general contractor" not necessarily determinative where defendant had authority to control activities at work site and to stop any unsafe work practices). *See also Miller v. Gedola*, 44 A.D.3d 1017, 845 N.Y.S.2d 109 (2d Dep't 2007) (subcontractor liable where it had authority to supervise and control the work which gave rise to the plaintiff's injuries and thus was statutory agent of owner or general contractor). Also, the fact that they did not perform the work is not dispositive. *See Kenny v. Fuller Co.*, 87 A.D.2d 183, 450 N.Y.S.2d 551 (2d Dep't 1982).

Practice Tip: Even a subcontractor can be held liable for violations of the Labor Law. In order to determine whether a subcontractor is liable, the same analysis (as discussed above) should be utilized. The plaintiff must establish that the subcontractor had the authority to supervise and control either the site where the accident occurred or the plaintiff's activities. *Lickers v. Albert Elia Building Co., Inc.*, 105 A.D.2d 1069, 482 N.Y.S.2d 596 (4th Dep't 1984).

[4] Agents Absolutely Liable

Labor Law §240's absolute liability also extends to the agent(s) of the owner and general contractor where they have authority to supervise and control the activity which resulted in the injury. *Kopacz v. Airco Carbon Division of Airco, Inc.*, 104 A.D.2d 722, 480 N.Y.S.2d 652 (4th Dep't 1984). An "agent" is defined as any individual or company which acts in the place of the owner or the contractor regarding the right to perform or control the work. It is not the word "contractor" or "subcontractor" that is dispositive, but rather the authority to supervise and control the work which is important. *See Soltes v. Brentwood Union Free School District*, 47 A.D.3d 804, 849 N.Y.S.2d 628 (2d Dep't 2008). Only upon obtaining the authority to supervise and control does the third party qualify as an "agent" under *§§240* and *241*. *Russin v. Louis N. Picciano and Son*, 78 A.D.2d 467, 436 N.Y.S.2d 370 (3d Dep't 1981), *aff'd*, 54 N.Y.2d 311, 445 N.Y.S.2d 127 (1981).

§ 6.14 Establishing Absolute Liability Under *Labor Law §240*

[1] Establishing Violation of *Labor Law §240*

[a] Establishing Work Performed on "Building" or "Structure"

Labor Law §240 only applies to work being performed on "a building or structure". The word "structure" has been interpreted liberally by the courts to include substantially more than just buildings. *Izrailev v. 1000 Sunrise Highway, Inc.*, 70 N.Y.2d 813, 523 N.Y.S.2d 432 (1987) (electrical sign affixed flat against building found to be structure); *Kahn v. Gates Construction Corp.*, 103 A.D.2d 438, 480 N.Y.S.2d 351 (2d Dep't 1984) (undersea pipeline constituted structure under *Labor Law §240*); *Lewis-Moors v. Contel of New York, Inc.*, 78 N.Y.2d 942, 573 N.Y.S.2d 636 (1991) (telephone pole held to be structure under *Labor Law §240[1]*).

[b] Establishing Specific Nature of Work Covered By Statute

Labor Law §240 applies to "erection, demolition, repairing, altering, painting, cleaning, or pointing" of a building or structure. *See Labor Law §240*. Routine maintenance is not included. *Esposito v. New York City Industrial Development Agency*, 305 A.D.2d 108, 760 N.Y.S.2d 18 (1st Dep't 2003), *aff'd*, 1 N.Y.3d 526, 770 N.Y.S.2d 682 (2003) (replacement of components that are expected to require replacement in normal wear and tear constitutes routine maintenance and is not within the purview of statute); *see also Panek v. County of Albany*, 99 N.Y.2d 452 (2003) ("alteration" requires "significant physical change to the building or structure") .

Demolition work includes "work incidental to or associated with the total or partial dismantling or razing of a building or other structure including the removing or dismantling of building or other equipment." *12 NYCRR §23-1.4(b)(16)*. "Repairing" and "altering" include all forms of remodeling, maintenance, fixing or modification of either a building or structure. *See Parsolano v. Nassau,* 93 A.D.2d 815, 460 N.Y.S.2d 823 (2d Dep't 1983).

Labor Law §240 also applies to site preparation which is incidental and necessary to the erection of a building. *See Lombardi v. Stout,* 80 N.Y.2d 290, 590 N.Y.S.2d 55 (1992) (removal of tree found to be site preparation). *Labor Law §240,* however, does not include the removal of debris from a work site, after the work covered by statute has been completed, if the person doing so was not otherwise involved in the underlying construction activity. *See Beehner v. Eckert Corp.,* 3 N.Y.3d 751, 788 N.Y.S.2d 637 (2004)*; see also Sandi v. Chaucer Assoc.,* 170 A.D.2d 663, 566 N.Y.S.2d 935 (2d Dep't 1991).

[c] Establishing Elevated Height Requirement

[1] Establishing Worker Fell from Elevated Height

In order to prevail under *Labor Law §240*, the plaintiff must establish that the injury was elevation-related. *Rocovich v. Consolidated Edison Co.,* 78 N.Y.2d 509, 577 N.Y.S.2d 219 (1991). The statute covers both "falling worker" cases and "falling objects" cases. Common types of "falling worker" cases involve falls from scaffolds (e.g., construction worker, window washer) and ladders. The courts have basically held that workers engaged in activities that include a substantial inherent risk resulting from the relative elevation at which the activities must be performed (or at which materials or loads must be positioned or secured) are entitled to the protection of *Labor Law §240(1)* because the contemplated hazards are related to the effects of gravity. *Id.* The statute was created to prevent accidents where the protection device(s) were inadequate to protect the injured worker from "harm directly flowing from the application of the force of gravity to an object or person." *Ross v. Curtis-Palmer Hydro-Electric Co.,* 81 N.Y.2d 494, 601 N.Y.S.2d 49 (1993). The plaintiff must prove that s/he needed to be at an elevated height in order to perform the particular task s/he was engaged in at the time of the accident. *Broggs v. Rockefeller Group,* 8 N.Y.3d 675, 839 N.Y.S.2d 714 (2007) (window-washing task that caused accident did not create elevation-related risk, precluding plaintiff from establishing task could not be done without ladder or other safety device).

[2] Establishing Material Fell from Elevated Height

The plaintiff may also recover under *Labor Law §240(1)* where the injury was caused by a "falling object". The Court of Appeals held in *Rocovich v. Consolidated Edison Co.,* 78 N.Y.2d 509, 577 N.Y.S.2d 219 (1991), "The contemplated hazards (of *§240* include) those related to the effects of gravity where protective devices are called for … because of a difference between the elevation level where the worker is positioned and the higher level of the materials or load being hoisted or secured." *See also Quattrocchi v. F.J. Sciame Construction Corp.,* 44 A.D.3d 377, 843 N.Y.S.2d

564 (1st Dep't 2007). "Falling object" cases typically involve devices such as ropes, pulleys, and irons. These devices are enumerated in the statute.

Simply because an injury is caused by something falling does not mean that it is the type of accident contemplated under *Labor Law §240(1)*. *See Vitaliotis v. Village of Saltaire*, 229 A.D.2d 575, 646 N.Y.S.2d 356 (2d Dep't 1996) (plaintiff injured when side of trench he was digging and part of nearby retaining wall collapsed on him, could not recover under *Labor Law §240[1]*, for it was not type of "gravity-related accident" contemplated under *§240[1]*). Rather, a plaintiff must show that the object fell while being hoisted or secured as a result of the absence or inadequacy of a safety device of the type enumerated in the statute. *See Pope v. Supreme-K.R.W. Constr. Corp.*, 261 A.D.2d 523, 690 N.Y.S.2d 587 (2d Dep't 1999) (plaintiff entitled to summary judgment where struck in head by beam being hoisted and installed one level above where he was working); *Baker v. Barrons Educ. Serv. Corp.*, 248 A.D.2d 655, 670 N.Y.S.2d 587 (2d Dep't 1998) (plaintiff entitled to summary judgment where struck in head by cinder block ceiling lowered by rope and derrick from roof); *Roberts v. General Electric Co.*, 97 N.Y.2d 737, 742 N.Y.S.2d 188 (2002) (where piece of asbestos dropped onto plaintiff, *Labor Law §240[1]* did not apply since material was not being hoisted or secured); *Narducci v. Manhattan Bay Assocs.*, 96 N.Y.2d 259, 727 N.Y.S.2d 37 (2001) (*§240[1]* liability for falling objects arises only for failure to use proper hoisting or securing devices).

[d] Establishing Breach of Duty
[1] Establishing Breach of Duty Under *Labor Law §240(1)*
[a] Establishing Breach of Duty to Provide Devices

Labor Law §240 requires that all owners, contractors and their agents "furnish or erect, or cause to be furnished or erected … scaffolding, hoists, stays, ladders, slings, hangers, blocks, pulleys, braces, irons, ropes, and other devices which shall be so constructed, placed and operated as to give proper protection…" *See Beehner v. Eckert Corp.*, 3 N.Y.3d 751, 788 N.Y.S.2d 637 (2004) (bright-line separating enumerated versus non-enumerated activities).

When no safety devices are provided, the statute is violated and the defendant(s) are liable – regardless of other considerations, such as rules, regulations, contracts, or custom and usage within the industry. *See Zimmer v. Chemung County Performing Arts*, 65 N.Y.2d 513, 493 N.Y.S.2d 102 (1985); *see also Hunt v. Spitz Constr. Co.*, 65 N.Y.2d 513, 493 N.Y.S.2d 102 (1985).

[b] Establishing Breach of Duty to Properly Place Devices

Where a safety device – whether it is one specifically enumerated in the statute or any "other device" – is provided, the plaintiff must show that the device was not properly "erected, constructed, placed and operated so as to give proper protection." The duty consists of two parts (i.e., providing the device *and* properly placing the device), both of which must be satisfied by the defendant(s). *Bland v. Manocherian*, 93

A.D.2d 689, 462 N.Y.S.2d 881 (1st Dep't 1983), *aff'd*, 66 N.Y.2d 452, 497 N.Y.S.2d 880 (1985). The defendant is not absolved from liability by demonstrating that it has provided, or made available, safety devices at the work site. The duty also requires that these safety devices be used and placed properly so as to afford adequate protection.

Practice Tip: Where the plaintiff is injured by a fall or by falling material, it should be alleged that, *by definition*, the safety device(s) provided (if any) were clearly not adequate and, thus, the defendants breached the statute. Simply, had the safety devices been adequate, there would not have been an accident.

Practice Tip: It is best to establish the device as one specifically named in the *Labor Law §240* (e.g., a scaffold) in order to make the court's decision a matter of law. *See Evans v. NAB Construction Corp.*, 80 A.D.2d 841, 436 N.Y.S.2d 774 (2d Dep't 1981).

Example: Where the plaintiff fell from a ladder because one of the rungs or rails on the ladder broke or the ladder collapsed, s/he will have shown that the ladder was a defective and/or inadequate safety device. The plaintiff will have made out a *prima facie* case merely by demonstrating that the ladder broke. *See Cummings v. Kelly*, 97 A.D. 114, 89 N.Y.S. 579 (2d Dep't 1904). Where the ladder did not break, but instead slid out from underneath the plaintiff or tipped over, a violation of *Labor Law §240(1)* can also be established, for the accident was caused as a result of the *improper placement* of the ladder. *See Haimes v. New York Telephone Company*, 59 A.D.2d 813, 299 N.Y.S.2d 77, *aff'd*, 46 N.Y.2d 132, 412 N.Y.S.2d 863 (1978).

[2] Establishing Breach of Duty Under *Labor Law §240(2)* or *(3)*

[a] Establishing Breach of Duty to Provide Safety Rails on Scaffolding More Than Twenty Feet High

Labor Law §240(2) requires safety rails on scaffolding or staging greater than twenty feet high. Establishing that the scaffold was in excess of twenty feet in height, that it lacked safety rails, and that the lack of the required safety rails was a proximate cause of the injuries will result in absolute liability against the owner and general contractor.

Practice Tip: If the scaffold is less than twenty feet high, the plaintiff should still show that, due to the lack of guard rails, the scaffold failed to provide adequate protection. Hence, *Labor Law §240(1)* requires guard rails on scaffolds *less* than twenty feet in height whenever a danger to workers exists. *Wright v. State*, 66 N.Y.2d 452, 497 N.Y.S.2d 880 (1985).

[b] Establishing Breach of Duty to Properly Secure Scaffolding

Labor Law §240(2) also requires that "such scaffolding or staging shall be so fastened as to prevent it from swaying from the building or structure." Further, *Labor Law §240(3)* requires that "all scaffolding shall be so constructed as to bear four times the maximum weight required to be dependent therefrom or placed thereon when in use." Thus, where the swaying of the scaffold and/or the fact that it did not support four times the maximum weight required to be used is a proximate cause of the plaintiff's injuries, a *prima facie* entitlement to absolute liability is established under *Labor Law §240(2)* or *§240(3), or both. Chacon v. New York University*, 258 A.D.2d 430, 685 N.Y.S.2d 96 (2d Dep't 1999).

> **Practice Tip:** To establish a breach of duty under *Labor Law §240*, the plaintiff need only prove that either *§240(1)* or *§240(2)* or *§240(3)* was violated.

[e] Establishing Proximate Cause

To prove a cause of action under *Labor Law §240*, beyond demonstrating that the statute was violated, the plaintiff must also show that the violation was a proximate cause of the injuries sustained. *See Haimes v. New York Telephone Co.*, 59 A.D.2d 813, 399 N.Y.S.2d 76, *aff'd*, 46 N.Y.2d 132, 417 N.Y.S.2d 863 (1978); *see also Mack v. Altmans Stage Lighting Co., Inc.*, 98 A.D.2d 468, 470 N.Y.S.2d 664 (2d Dep't 1984); *see also Golaszewski v. Cadman Plaza North, Inc.*, 136 A.D.2d 596, 523 N.Y.S.2d 581 (2d Dep't 1988) (plaintiff failed to explain how he fell, making it unclear whether alleged violation was proximate cause of accident).

> **Practice Tip:** In setting forth a *Labor Law §240* claim, the plaintiff must be able to show (under the specific facts of the case) that the injuries were caused by a *§240* violation. For example, the scaffold's unsupported plank collapsed, causing the plaintiff to fall and become injured; or the ladder slid or tipped, causing the plaintiff to lose his balance, fall, and sustain injuries.

§ 6.15 Defenses to *Labor Law §240* Claim

[1] Comparative Negligence and Assumption of Risk

Comparative negligence and assumption of risk are not defenses to a violation of *Labor Law §240. Haimes v. New York Telephone Co.*, 59 A.D.2d 813, 399 N.Y.S.2d 76 (1977), *aff'd*, 46 N.Y. 2d 132, 412 N.Y.S.2d 863 (1978); *see also Bombard v. Christian Missionary Alliance of Syracuse*, 292 A.D.2d 830, 739 N.Y.S.2d 516, 517 (4th Dep't 2002). The injured worker's fault, if any, does not decrease the owner's or general contractor's liability for failing to provide adequate devices. *Stalt v. General Foods Corp.*, 81 N.Y.2d 918, 597 N.Y.S.2d 650 (1993). Comparative negligence is not applicable to a *Labor Law §240* action. *See Glielmi v. Toys "R" Us, Inc.*, 94 A.D.2d 663, 462 N.Y.S.2d 255 (1st Dep't 1983), *aff'd*, 62 N.Y.2d 664, 476 N.Y.S.2d

283 (1984). However, *see Blake v. Neighborhood Housing Services of New York City*, 1 N.Y.3d 280, 771 N.Y.S.2d 484 (2003), as discussed in [3] below.

> **Practice Tip:** In connection with a motion for summary judgment (either brought by plaintiff or defendant), the defendant will usually attempt to point to something improper done by the plaintiff (e.g., see section [3] below). The plaintiff's attorney should, in responding to same, state that such conduct at most rises to comparative negligence (which is not a defense to *a Labor Law §240* claim and, hence, moot).

[2] Recalcitrant Worker Defense

Labor Law §240 does not impose liability where a worker has been provided adequate safety equipment and s/he refuses to use it. The existence of safe and adequate equipment available for use by a worker who refuses to use it amounts to a "*recalcitrant worker*". See *Jastrzebski v. North Shore Sch. Dist.*, 88 N.Y.2d 946, 647 N.Y.S.2d 708 (1996).

The "recalcitrant worker" defense is only applicable when the worker has been injured as a result of a refusal to use an available safety device provided by his or her employer or the owner. *Enright v. Buffalo Tech. Bld. "B" Pshp.*, 278 A.D.2d 927, 718 N.Y.S.2d 764 (4th Dep't 2000). *See also Cahill v. Triborough Bridge and Tunnel Authority*, 4 N.Y.3d 35, 790 N.Y.S.2d 740 (2004). The defense is not available where an employer or owner fails to supply adequate safety devices. *See Hagins v. State*, 81 N.Y.2d 921, 597 N.Y.S.2d 651 (1993). Where the worker refuses to use the safety equipment, s/he is considered a "recalcitrant worker" and, hence, is subject to comparative negligence; where the worker simply fails (as opposed to "refuses") to use the safety equipment, the "recalcitrant worker" defense does not apply. *See Neville v. Deters*, 175 A.D.2d 597, 572 N.Y.S.2d 256 (4th Dep't 1991). The trend of the courts has been to analyze cases in terms of the "sole proximate cause" defense discussed in [3] below, encompassing the "recalcitrant worker" defense therein.

[3] Sole Proximate Cause Defense

Where the facts show the plaintiff to be *solely* at fault in an accident, <u>and</u> there is no causation to trace to any *Labor Law §240* omission on the part of the owner or general contractor (e.g., absence of, defect in, or improper placement of safety device), the plaintiff will not be granted partial summary judgment on the issue of liability under *Labor Law §240*. Rather, where there is a judicial determination, as a matter of law, that the injured worker's conduct was the sole proximate cause of the accident, the plaintiff's case will be dismissed by the judge (either on summary judgment or at trial). *See Blake v. Neighborhood Housing Services of New York City*, 1 N.Y.3d 280, 771 N.Y.S.2d 484 (2003) (judgment against plaintiff affirmed due to plaintiff's "misuse" of ladder, i.e., failure to lock extension clips in place). The court in *Blake* specifically refers to the "recalcitrant worker" defense (as discussed above) in its analysis. *See also Robinson v. East Medical Center, LP*, 847 N.E.2d 1162, 6 N.Y.3d 550 (2006); *see also Molyneaux v. City of New York*, 28 A.D.3d 438, 813 N.Y.S.2d 729 (2d Dep't 2006), *lv. denied*, 7 N.Y.3d 705, 853 N.E.2d 244, 819 N.Y.S.2d 873 (2006); *see also Cahill v.*

Triborough Bridge & Tunnel Authority, 31 A.D.3d 347 (1st Dep't 2006). Where there is an issue of fact as to whether the injured worker was the sole proximate cause of the accident, the issue is left for the trier(s) of fact.

> **Practice Tip:** In light of the sole proximate cause defense, on a motion for summary judgment under *Labor Law §240(1)*, the plaintiff's attorney should articulate how the device (e.g., ladder) was not constructed, placed, and operated so as to afford proper protection to the worker. Demonstrating that a specific OSHA regulation and/or specific New York State Industrial Code provision was not met will make it extremely difficult for the defendant to successfully oppose the plaintiff's motion for summary judgment.

PART G: *LABOR LAW §241(6)* CLAIM

§ 6.16 Determining Whether Injured Party Protected By *Labor Law §241(6)*

Labor Law §241(6)'s language seems to provide protection to a greater class of workers than that of *Labor Law §240*. While each statute covers anyone who is "permitted or suffered to work on the project" (*Haimes v. New York Telephone Co.*, 46 N.Y.2d 132, 412 N.Y.S.2d 863 [1978]), *Labor Law §241(6)* also applies to those "lawfully frequenting such places." However, in *Mordkofsky v. V.C.V. Dev. Corp.*, 76 N.Y.2d 573, 561 N.Y.S.2d 892 (1990), the Court of Appeals held that *§241(6)* applied only to employees, mechanics, workers, or laborers "permitted or suffered to work" at the site.

> **Practice** Tip: A plaintiff who was not at the work site to *work* should not base a claim exclusively upon *§241(6)*, but rather should also make a claim for common-law negligence. Specific violation(s) of the NYS Industrial Code must be used to properly demonstrate such a claim.

> **Warning:** Like *Labor Law §240*, *§241(6)* does not provide protection to volunteer workers. *See Harrison v. City of New York*, 248 A.D.2d 592, 60 N.Y.S.2d 527 (2d Dep't 1998).

§ 6.17 Parties Liable Under *Labor Law §241(6)*

As with *Labor Law §240*, *Labor Law §241(6)* also imposes a non-delegable duty upon all owners, contractors and their agents. An owners and general contractor may delegate the work to others, but if there is a breach of *Labor Law §241(6)*, the owner and general contractor will ultimately still be responsible. Hence, owners, contractors, and their agents may delegate the *work*, but not their *responsibility*. *Kemp v. Lakelands Precast, Inc*, 84 A.D.2d 630, 444 N.Y.S.2d 274 (3d Dep't 1981), *modified*, 449 N.Y.S.2d 710 (1982). This is the most significant difference between a *§200* claim and a *§241(6)* claim. See §6.13[2] above.

Practice Tip: Under *Labor Law §241(6)*, there is no exemption for owners of one and two-family homes who contract for, but do not direct or control, the work. Hence, an owner of a one or two-family home is responsible to comply with the NYS Industrial Code, regardless of whether s/he directs or controls the work. *Ferrero v. Best Modular Homes, Inc.*, 33 A.D.3d 847, 823 N.Y.S.2d 477 (2d Dep't 2006).

§ 6.18 Establishing Liability Under *Labor Law §241(6)* Claim

[1] Establishing Violation of *Labor Law §241(6)*

[a] Establishing Work as Construction, Demolition, or Excavation

Labor Law §241(6) was enacted in order to provide additional protection from the dangers associated with construction, demolition and excavation. *Allen v. Cloutier*, 44 N.Y.2d 290, 405 N.Y.S.2d 630 (1978). *Labor Law §241(6)* only applies where construction, demolition, or excavation is being performed. *Nagel v. D & R Realty Corp.*, 99 N.Y.2d 98, 752 N.Y.S.2d 581 (2002). For a definition of construction work, demolition work, and excavation work, see *12 NYCRR §23-1.4(13)*, *12 NYCRR §23-1.4(16)*, and *12 NYCRR §23-1.4(19)*, respectively.

Practice Tip: *Labor Law §241(6)* applies to workers employed in construction, demolition, and excavation who are exposed not only to gravity-related dangers, but also to those dangers associated with many other things, including vehicles, machinery, equipment, fire, explosion, electricity, tools, machines, materials, and exposure to the elements and air contaminants. *See 12 NYCRR §23-1.2.*

[b] Establishing Unsafe Condition(s) at Work Site

Under *Labor Law §241(6)*, the plaintiff simply needs to show that the work site was *unsafe* (i.e., not that the owner or general contractor created, or had notice of, the condition). The plaintiff is not required to prove negligence or notice on the part of the defendant. *Rizzuto v. L.A. Wenger Contracting Co., Inc.*, 91 N.Y.2d 343, 670 N.Y.S.2d 816 (1998) (plaintiff need not prove defendant had actual or constructive notice of the dangerous condition in issue). *See also Wrighten v. ZHN Contracting Corporation*, 32 N.Y.3d 1019, 822 N.Y.S.2d 115 (2d Dep't 2006) (actual or constructive notice irrelevant under *Labor Law §241[6]* since liability is vicarious).

Practice Tip: Under *Labor Law §241(6)*, owners and general contractors may *not* escape liability by delegating their duties, unlike under *§200*. Since the duty is non-delegable, regardless of their control or supervision of the job site, *notice* is not an element of a *Labor Law §241(6)* claim. *Allen v. Cloutier*, 44 N.Y.2d 290, 405 N.Y.S. 630 (1978).

Warning: The issue of whether a condition at the work site is safe or unsafe generally presents a factual question. *Belcastro v. Hewlett-Woodmere Union Free Sch. Dist. No. 14*, 286 A.D.2d 744, 730 N.Y.S.2d 535 (2d Dep't 2001) (plaintiff's motion for summary judgment denied because *§241[6]* violation was only some evidence of negligence and jury needed to determine whether equipment, operation, or conduct at work site was reasonable and adequate under specific circumstances). Hence, a claim under *§241(6)* is generally not one in which the plaintiff will successfully bring a motion for summary judgment. However, the First and Second Departments have awarded summary judgment to plaintiffs under *§241(6)* where the evidence was uncontroverted that a *specific* NYS Industrial Code provision was a substantial factor in causing the accident. See §[3] below.

[c] Establishing Specific Safety Violation

While the duty imposed under *Labor Law §241(6)* is essentially the same duty imposed by *Labor Law §200* (i.e., to provide a safe work place), a *§241(6)* claim must allege that the defendant violated a *specific* applicable safety regulation of the New York State Industrial Code. *See Mancini v. Pedra Constr.*, 293 A.D.2d 453, 740 N.Y.S.2d 387 (2d Dep't 2002) (Industrial Code provision relied on established *general* safety standard, insufficient to give rise to nondelegable duty as required by *Labor Law 241[6]*). *See also Kwang Ho Kim*, 47 A.D.3d 616, 852 N.Y.S.2d 138 (2d Dep't 2008). *See also Ross v. Curtis-Palmer Hydro-Electric Co.*, 81 N.Y.2d 494, 601 N.Y.S.2d 49 (1993).

Practice Tip: The best way to establish an unsafe condition is by relying on one or more rules promulgated under *Industrial Code Rule 23.* The NYS Industrial Code can be found on the NYS Department of Labor website at www.labor.state.ny.us/workerprotection/safetyhealth/sh23.shtm. *See also PJI §2:216A.*

Practice Tip: Provisions of the NYS Industrial Code which refer only to the duty of employers, also impose a duty on owners. *Rice v. City of Cortland*, 262 A.D.2d 770, 691 N.Y.S.2d 616 (3d Dep't 1999). *See also Halftown v. Triple D Leasing Corp.*, 89 A.D.2d 794, 453 N.Y.S.2d 514 (4th Dep't 1982).

Warning: Only a violation of the NYS Industrial Code (i.e., regulations set forth by the NYS Industrial Board of Appeals) may be used as a basis for *Labor Law §241(6)* liability. *Heller v. 83rd Street Investors Ltd. Partnership*, 228 A.D.2d 371, 645 N.Y.S.2d 8 (1st Dep't 1996) (violation of NYC Administrative Code not proper basis for *Labor Law §241(6)* claim).

[2] Establishing Proximate Cause

The plaintiff must establish that the *specific* safety violation was a proximate cause of his or her injuries. *See Shandraw v. Tops Market, Inc.*, 244 A.D.2d 997, 665 N.Y.S.2d 486 (4th Dep't 1997) (code violation alleged did not apply to facts of case and thus *Labor Law §241(6)* claim did not exist).

[3] Violation of *Labor Law §241(6)* Merely Evidence of Negligence

Unlike the absolute liability provisions of *Labor Law §§240, 241(1) - (5)*, and *§241-a*, which set forth the specific requirements, the NYS Industrial Board of Appeals is given the authority to carry out the intent of *§241(6)*. A violation of the NYS Industrial Board of Appeals' rules and regulations (i.e., a specific NYS Industrial Code violation), though, is merely evidence of negligence. *See Irwin v. St. Joseph's Intercommunity Hosp.*, 236 A.D.2d 123, 665 N.Y.S.2d 773 (4th Dep't 1997) (summary judgment denied as questions of fact existed regarding comparative negligence). The First and Second Departments have differed, though, and granted summary judgment under *Labor Law §241(6)* where it was clear that a violation of an Industrial Code provision was a substantial factor in causing the accident. *See Harris v. Arnell Construction Corporation*, 47 A.D.3d 768, 850 N.Y.S.2d 547 (2d Dep't 2008); *see also Auluaga v. PPC Construction, LLC*, 45 A.D.3d 479, 847 N.Y.S.2d 30 (1st Dep't 2007).

§ 6.19 Comparative Negligence and Assumption of Risk

Comparative negligence and assumption of risk are applicable defenses to a *Labor Law §241(6)* cause of action. *See Long v. Forest-Fehlhaber*, 55 N.Y.2d 154, 448 N.Y.S.2d 132 (1982). *See CPLR §1411. Labor Law §241(6)* is *not* a self-executing statute resulting in absolute liability. *See Uluturk v. City of New York*, 748 N.Y.S.2d 371 (1st Dep't 2002) (comparative negligence available as affirmative defense in action based on *Labor Law §241[6]*).

> **Practice Tip:** The plaintiff wants to depict the claim as a violation of *Labor Law §240, §241(1) - (5)*, or *§241-a*, generally making the plaintiff's own negligence irrelevant (except where plaintiff's conduct is the sole proximate cause of the accident). The defendant, on the other hand, will try to shape the claim into one under *§200* or *§241(6)* (i.e., where the plaintiff's comparative negligence can proportionately diminish an award).

PART H: *LABOR LAW §241(1) - (5)* CLAIM

§ 6.20 Determining Whether Injured Party Protected by *Labor Law §241 (1) - (5)*

The parties protected by *Labor Law §241(1) - (5)* are the same as those protected under *Labor Law §240* (i.e., any "person so employed" on a construction project). See §6.12 above.

§ 6.21 Determining Parties Liable Under *Labor Law §241(1) - (5)*

As with *Labor Law §240, Labor Law §241(1) - (5)* imposes absolute liability upon "all contractors and owners and their agents" for any violation of *§241(1), (2), (3), (4), or (5),* even if they do not control or supervise the work. The exemption for owners of one or two-family dwellings under *§240* is the same under *§241.* Under both statutes, an owner of a one or two-family dwelling who contracts for but does not direct or control the work is not liable for violations of the statutes. *See Labor Law §241.* See §6.13 above.

> **Practice Tip:** The defense is **not** available for *Labor Law §241(6)* claims. Hence, when faced with a case against an owner of a one or two-family dwelling, the plaintiff's attorney must generally focus on violation(s) of the NYS Industrial Code (i.e., in setting forth a *prima facie* case under *Labor Law §241[6]*).

§ 6.22 Establishing Absolute Liability Under *Labor Law §241(1) - (5)*

[1] Establishing Violation of *Labor Law §241(1) - (5)*

[a] Establishing Work as Construction, Demolition, or Excavation

Labor Law §241(1),(2),(3),(4), and *(5)* apply to construction, demolition, and excavation work. For a definition of construction work, demolition work, and excavation work, *see 12 NYCRR §23-1.4(13), 12 NYCRR §23-1.4(16)*, and *12 NYCRR §23-1.4(19)*, respectively. See §6.14[1][b] above.

[b] Establishing Violation of *Labor Law §241(1), (2), (3), (4), or (5)*

Labor Law §241(1) - (5) and *§240* are similar in that they each protect workers from falling hazards; the statutes differ, however, as to the scope of the falling hazards covered. *Labor Law §241(1) - (5)* protects against falls through the open spaces *within* the building where the permanent floors are planned to be installed. *Labor Law §241(1) - (4)* requires owners and contractors to comply with specific requirements for constructing the flooring in multi-story buildings as the work progresses.

Labor Law §241(5) requires all elevator and elevating machine shafts and openings on each floor to be fenced or enclosed. The fencing or enclosure must include a barrier of suitable height on all sides; two sides, however, may be used for placing and removing materials (and those sides must be guarded by an adjustable barrier between three and four feet from the floor and at least two feet from the edges of such shafts or openings).

[2] Establishing Proximate Cause

A violation of any one of subsections (1) through (5) of *Labor Law §241*, so long as a proximate cause of the injuries sustained, results in absolute liability. *Long v. Forest-Fehlhaber*, 55 N.Y.2d 154, 448 N.Y.S.2d 132 (1982).

§ 6.23 Comparative Negligence and Assumption of Risk

Since *Labor Law §241(1) - (5)* sets forth specific responsibilities, a violation of any subsection results in absolute liability for which comparative negligence and assumption of risk are not viable defenses.

Warning: Where the facts show the plaintiff to be *solely* at fault in an accident, and there is no causation to trace to any *Labor Law §241 (1) - (5)* omission on the part of the owner or general contractor (e.g., absence of, defect in, or improper placement of safety device), the defendants will argue that the plaintiff's motion for summary judgment should be denied and that the case should be dismissed, pursuant to *Blake v. Neighborhood Housing Services of New York City*, 1 N.Y.3d 280, 771 N.Y.S.2d 484 (2003) (*Labor Law §240(1)* case). See §6.15[1] above.

PART I: *LABOR LAW §241-a* CLAIM

§ 6.24 Determining Whether Injured Party Protected By *Labor Law §241-a*

Labor Law §241-a protects workers working in or at elevator shaftways, hatchways, and stairwells of buildings in the course of construction or demolition.

§ 6.25 Parties Absolutely Liable Under *Labor Law §241-a*

Labor Law §241-a imposes a *non-delegable* duty upon all owners and contractors. *See Horan v. Dormitory Authority*, 43 A.D.2d 65, 349 N.Y.S.2d 448 (3d Dep't 1973). Just like *§240 and §241,* owners and contractors are required to comply with *§241-a* whether or not they are in control of the work site. Further, the homeowner's exemption (for one and two-family dwellings) set forth in *Labor Law §241* should be read into *§241-a. See Khela v. Neiger*, 85 N.Y.2d 333, 624 N.Y.S.2d 566 (1995). See §6.13 above.

§ 6.26 Establishing Absolute Liability Under *Labor Law §241-a*

[1] Establishing Violation of *Labor Law §241-a*

[a] Establishing Work Being Performed in Elevator Shaftway, Hatchway, or Stairwell

Labor Law §241-a provides protection to any person "working in or at elevator shaftways, hatchways and stairwells of buildings" while in the course of construction or demolition. *Labor Law §241-a* protects workers injured as a result of a fall, or falling object, through an opening which is designed and intended to remain open; it applies to elevator shaftways, hatchways and stairwells which are designed to remain open after the construction of the building is completed. This statute, however, has been very narrowly interpreted by the courts. *See Silvers v. Howell, Inc.*, 129 A.D.2d

694, 514 N.Y.S.2d 455 (2d Dep't 1987) (ventilation shaft not hatchway for *Labor Law §241-a* purposes). The statute does not apply where it is necessary for the shaft to remain open. *Boyle v. 42nd Street Development Project, Inc.*, 38 A.D.3d 404, 835 N.Y.S.2d 7 (1st Dep't 2007).

[b] Establishing Breach of Duty

Labor Law §241-a requires planking for elevator shafts, hatchways and stairwells. *Bruno v. Almar Residence Corp.*, 13 A.D.2d 232, 216 N.Y.S.2d 157 (1st Dep't 1961); *Silvers v. Howell, Inc.*, 129 A.D.2d 694, 514 N.Y.S.2d 455 (2d Dep't 1987). *Labor Law §241-a* requires the use of sound planking at least two-inches thick over the opening at heights not greater than two stories above, or one story below, the workers to protect them from "falling" hazards. *See Baum v. Ciminelli-Cowper Co.*, 300 A.D.2d 1028, 755 N.Y.S.2d 138 (4th Dep't 2002) (plaintiff's motion for summary judgment, pursuant to *Labor Law §241-a*, granted where plaintiff fell into elevator shaft while welding and planking required by statute was missing). By requiring planking two stories *above* the workers, *Labor Law §241-a* provides protection from falling objects, in addition to falls from elevated heights.

> **Practice Tip:** Under *Labor Law §241-a*, notice is not a required element. *Duncan v. Twin Leasing Corp.*, 283 A.D. 1080, 131 N.Y.S.2d 423 (2d Dep't 1954).

[2] Establishing Proximate Cause

In order to establish liability under *Labor Law §241-a*, the plaintiff must prove that the violation of *Labor Law §241-a* was a proximate cause of the accident.

§ 6.27 Comparative Negligence / Assumption of Risk

A violation of *Labor Law §241-a* results in absolute liability, rendering the defenses of comparative negligence and assumption of risk inapplicable. *Doucoure v. Atlantic Development Group, LLC*, 18 A.D.3d 337, 796 N.Y.S.2d 48 (1st Dep't 2005); *Koploff v. St. Vincent Ferrier Church*, 39 A.D.2d 581, 332 N.Y.S.2d 388 (2d Dep't 1972).

> **Warning:** Where the facts show the plaintiff to be *solely* at fault in an accident, <u>and</u> there is no causation to trace to any *Labor Law §241-a* omission on the part of the owner or general contractor (e.g., absence of, defect in, or improper placement of safety device), the defendants will argue that the plaintiff should not prevail on a motion for summary judgment brought under *Labor Law §241* and that the case should be dismissed, pursuant to *Blake v. Neighborhood Housing Services of New York City*, 1 N.Y.3d 280, 771 N.Y.S.2d 484 (2003) (*Labor Law §240(1)* case). See §6.15[1] above.

PART J: *LABOR LAW §202* CLAIM

§ 6.28 Determining Whether Injured Party Protected By *Labor Law §202*

Labor Law §202 protects window washers, and their employees, engaged in cleaning windows and exterior surfaces of commercial / public buildings from the outside.

§ 6.29 Parties Liable Under *Labor Law §202*

Labor Law §202 holds the owner, lessee, agent, and manager of every public building responsible to comply with the statute.

§ 6.30 Establishing Liability Under *Labor Law §202*

[1] Establishing Breach of Duty Under *Labor Law §202*

Labor Law §202 requires the responsible parties to "provide such safe means for the cleaning of the windows and of the exterior surfaces of such buildings as may be required by the board of standards and appeals." *See Labor Law §202*, as amended in 1970, ch. 822, §1. There are three ways to breach *Labor Law §202*: failure to provide any safety devices, supplying device(s) not approved by the NYS Industrial Board of Appeals, or inadequate maintenance of such devices. A plaintiff may simultaneously maintain causes of action under both *Labor Law §202* and *Labor Law §240. See Bauer v. Female Academy of the Sacred Heart*, 95 N.Y.2d 445 (2002).

[2] Establishing Proximate Cause

In order to establish liability under *Labor Law §202*, the plaintiff must prove that the defendant's negligence, including any violation of *Labor Law §202,* was a proximate cause of the accident.

§ 6.31 Comparative Negligence / Assumption of Risk

As the statute, amended in 1970, refers to the board of standards and appeals, a breach of same only amounts to some evidence of negligence; this is not an absolute liability provision (although, at one time, it was). *See Stanley v. Carrier Corporation*, 303 A.D.2d 1022, 756 N.Y.S.2d 689 (4th Dep't 2003).

PART K: LITIGATING LABOR LAW ACCIDENT CASE

§ 6.32 Requesting Documents Once Retained

The plaintiff's attorney may wish to obtain some, or all, of the following documents once s/he has been retained:

- copy of the deed to the premises, as well as a search for leases and liens affecting the property;
- copies of all accident reports, including the C-2 form (employer's workers' compensation report), the C-3 (employee's workers' compensation application), and the ambulance call report;
- copies of OSHA regulations and state and local building codes in effect on the date of the accident[7];
- any reports or records filed with the Workers' Compensation Board, including transcripts of any testimony given; and

---

7   Certified copies of OSHA standards (29 CFR 1910) can be obtained from the Superintendent of Documents, US Government Printing Office, Washington, D.C. 20402. A certified copy of Industrial Code Rule 23 can be obtained from the New York State Department of State, Division of Information Services, 162 Washington Avenue, Albany, New York 12231.

- all of the plaintiff's medical records, including the ambulance report, hospital records, and other medical records.

Freedom of Information Law (FOIL) requests should be made to the government / municipal agencies which issue building permits (to obtain the complete building permit file), as well as to OSHA (U.S. Department of Labor Form DL1-520) for their entire file, if any (regarding any inspection they conducted, including copies of photographs, violations, and prior investigations and violations involving the same owner and contractors).

§ 6.33 Preparing Complaint in Labor Law Accident Case

[1] Naming Various Parties as Defendants

The plaintiff's attorney should name the owner, general contractor (or any other contractor, other than plaintiff's employer or co-employee, with supervisory control), and agents of both (such as the managing agent) as defendants. Further, if plaintiff's counsel anticipates that the owner and general contractor will commence third-party actions against other defendants, the plaintiff may wish to name all possible defendants in the original action.

[2] Required Elements of Labor Law Accident Complaint

In preparing the Labor Law accident complaint, the plaintiff's counsel should allege the following, in separate paragraphs, with respect to each defendant on the date of the accident:

- owner of the premises;
- lessor of the premises;
- lessee of the premises;
- possessor of the premises;
- control of the premises;
- control of the plaintiff's work at the job site;
- supervision of the plaintiff's work at the job site;
- general contractor of the job;
- contract between plaintiff's employer and defendant;
- contract between general contractor and defendant; and
- contract between owner and defendant.

The complaint should allege separate causes of action, where applicable, for:

- common-law negligence;
- *Labor Law §200*;
- *Labor Law §240* (subdivisions 1 - 3);
- *Labor Law §241* (subdivisions 1 - 5);
- *Labor Law §241* (subdivision 6);
- *Labor Law §241-a*;

- *Labor Law §202* (in the case of a window washer); and
- *General Municipal Law §205(a)* or *§205(e)* (in the case of a firefighter or police officer who is making a claim against his or her employer).

[3] Pleading Applicable *CPLR §1602* Exceptions

The plaintiff's attorney should allege that the provisions of *CPLR §1601* (limitations on joint and several liability regarding non-economic losses) do not apply by reason of one or more of the exceptions set forth in *CPLR §1602*. The specific exceptions possibly applicable to the case must be alleged in the complaint. See chapter 5, §5.17[4].

[4] Choosing Best Venue

The plaintiff's attorney controls the venue of the case at the outset, choosing where to file the lawsuit. The plaintiff may bring the action in any county in which any one of the parties maintains a residence on the date the lawsuit is commenced. Further, a party may have more than one residence; any one of them is a proper venue, increasing plaintiff's venue options. *See CPLR §§503, 504, 505*. See also §5.04[3] above.

In the area of Labor Law accident cases, the Appellate Divisions' decisions vary on many legal issues related to liability. The plaintiff's attorney should research the issues relevant to the particular case before commencing an action, as forum shopping is important in this area. In general, but not always, the First Department is the most plaintiff-friendly. Choosing the proper Department to venue the specific case can be dispositive. See §6.32[4] above.

§ 6.34 Demanding Discovery in Labor Law Accident Case

[1] General Demands for Disclosure

Upon receipt of each defendant's answer, the plaintiff's attorney should, as in all cases, immediately serve demands for:

- insurance information (including primary, excess, and umbrella policies);
- statements attributable to the plaintiff (written or recorded);
- photographs;
- accident reports;
- surveillance material (of the plaintiff, as well as of the accident, if any);
- expert disclosure; and
- witness information.

See CPLR §3101.

[2] Demanding Specific Documents Relating to Labor Law Accident Case

The plaintiff's attorney should also serve a demand requesting production of some or all of the following documents:

- leases and subleases affecting the premises on the date of the accident;

- contracts, subcontracts, agreements and/or purchase orders relating to work performed by, or for, any defendant relating to the premises;
- photographs, films, and videotapes (including progress photographs, films, and videotapes) of the premises;
- daily progress reports, daily logs, and field reports relating to the job;
- minutes of all job meetings;
- documents signed by, or on behalf of, the plaintiff relating to the project;
- plans, specifications, blueprints, drawings, permits, and applications relating to the project;
- inventories of safety equipment owned, leased, or available for use by the defendant or its employees on the project;
- site safety plan prepared regarding the job;
- daily safety reports and/or safety meeting minutes regarding the job;
- financing agreements relating to the property on the date of the accident;
- payroll records relating to work performed at the premises, reflecting the identity of any employees on site;
- entire contents of the job file; and
- for *§200* and *§241(6)* causes of action, see chapter 5, §5.18 for additional documents and information to be requested.

Additionally, pursuant to *CPLR §3120*, the plaintiff is entitled to an inspection and testing of land (e.g., ladder, scaffolding, etc.), relevant to the case.

> **Practice Tip:** The plaintiff's attorney should attempt to have all outstanding discovery requests court-ordered at the preliminary conference. The plaintiff's attorney should make sure to receive requested documents, and to conduct any expert inspection, prior to commencement of examinations before trial. This should be clearly set forth in the preliminary conference order.

See chapter 11, §11.04 for a preliminary conference checklist for construction (or Labor Law) accident cases.

§ 6.35 Conducting Examinations Before Trial in Labor Law Accident Case
[1] Preparing Plaintiff
[a] Discussing Documents

The contents of relevant documents such as accident reports – including the employer's accident report (C-2 form), employee's workers' compensation application (C-3 form) –, photographs, witness statements, the bill(s) of particulars, the ambulance call report, emergency room records, and all of the plaintiff's other medical records should be discussed with the plaintiff prior to the examination before trial.

[b] Liability

In a Labor Law accident case, the plaintiff should be prepared as to what the law requires as far as proving absolute liability. The plaintiff should be prepared for the "recalcitrant worker" and "sole proximate cause" defenses (see §6.15 above). Further, the plaintiff should be prepared to combat any defense of comparative negligence – which will only be relevant if the case falls outside the purview of the absolute liability provisions of the Labor Law.

[c] Damages

[1] Pain and Suffering

The plaintiff should be prepared to answer questions regarding pain, medical treatment, objective testing, surgeries undergone and future surgeries, scarring, hospital stays, pain medications (prescription and non-prescription), and casts and other prescribed medical devices (e.g., canes, crutches, and walkers).

[2] Prior and Subsequent Accidents and Injuries

The plaintiff should be prepared to answer questions regarding prior and subsequent accidents and injuries. The insurance companies have access to a system whereby they can obtain information regarding prior claims the plaintiff has made. The plaintiff should also be prepared for questions regarding whether the plaintiff re-injured himself / herself after the accident. See chapter 5, §5.19[b][2].

[3] Economic Losses

The Labor Law accident plaintiff typically has had all of his or her medical expenses and some of his or her loss of earnings paid for by workers' compensation. The plaintiff should be well-prepared to testify about earnings history, past loss of earnings and potential future loss of earnings (including loss of pension, annuities, health insurance, etc.) and any other economic loss sustained. The plaintiff should be familiarized with the approximate amount of the medical bills workers' compensation has paid (as workers' compensation has a statutory lien on the file and, hence, plaintiff can recoup that money at trial). The plaintiff should also anticipate questions regarding why s/he is unable to work, attempts to work, attempts to seek alternative employment, job applications, whether the assistance of a vocational rehabilitation professional (i.e., job counselor) was sought, his / her educational background, his / her other skills, whether s/he applied for disability, and how s/he is presently supporting him / herself.

Practice Tip: Many of the largest cases are Labor Law accident cases wherein a plaintiff is never able to return to work, making for a potentially huge loss of earnings claim. These cases scare insurance carriers because even a large verdict for economic losses will be affirmed on appeal.

See chapter 11, §11.10 for a checklist of preparation topics for a construction accident examination before trial.

[2] Conducting Labor Law Accident Examinations Before Trial

The plaintiff's attorney should be prepared to ask questions to establish the names of the owners, contractors, and their agents. The plaintiff's attorney wants to establish who owned the premises on the date of the accident, the names of the contractor(s) with supervisory control (usually the general contractor), and the identity of their agents.

Most importantly, the plaintiff's attorney needs to use the examinations before trial to establish all of the elements necessary for absolute liability (as discussed in great detail throughout this chapter), thus enabling the plaintiff to succeed on its future motion for summary judgment. See §6.32 above. Further questions must be asked in order to establish liability in the non-absolute liability causes of actions – *Labor Law §200, Labor Law §241(6)*, and common-law negligence – just in case the plaintiff's motion for summary judgment is denied. See §§6.10 - 6.11, §§6.16 - 6.19 above; see also chapter 5, §5.02.

The examination before trial of the defendants should further be used to determine that the proper parties have been sued or, if not, can be sued. The plaintiff's attorney should also attempt to ascertain the existence of documents, as well as to explore the authenticity and reliability of documents previously exchanged. The plaintiff's attorney should further determine what knowledge the witness has of the accident, as well as attempt to determine the identity and accounts of other witnesses. See chapter 11, §11.07 for a checklist of topics for conducting a construction accident examination before trial.

§ 6.36 Making Motion for Summary Judgment in Labor Law Accident Case

The plaintiff's attorney's goal in most Labor Law accident cases should be to make a motion for summary judgment on the issue of liability pursuant to the absolute liability provisions of *Labor Law §240, §241(1) - (5)*, or *Labor Law §241-a*. Each step of the case should be handled with this in mind. If the plaintiff can prove each element necessary under any of the absolute liability statutes (as discussed in this chapter), summary judgment should be awarded; the only issue for the jury will be an assessment of damages. Besides removing the issue of liability from the case, a successful motion for summary judgment will entitle the plaintiff to interest from the date of the liability decision. *CPLR §5002. See Van Nostrand v. Froehlich*, 44 A.D.3d 54, 844 N.Y.S.2d 293 (2d Dep't 2007). If the defendant establishes as a matter of law that the accident was not caused by any statutory violation, or that the plaintiff was the "sole proximate cause" of the accident, the defendant can obtain summary judgment.

§ 6.37 Dealing with Workers' Compensation Liens

The workers' compensation insurance carrier, by statute, has a lien against the proceeds of a third-party negligence action. Prior to settling the negligence case, the plaintiff's attorney must obtain the consent of the workers' compensation insurance carrier. Then, upon settling the negligence case, the workers' compensation carrier's lien must be paid. See chapter 8, §8.32 for an extensive discussion regarding workers' compensation liens, including the statutory reduction and the *Kelly* calculation.

CHAPTER 7

GOVERNMENT LIABILITY

PART A: OVERVIEW

§ 7.01 Overview – Government Liability

Claims against municipalities (i.e., municipal corporations, districts, and public benefit corporations) encompass numerous procedural prerequisites, shortened statutes of limitations, and more stringent levels of proof for the claimant's / plaintiff's attorney to comply with. This chapter discusses the procedural requirements of *General Municipal Law (GML) §50-e* and *§50-h*, the most ubiquitous statutes in the government liability arena. Further discussed are the requirements for claims against the State of New York, pursuant to the *Court of Claims Act*.

PART B: MEETING PROCEDURAL REQUIREMENTS

§ 7.02 Identifying Proper Government Entities

Identification of the proper responsible government entity or entities is often a difficult task. In the City of New York, for example, *The Green Book: Official Directory of the City of New York* should be consulted. This directory lists all the various municipalities in the City of New York, and contains their addresses for service. Examples of public benefit corporations within the City of New York include:

- Battery Park City Operating Authority
- City University of New York (CUNY)
- Department of Education of the City of New York
- Dormitory Authority of the State of New York
- Long Island Railroad (LIRR)
- Manhattan and Bronx Surface Transit Authority (MABSTOA)
- Metro-North Commuter Railroad
- Metropolitan Assistance Corp. for the City of New York
- Metropolitan Transportation Authority (MTA)
- New York City Health and Hospitals Corp. (NYCHHC)
- New York City Housing Authority (NYCHA)

- New York City Municipal Water Finance Authority
- New York City Off-Track Betting Corp. (OTB)
- New York City School Construction Authority
- New York City Transit Authority (NYCTA)
- New York City Municipal Water Board
- New York City Convention Center Development Corp.
- Port Authority of New York and New Jersey
- Roosevelt Island Operating Corp.
- Triboro Bridge and Tunnel Authority (TBTA)
- United Nations Development Corp.

§ 7.03 Notice of Claim
[1] Notice of Claim Requirements

Prior to commencing an action against a municipality, the claimant's attorney must serve a notice of claim on the municipality. The rationale behind this requirement is to provide municipalities with an opportunity to investigate any claims prior to the commencement of an action.

Pursuant to *GML §50-e*, the following are required with respect to a notice of claim:

- the notice must be in writing, sworn to by or on behalf of the claimant(s);
- the name and address of the claimant (as well as any claimants with derivative claims) and the claimant's attorney must be specified;
- the nature of the claim (e.g., personal injuries) must be specified;
- the time, date, and place of the occurrence must be specified; and
- the items of damage or injuries claimed to have been sustained, so far as practicable, must be specified.

Practice Tip: If the municipality cannot, based solely on the notice of claim, go to the exact location of the accident, the notice of claim may be found to be prejudicial to the municipality (ultimately resulting in dismissal of the case). *See Lupo v. City of New York*, 160 A.D.2d 773, 554 N.Y.S.2d 60 (2d Dep't 1991). Hence, it is good practice to include meets and bounds estimates (e.g., approximately ten feet from pole, fifteen feet from curb) and attach photographs (with arrows, etc.) to the notice of claim.

Practice Tip: A notice of claim should be served upon all potential municipal defendants in order to preserve the claimant's right to commence an action against each of those municipalities.

[2] 90-Day Time Limit for Serving Notice of Claim

Pursuant to *GML §50-e*, a pre-action notice of claim must be served on any potentially liable municipality within 90 days of the accident.[8] *See also Pub. Hous. Law §§157, 402-a(13).* Otherwise, the claimant will be barred from suing the municipality. In a wrongful death case, a notice of claim must be served within 90 days of the appointment of the administrator / executor of the estate. *Gibbons v. City of Troy*, 91 A.D.2d 707, 457 N.Y.S.2d 950 (3d Dep't 1982). The notice of claim must be served on each potential municipal defendant by personal service, registered mail, or certified mail upon the corporation or its attorney. *See GML §50-e 3(a).* If the notice of claim is served by registered or certified mail, the date of service will be the date of mailing. If the ninetieth day falls on a weekend or a holiday, the time limit is extended to the next business day.

[3] Curing Improperly Served Notice of Claim

If the notice of claim is served improperly (i.e., by regular mail), but within the 90-day time limit, it will be deemed proper service if:

- the municipality fails to return the notice of claim within 30 days of receipt; or
- the notice of claim is returned by the municipality within 30 days of its receipt and the notice of claim is re-served properly within 10 days; or
- the municipality demands an examination (i.e., an oral or physical examination pursuant to *GML §50-h*).

See GML §50e 3(c)-(d).

[4] Curing Defective Notice of Claim

A notice of claim may be amended without court order if still within the 90-day time period. Otherwise, the court's permission is required (and the claimant must seek to have the notice of claim relate back, *nunc pro tunc*). Pursuant to *GML §50-e*, it is within the court's discretion to allow an amended notice of claim (i.e., after the 90-day period has expired) for a mistake made in good-faith, so long as the municipality is not prejudiced. If the municipality did not yet investigate the matter prior to an attempt to amend the notice of claim, there is clearly no prejudice in allowing the amended notice of claim. Prejudice must be conclusively established (e.g., the municipality conducted a timely investigation at the wrong site due to the mistake). With respect to transitory conditions (e.g., snow and ice), it is highly unlikely that the municipality would be prejudiced. Court approval should be sought promptly, for the court can only grant this permission in the event the statute of limitations on the action has not passed (i.e., one year and 90 days from the date of the accident, generally).

---

8   The Long Island Railroad does not have a notice of claim requirement, but requires a demand within one year, and commencement of an action within one year and 30 days, or two years for wrongful death. *Pub. Auth. Law §§1276(1)(2), 2981-2982.* The Port Authority of New York and New Jersey mandates commencement of a lawsuit (for personal injury or wrongful death) within one year, and a notice of claim at least sixty days prior thereto. *Unconsol. Law §7107.*

[5] Late Notice of Claim
[a] Late Notice of Claim – In General

An untimely notice of claim is a nullity without leave of the court. *Chikara v. City of New York*, 10 A.D.2d 862, 199 N.Y.S.2d 829 (2d Dep't 1960). Being a legal nullity, it has no effect of conferring actual knowledge upon the municipality. *Mack v. City of New York*, 696 N.Y.S.2d 206, 265 A.D.2d 308 (4th Dep't 2006). In order to file a late notice of claim, the claimant must:

- offer a reasonable excuse for the delay in filing the notice of claim;
- establish that the defendant had actual or constructive knowledge of the facts of the claim; and
- establish that the defendant is not substantially prejudiced (by being denied an opportunity to fully investigate, e.g., witnesses, accident report).

See GML §50-e(5) and §50-e(1)(a).

Practice Tip: An application for leave to serve a late notice of claim must be supported by factual evidence such as affidavits, certified medical records, etc. A denial of the motion will result in the claim being barred.

An application for a leave to file a late notice of claim must be made within the statute of limitations period for commencing an action against the municipality. Once the application is made, the statute of limitations is tolled until the court issues a decision.

Where a notice of claim was timely served, however, an amended notice of claim after the 90-day period is permitted. *Goodwin v. New York City Hous. Auth.*, 42 A.D.3d 63, 834 N.Y.S.2d 181 (1st Dep't 2007).

[b] Incapacitated Claimant

Physical, mental, or emotional incapacity, supported by proper evidence (including medical records), is an excuse often accepted by the courts in allowing the filing of a late notice of claim. *Myette v. New York City Housing Auth.*, 611 N.Y.S.2d 521, 204 A.D.2d 54 (1st Dep't 1994).

[c] Infancy

Pursuant to *GML §50(e)*, the 90-day notice of claim requirement is not tolled by *CPLR §208*, for the *CPLR* does not mention tolling a "condition precedent" to an action (i.e., the notice of claim requirement), only "commencement" of an action. Courts do have some discretion, though, allowing them to toll the notice of claim requirement at times. The plaintiff's attorney must attempt to show a nexus between the delay and the state of infancy which would excuse the delay. *Knightner v. City of New York*, 702 N.Y.S.2d 643, 269 A.D.2d 397 (2d Dep't 2000). Absent a showing of prejudice, the courts generally grant such motions with regularity. *Clark v. City of Ithaca*, 652 N.Y.S.2d 819, 235 A.D.2d 746 (3d Dep't 1997). The one year and 90 day statute of limitations contained in the General Municipal Law in which to commence a personal injury action (or two years for wrongful death) *is* tolled by *CPLR §208*.

Warning: The extension of time granted to the infant does not extend to his or her parent's derivative claim, if any.

[d] Law Office Failure

Law office failure is an inadequate excuse to file a late notice of claim. *Jensen v. City of Saratoga Springs,* 203 A.D.2d 863, 611 N.Y.S.2d 330 (3d Dep't 1994).

§ 7.04 *50-h* Examination

[1] *50-h* – In General

Pursuant to *GML §50-h*, municipal corporations, fire districts, ambulance districts, and school districts have the right to demand that the claimant appear for:

- an oral examination "relative to the occurrence and extent of the injuries and damage to which the claim is made"; and
- a physical examination by a duly qualified physician.

Warning: Cases are often lost at the *50-h* hearing due to improper preparation of the case and the claimant. This testimony, which can be used at the time of trial, is closest to the date of the incident and, thus, perceived as the most reliable.

The demand for the hearing must be served, in writing, within 90 days from the filing of a notice of claim (regardless of whether a lawsuit has been filed). After the expiration of the 90 days, the municipality has no right to demand such a hearing. Further, pursuant to *GML §50-h(2)*, the demand must give the claimant reasonable notice of the examination, must set forth the date, time, and place of the examination, and if a physical examination is required it must state so.

Warning: Not all municipalities are governed by *GML §50-h*. Hence, the specific statute applying to the specific municipality must be consulted. See Public Authorities Law and Public Housing Law, among others.

Practice Tip: Questioning of the claimant should be limited to what is allowed pursuant to statute, with proper objections being made. Further, according to the statute, the claimant is not to be treated as an adverse party. Questions which are beyond the scope should not be answered. However, the claimant's attorney must be careful not to obstruct the examination to such an extent that the municipality declares a default.

Practice Tip: The municipal hearing emanates from statute; thus, the *CPLR* does not apply. Hence, the claimant need not execute *50-h* transcripts, and the transcripts are generally not discoverable by co-defendants. Further, pursuant to *GML §50-h*, the hearing transcript may be used as evidence-in-chief by *any* party (as opposed to the limitation under the *CPLR* which only allows an adverse party to use an EBT transcript as evidence-in-chief).

[2] *50-h* as Condition Precedent to Commencing Action

Where a demand for examination pursuant to *GML §50-h* has been properly made, the examination is a condition precedent to the filing of an action. Where the governmental entity fails to demand an examination within 30 days, the claimant may commence an action. *GML §50-i*. Where the demand is properly made, and the examination (through no fault of the claimant) is not conducted within 90 days of the demand, the claimant may commence an action. *GML §50-h*.

[3] Various Statutes Re: Pre-Action Examinations

Public benefit corporations (see §7.02 above) are not granted the right to examine claimants under *GML §50-h*. Any statutory authority that they have to require the claimant to appear for such an examination is provided to them in other statutes. For example, the New York City Transit Authority has the right to demand that the claimant appear for an oral examination, but not a physical examination. *Pub. Auth. Law §1212*. The New York City Housing Authority, on the other hand, has the right to demand both an oral and physical examination of the claimant. *Pub. Hous. Law §157(2)*.

§ 7.05 Statute of Limitations

A lawsuit against a municipality (i.e., municipal corporation, district, or public benefit corporation) generally must be commenced within one year and 90 days from the date of the accident.[9] However, in a wrongful death action, the statute of limitations is two years.[10] *See EPTL §5-4.1; Pub. Auth. Law §§2981-2982, 1744; GML §50-i*. The statute of limitations is tolled for infants, pursuant to *CPLR §208*.

§ 7.06 Pleading Requirements

Pursuant to *GML §50-e* and *§50-i*, where a defendant is a municipality, a complaint served in a tort action must allege:
- that a notice of claim was served on the municipality within the statutory time period (usually 90 days after the date of the accident);
- that at least 30 days has elapsed from the filing of the notice of claim without settlement;
- that a municipal hearing (e.g., *50-h* hearing) was held or waived by the defendant; and
- that the action is being commenced within the statutory time period (generally, within one year and 90 days of the accident date, or two years where it is a wrongful death action, unless tolled).

---

9   Claims against Port Authority of New York and New Jersey must be commenced within one year. *Unconsol. Law §7107*. Similarly, claims against many public authorities must be commenced within one year. See Public Authorities Law. Claims against the Long Island Railroad must be commenced within one year and 30 days. *Pub. Auth. Law §1276(1), (2)*.

10   The statute of limitations on a wrongful death claim against the Port Authority of New York and New Jersey is one year. *Unconsol. Law §7107*.

Practice Tip: Where the court has granted leave to serve a late notice of claim, an allegation to that effect should be contained in the complaint, including the name of the judge and the date of the order. The order should be attached to the complaint as an exhibit.

Warning: Where the complaint fails to allege compliance with the statutory prerequisites of *GML §50-e* and *§50-i*, it will be dismissed, on motion of the defendant, for failure to state a cause of action. *Caruso v. City of Buffalo Urban Renewal Agency*, 159 A.D.2d 996, 553 N.Y.S.2d 254 (4th Dep't 1990).

See §7.20 below for a discussion of Big Apple Sidewalk and Protection Committee maps, which may have to be referred to in, and attached to, the complaint in a sidewalk or crosswalk case where the City of New York is a defendant.

§ 7.07 Venue in Government Liability Actions

[1] Actions Against County

Pursuant to *CPLR §504*, the proper venue for an action against a county is in that county.

[2] Actions Against City, Town, Village, School District, or District Corporation

Pursuant to *CPLR §504*, the proper venue for an action against a city (other than the City of New York), town, village, school district, or district corporation is the county where the city, town, village, school district, or district corporation is located. Where situated in more than one county, either county is a proper venue. In actions against the City of New York, the proper venue is the county in which the cause of action arose; if it arose outside the City of New York, New York County is the proper venue. *CPLR §504*.

[3] Actions Against Public Authorities

Pursuant to *CPLR §505*, the proper venue for an action against a public authority is the county where the authority has its principal office or where it has facilities involved in the action. In an action against the New York City Transit Authority (NYCTA), the proper venue is the county within New York City in which the cause of action arose; if it arose outside New York City, New York County is the proper venue. *CPLR §505*.

PART C: CLAIMS AGAINST STATE OF NEW YORK

§ 7.08 Jurisdiction of Claims Against State

All actions against the State of New York and its officers and employees acting within the scope of their employment are under the sole jurisdiction of the *Court of Claims Act*.

THE LAWYERS' GUIDE TO PERSONAL INJURY LAW

Warning: Some entities that fall within the *Court of Claims Act* (e.g., CUNY - Senior Institutions, Saratoga Springs Authority) do not contain the name "New York State" in their title. Other entities contain the name in their title, but do not fall within the *Court of Claims Act* (e.g., Dormitory Authority of the State of New York). Hence, the claimant's attorney must be very careful in determining the proper entities upon which to serve a notice of intention; the name of the entity is not conclusive.

§ 7.09 Statutory Prerequisites for Action Against State

A claim or a notice of intention to file a claim must be timely filed. If a notice of intention is filed, a claim must later be filed within the statute of limitations for the action.

§ 7.10 Service of Claim or Notice of Intention to File Claim on State

Typically, the claim or notice of intention must be filed with the Court of Claims and served upon the Attorney General. *Court of Claims Act §11-a(1)*. There are, however, a few entities requiring service upon themselves (e.g., claims against CUNY - Senior Institutions). The claim or notice of intention can be served personally or via certified mail return receipt requested. *Court of Claims Act §11-a(1)*. Service via certified mail return receipt requested is not deemed complete until received by the Attorney General's office.

§ 7.11 Requirements of Claim and Notice of Intention to File Claim Against State

[1] Requirements of Notice of Intention to File Claim

A notice of intention to file a claim must state:

- the date and time when the claim arose;
- the place where the claim arose; and
- the nature of the claim. ˙

The notice of intention must also be verified. *Court of Claims Act §11-b.*

[2] Requirements of Claim Against State

A claim against the State of New York must state:

- the date and time when the claim arose;
- the place where the claim arose;
- the items of damage or injury claimed to have been sustained; and
- the total sum claimed.

The claim must also be verified. *Court of Claims Act §11-b.*

§ 7.12 Statutes of Limitations in Claims Against State

[1] Negligence Actions Against State

A claim or notice of intention must be served within 90 days of the date of the accident. Where a notice of intention is filed, a claim must be filed within two years of the date of the accident. *Court of Claims Act §10(3)-(3a)*.

[2] Property Damage and Intentional Tort Actions Against State

A claim or notice of intention must be served within 90 days of the date of the accident. Where a notice of intention is filed, a claim must be filed within one year of the date of the accident. *Court of Claims Act §10(3b)*.

[3] Wrongful Death Actions Against State

A claim or notice of intention must be served within 90 days of the appointment of an administrator. Where a notice of intention is filed, a claim must be filed within two years of the date of death. *Court of Claims Act §10(2)*.

§ 7.13 Defects in Filing and Service

Defenses based upon defects in filing and/or service of the notice of intention, or the claim, are waived unless raised with specificity in the answer or by motion to dismiss prior to service of the answer. *Court of Claims Act §11-c*.

§ 7.14 Late Claims Against State

[1] Application for Permission to File Late Claim

The Court of Claims has discretion to grant permission to file late claims against the State of New York. The late claim, however, must be filed within the statute of limitations period. *Court of Claims Act §10(6)*. An application for permission to file a late notice of claim should address the following factors:

- a reasonable excuse for the delay;
- lack of prejudice to the State;
- a showing that the claim is meritorious; and
- a lack of other remedies available to the claimant.

The application must also contain a copy of the proposed claim.

[2] Disabilities as Toll of Statute of Limitations

Legal disabilities (e.g., infancy or incompetence) toll the statute of limitations until the disability no longer exists. The claim must be made within two years of the removal of the disability. *Court of Claims Act §10(5)*.

§ 7.15 Venue of Claims Against State

All tort actions against the State of New York must be heard in the Court of Claims. *Court of Claims Act §19*. For example, the Court of Claims has exclusive jurisdiction where the defendant is the New York State Thruway Authority, Jones Beach State Parkway Authority, and the Saratoga Springs Authority. Claims in the Court of Claims are determined solely by a judge, without any jury.

PART D: PRIOR WRITTEN NOTICE REQUIREMENT

§ 7.16 Prior Written Notice – In General

Pursuant to *GML §50-g*, cities are granted the right to enact laws establishing prior written notice prerequisites to actions based on defects in streets and sidewalks. Various municipalities have enacted greater-encompassing prior written notice ordinances. The specific prior written notice ordinance for the City of New York is located in the *New York City Administrative Code §7-201* (discussed in §7.17 below). Outside the City of New York, there are a slew of prior written notice ordinances enacted by various counties, villages, towns, and cities under numerous statutes. The purpose of prior written notice provisions is to impose liability only for those defects or dangerous conditions of which the municipality has actual knowledge.

§ 7.17 Prior Written Notice – City of New York

Pursuant to the *Administrative Code of the City of New York §7-201*, the claimant must generally be able to prove the City had prior *written* notice of the defect where the accident occurred in any of the following:

- street (including curbstones, underpasses, avenues, roads, alleys, boulevards, concourses, roads or paths within a park, driveways, thoroughfares, and public ways, public squares, public parking areas);
- highway;
- bridge (including overpasses and viaducts);
- culvert;
- crosswalk; or
- sidewalk (including boardwalks, underpasses, pedestrian walks or paths, steps and stairways).

See Bruni v. City of New York, 2 N.Y.3d 319, 778 N.Y.S.2d 757 (2007) (defendant-city's internal inspection report qualified as prior written notice). Thus, for example, if the accident occurred in a New York City school or playground, the prior written notice requirement would not apply since schools and playgrounds are not enumerated in the code. See §7.20 below for a discussion of Big Apple notice.

§ 7.18 Prior Written Notice Not Required

In cases against municipalities, prior written notice is not required when:

- the municipality *created* the dangerous or defective condition (*See Kiernan v. Thompson*, 73 N.Y.2d 840, 537 N.Y.S.2d 122 [1988]);

Warning: The First Department has limited the rule that the municipality's affirmative negligence obviates the need for prior written notice of a defect. The court limited the exception to work done by the municipality which *immediately* results in the existence of a dangerous condition. *Yarborough v. City of New York*, 10 N.Y.3d 726 (2008); *see also Bielecki v. City of New York*, 14 A.D.3d 301, 788 N.Y.S.2d 67 (1st Dep't 2005).

- where a "special use" confers a special benefit upon the municipality (*see Poirier v. City of Schenectady*, 85 N.Y.2d 310, 624 N.Y.S.2d 555 [1995]); or
- the alleged defect does not fall into any of the relevant enumerated prior written notice categories.

See Amabile v. City of Buffalo, 93 N.Y.2d 471, 693 N.Y.S.2d 77 (1999); *see also Yarborough v. City of New York*, 10 N.Y.3d 726 (2008).

Where prior written notice is *not* required, liability against the municipality is generally determined by the same rules and principles that govern liability of private landowners. *See Stevens v. Central Sch. Dist. No. 1*, 25 A.D.2d 871, 270 N.Y.S.2d 23 (2d Dep't 1966), *aff'd*, 21 N.Y.2d 780, 288 N.Y.S.2d 475 (1968). Prior written notice requirements do not apply to public school districts, other districts, and public benefit corporations. However, public authorities are required to establish and maintain records of alleged defects, including written notice of such defects. *See GML §50-f.*

§ 7.19 Freedom of Information Laws (FOIL)

The claimant's attorney should send a FOIL request to each governmental agency relevant to the particular accident. The request should seek items relevant to the claim, such as prior complaints, inspection reports, logs, work orders, work permits, street opening permits, road paving permits, citations / complaints to the abutting landowner, prior notices of claim, etc. Pursuant to FOIL, the municipality must promptly respond. The plaintiff's attorney should use these FOIL requests to help prove prior written notice and/or creation of the dangerous condition. The claimant's attorney should consult www.nyc.gov or *The Green Book: The Official Directory of the City of New York* for a list of all the government agencies in the City of New York.

§ 7.20 Big Apple Pothole and Sidewalk Protection Committee

The Big Apple Pothole and Protection Committee, a division of the New York State Trial Lawyers Association (NYSTLA), prepares maps of the entire city of New York (depicting every defect on all sidewalks and crosswalks). The maps are then served on the New York City Department of Transportation, and thus serve as prior written notice (at least insofar as defeating a motion for summary judgment on the issue of prior written notice). The map can be obtained from NYSTLA (for a fee) or the NYC Department of Transportation (through a FOIL request). When utilizing such a map to prove prior written notice, it should be specifically referred to in the complaint and a copy of the map should be attached to the complaint as an exhibit. Mention of one type of defect on the map (in the area of the accident) does not, however, constitute notice of a different type of defect in the area. *Roldan v. City of New York*, 36 A.D.3d 484, 831 N.Y.S.2d 110 (1st Dep't 2007).

PART E: SPECIFIC CASES AGAINST MUNICIPALITIES

§ 7.21 Sidewalk Cases

[1] General Rule

Public sidewalks are generally the responsibility of the municipality. *See Tremblay v. Harmony Mills*, 171 N.Y. 598, 601, 64 N.E. 501 (1902). The owner, or person in possession, of property abutting a public sidewalk is generally not liable to the claimant for an accident occurring on the public sidewalk unless:

- the local ordinance gives the abutting landowner the responsibility to maintain the sidewalk *and* imposes tort liability on the abutting landowner for failure to do so; or
- the abutting landowner *created* the dangerous condition (e.g., patchwork on the sidewalk); or
- the abutting landowner utilized that part of the sidewalk for a "special use" (e.g., a newspaper vending machine, basement trap door, or driveway).

See Bloch v. Potter, 204 A.D.2d 672, 673, 612 N.Y.S.2d 236, 237 (2d Dep't 1994) (setting forth standard). See chapter 5, §5.08[3] for a discussion on "de minimis defect" and "open and obvious" defenses.

[2] Sidewalk Claims Against City of New York

For all accidents occurring after September 14, 2003, the City of New York has shifted the responsibility (along with tort liability) for sidewalk maintenance onto the abutting landowners, except with regard to one, two, or three-family residential properties that are at least partially owner-occupied and used exclusively for residential purposes. *NYC Administrative Code §7-210.* Where the abutting landowner is either uninsured or under-insured, a claimant may qualify for a city disbursement. The City of New York, however, remains responsible for trees and tree wells, as they are not intended for pedestrian use and are, therefore, not considered part of the sidewalk. *Vucetovic v. Epsom Downs, Inc.*, 45 A.D.3d 28, 841 N.Y.S.2d 301 (1st Dep't 2007). See chapter 5, §5.08

§ 7.22 Snow and Ice Cases Against Municipality

The duty to remove snow and ice from streets and sidewalks is primarily that of the municipality. *City of Rochester v. Campbell*, 123 N.Y. 405, 25 N.E. 937 (1890). One means of carrying out its duty is via an ordinance requiring the abutting property owner to clear snow and ice from the sidewalk. In such a case, the municipality's effort to enforce such an ordinance is relevant in determining whether the municipality acted with reasonable care.

In determining whether the municipality acted with reasonable care under the circumstances, and within a reasonable time, the following factors must be considered:

- efforts made by the municipality to have the abutting property owner clean the sidewalk;
- the temperature since the snow ended (i.e., could be reasonable to await a thaw; continuous freezing temperatures may have made removal more difficult); and
- the number of miles of streets and sidewalks to be cleaned, the amount of snow to be removed, the equipment and workers available, and the position of the area in question in terms of the order of priority of the work to be done.

When evidence of the enormous magnitude of the work and efforts made by the municipality is shown, it is often held, as a matter of law, that the municipality was not negligent. Municipalities are generally afforded more leeway in terms of the amount of time they are given to clear snow and ice. *See Garricks v. City of New York*, 1 N.Y.3d 22, 769 N.Y.S.2d 152 (2003); *see also Martinez v. Columbia Presbyterian Med. Ctr.*, 238 A.D.2d 286, 656 N.Y.S.2d 271 (1st Dep't 1997) (city not obligated to clear snow within 48 hours where two large snow storms struck in a row). *See also PJI §2:225 D.* See chapter 5, §5.09 regarding non-municipal liability in snow and ice cases.

§ 7.23 School Accidents

The defendant (e.g., Department of Education) has the duty to provide adequate supervision of students and use reasonable care for the students' safety while under their control. The plaintiff must be able to prove:

- a dangerous condition existed before the plaintiff was injured;
- the defendant had actual or constructive notice of the dangerous condition; and
- the defendant's negligence was a substantial factor in causing the plaintiff's injuries.

Negligence, as it relates to a Board of Education, is the failure to use the same degree of care and supervision that a reasonably prudent parent would use under the same circumstances. *See PJI §2:227.* The Board (or Department) of Education must be named as a separate entity. *Torres v. City of New York*, 41 A.D.3d 378, 837 N.Y.S.2d 571 (1st Dep't 2007) (failure to name and sue Department of Education led to dismissal).

Notice is not required where the danger to the students is obvious and clear, and general supervision is required as a matter of law. *Coon v. Board of Educ.*, 160 A.D.2d 403, 554 N.Y.S.2d 110 (1st Dep't 1990). Further, where the defendant created the dangerous condition, notice is not required. *See Peralta v. Henriquez*, 100 N.Y.2d 139, 145, 760 N.Y.S.2d 741, 745 (2003) (defendant's creation of dangerous condition may relieve plaintiff's obligation of proving notice of that condition). The Board of Education is vicariously liable for the acts of its teachers. *Domino v. Mercurio*, 17 A.D.2d 342, 234 N.Y.S.2d 1011 (4th Dep't 1962), *aff'd*, 13 N.Y.2d 922, 244 N.Y.S.2d 69 (1963).

§ 7.24 Accidents Involving Common Carrier

[1] Common Carriers – Standard of Care

Common carriers (e.g., railroad, train, bus, airline) must use reasonable care in operating their vehicles for the safety of passengers, including providing a reasonably safe place to enter and exit the vehicle. Where there is actual or constructive notice of a passenger's disability (e.g., disabled, sick, intoxicated, child), additional care is required. *See PJI §§2:161 - 2:181.*

[2] Common Carriers – Sudden Jerk

Common carriers are not responsible for injuries to passengers which occur as a result of some jolting; this is to be expected. However, absent an emergency, a common carrier must avoid sudden, unusual, and violent jerks, lurches, or stops. *See PJI §2:165.* To sustain a verdict for the plaintiff, there must be evidence that the bus or train was propelled forward with unusual and unnecessary force, beyond the plaintiff's mere claim that it "lurched forward" with unnecessary force. *Taylor v. Westchester St. Transp. Co., Inc.*, 276 A.D. 874, 93 N.Y.S.2d 395 (2d Dep't 1949).

CHAPTER 8

SETTLING A NEGLIGENCE CASE

PART A: OVERVIEW

§ 8.01 Procedural Context – Settling a Negligence Case

There are many complex facets associated with settlement of a negligence case. Discussed below are ways to increase the case value, negotiate with insurance claims representatives, and ultimately settle for maximum value. Also discussed are special considerations that must be taken into account on different types of cases, including dealing with various types of liens.

PART B: MAXIMIZING CASE VALUE

§ 8.02 Conducting Proper Investigation

The case must be investigated properly from the start (i.e., photographs, witness statements, experts, etc.). Cases are often won or lost early-on – often before the defendant and/or the insurance carrier are even aware of the accident or the ensuing case. This is particularly true in the non-motor vehicle accident setting. If the plaintiff's investigation is properly conducted, the plaintiff will often have a decisive advantage over the defendant (and ultimately the insurance carrier), for the plaintiff will have the first opportunity to interview witnesses, take photographs, and hire an expert to inspect the accident site. A lack of investigation on behalf of the plaintiff, however, will generally yield a significant advantage to the defense; once they are aware of the claim, the insurance carriers will utilize their enormous resources to properly defend themselves.

§ 8.03 Considering Venue Options

The importance of venue in personal injury practice cannot be emphasized enough. The plaintiff's attorney must commence the lawsuit in the most plaintiff-friendly county possible. Many of the seven-figure cases in the City of New York, for example, would have resulted in defense verdicts if the lawsuits had been brought outside of the city (e.g., Westchester County or Nassau County).

Not only does the plaintiff win a far greater percentage of personal injury lawsuits in the City of New York, but the dollar amounts of the verdicts are, on average, several times greater than those outside the city. Even within the City of New York, there is a great dichotomy between the counties of Kings and Bronx versus the rest of the city. Venue is often the key, and it should not be taken lightly. It is certainly worth investigating ways to properly choose the best venue possible. *See CPLR §§503, 504, 505*; see also chapter 3, §§3.05[4] and §3.15[6]; see also chapter 5, §§5.04[3] and 5.17[3].

§ 8.04 Commencing Lawsuit and Pushing Case Forward

Prior to the commencement of a lawsuit, insurance companies will "dangle" the possibility of settlement for a long while, attempting to delay the proceedings and/or to pay a fraction of the true value of the case. Insurance claims representatives feel that plaintiffs' attorneys will be willing to settle for substantially less money prior to the filing of a lawsuit in exchange for avoiding years of work (as well as thousands of dollars in disbursements). This is why any sizeable case should be litigated from the outset. Attempting to settle the case prior to litigation is largely a waste of time. Commencing a lawsuit allows the insurance carrier to realize that the plaintiff's attorney is serious, while also avoiding delays. Once the lawsuit is brought, the plaintiff's attorney should attempt to avoid delays – requesting a preliminary conference as soon as the defendant's answer is received, pushing to complete depositions and discovery, and placing the case onto the trial calendar as swiftly as possible. Generally, the closer the case is to a trial, the more money the insurance company will be willing to pay.

> **Practice Tip:** In minimum insurance policy (i.e., $25,000) and/or minimum injury cases (e.g., soft-tissue injuries), prior to putting the case into a lawsuit, it is best to look for some alternative, such as arbitration, mediation, or settlement. Filing a lawsuit in these types of cases may well result in the investment of time (including possible trial) and money for a case without much upside.

§ 8.05 Making Strong Impression

Making a strong impression of the case on the claims representative, from the outset, is important. Very often, a claims representative will set the "reserve" on a file without having all of the appropriate information. Once a claims representative places a reserve on a claim, s/he is not likely to increase the figure without good cause. Therefore, if contacted by the claims representative early-on, the plaintiff's attorney should set forth the positive aspects of the case (e.g., huge damages) but should not disclose much information regarding the weaker parts of the case (e.g., alcohol involvement by plaintiff, specifics regarding liability, etc.).

§ 8.06 Utilizing Discovery to Strengthen Case Value

The plaintiff's attorney must utilize discovery to his or her advantage, requesting (and receiving) the appropriate documents and deposing the appropriate witnesses. The depositions are the most crucial part of discovery, and should not be taken lightly.

Preparing the plaintiff for his or her testimony is often the most essential part of the plaintiff's attorney's job. This is not something that should take place at the courthouse a half-hour before the deposition. Rather, this should occur a day or so in advance for at least a couple of hours; then, the plaintiff's attorney should meet the plaintiff again (about an hour) prior to the deposition, simply to review the issues. Further, the depositions of the defendant(s) and other witnesses are of great significance, as well. If the plaintiff's attorney neglects the deposition(s), s/he may well soon be wondering why such a paltry sum, if any, is being offered on the case. Insurance companies are not in the business of giving money away. Hence, if the case is not properly prepared for trial, the insurance carrier will be aware; it will surely be reflected in the offer.

§ 8.07 Formulating Demand

In evaluating a case, the plaintiff's attorney must take into account liability, damages, venue, and available insurance coverage. The demand must provide the plaintiff's attorney with sufficient room to maneuver (and to "meet in the middle"); as such, it is always better to be on the high side. It is very difficult to increase a demand, whereas demands can always be lowered at a later date. Initially, the plaintiff's attorney should generally assume 100% liability. As talks progress, the plaintiff's attorney may want to discount the demand based on liability problems (e.g., 50/50), depending on the venue.

Once the injuries and other damages are known, the case can be evaluated in terms of the potential jury verdicts (sustainable on appeal) in the venue where the case is pending. Once the range of possible settlements is determined, the plaintiff's attorney should establish a demand. Knowing reported verdicts and settlements from past issues of *Verdict Search* is important, and can be of great assistance in formulating a demand. *Verdict Search* does not indicate the rulings of the Appellate Division; thus, reading *Judicial Review of Damages* (or ordering an appellate search from *Verdict Search*) can be helpful in determining the amount the appellate courts will sustain for similar injuries. The plaintiff's attorney must utilize this proof in order to justify his or her settlement demands. Obviously, the age of the plaintiff must also be taken into account (i.e., the younger the plaintiff, the more valuable the future pain and suffering aspect of the case), as well as past and future economic losses (which can lead to some of the largest settlements – for they are concrete and, if believed by a jury, are unlikely to be reduced on appeal).

§ 8.08 Understanding and Utilizing Residual Effects of Injuries

The plaintiff's attorney should set forth the plaintiff's best arguments regarding residual effects of the injuries. Otherwise, there will be little, if any, money offered for future pain and suffering. Being cognizant of the residuals is what can turn a decent case into a significant one. Examples of residuals include shortening of a limb (following a fracture and surgery, or where the growth plate is affected as a result of a fracture of an infant), nerve damage (e.g., as result of a laceration, etc.), future surgery required (e.g., hardware loosened or hardware needs to be removed in a case with internal fixation), and arthritis (based on a recent x-ray) resulting in the need for a future joint replacement. Obviously, a medical expert will have to support the allegations.

§ 8.09 Utilizing Liens to Settle for More Money

Liens (such as medical, workers' compensation, Medicare, etc.) can have a large impact on the client's net settlement proceeds. The plaintiff's attorney should utilize these liens to the plaintiff's advantage. Medicaid, Medicare, and workers' compensation are exempt from the collateral source rule. *See CPLR §4545(c)*. As those entities are entitled to recoup their outlays, the plaintiff is allowed to collect same from the defendant in the third-party action.

Even where the lien is not exempt from the collateral source rule (and therefore not recoverable in the third-party action), the lien amount can be utilized as a tool to secure a greater settlement. Essentially, the argument must be set forth that, due to the amount of the lien, the plaintiff has no incentive to settle the claim for any amount less than $X. The higher the lien, the lower the plaintiff's share of the settlement, and hence the less incentive there will be for a plaintiff to accept an offer. The lien will typically allow for a higher offer. The plaintiff's attorney can then attempt to negotiate the lien. See §§8.33 - 8.40 below.

§ 8.10 Taking Case to End

In general, the closer the case is to trial, the more money the insurance companies will offer; this is particularly true in a plaintiff-friendly venue where the prospect of a large, runaway verdict draws near. Thus, the day of selecting a jury, the offer will typically increase; after selecting the jury / the day of trial, the offer will often increase further. Once a trial begins, however, offers can be increased, decreased, or withdrawn, depending on the judge's rulings, the evidence received, and the witnesses' testimony.

PART C: NEGOTIATING WITH INSURANCE CLAIMS REPRESENTATIVE[11]

§ 8.11 Being Prepared

Negotiating when unprepared sends a negative message, and can adversely impact the amount of the offer. Documents which should be reviewed prior to discussing the case with the claims representative are the police report or other accident reports, photographs, ambulance / hospital / medical records, and documents relating to lost time from work and lost wages, etc.

§ 8.12 Staying Firm

The claims representative should know that the plaintiff's attorney is willing to try the case. Where the plaintiff's attorney is not willing to try the case, s/he is doing

---

[11] See Landau, Kenneth. "Nine Ways to Settle Your Cases in '99." *Nassau Lawyer* December 1998; Landau, Kenneth. "Nine Ways to Settle Your Cases in '98." *Nassau Lawyer* January 1998.

a disservice to the plaintiff. If there is a sense that the plaintiff's attorney desperately wants to avoid trial, s/he will be taken advantage of. Weaving past, or upcoming, trials into the conversation can certainly be helpful to show that the attorney is willing to try the case.

§ 8.13 Knowing Insurance Policy Limits

The plaintiff's attorney's demand should be equal to, or less than, the limits of the applicable insurance policies (except, of course, where there is excess coverage or where the defendant is self-insured). Demands in excess of the insurance policy limits will generally thwart any possible settlement negotiations.

Further, to facilitate settlement, the plaintiff's attorney may wish to offer to save the claims representative some of the insurance policy limits by settling for less than the full policy (e.g., $22,500 or $95,000). Due to the expenses involved with the litigation (including expert witness fees), this can be a favorable outcome for all parties.

In cases where the insurance policy limits are substantial, the plaintiff's attorney may want to remind the claims representative of the potential exposure should the case proceed to trial. As discussed in §8.07 above, the plaintiff's attorney should, though, be prepared to buttress his or her demands with recently reported jury verdicts and settlements.

§ 8.14 Considering Mediation and Arbitration

The plaintiff's attorney may want to consider the possibility of mediation and/or arbitration. Advantages of alternate dispute resolution include resolving the matter within months rather than years, certainty and finality (i.e., no verdict or appeals), and saving money (i.e., no need for doctors / experts to testify, as reports are sufficient).

Arbitration is best suited for cases with minor injuries, limited insurance coverage, and only one defendant; the parameters should generally be based on the last demand and offer. Mediation is better suited for cases with serious injuries, multiple defendants, and/or substantial insurance coverage. Mediation also helps the claims representative justify settlements.

> **Warning: Where** a case is pending in a plaintiff-friendly venue, agreeing to arbitration takes the case away from a potential jury and plays into the insurance carrier's hands.

§ 8.15 Avoiding Ultimatums

The plaintiff's attorney should avoid "ultimatum" demands. The certainty of settlements, as opposed to trial (i.e., uncertain outcome, possibility of appeals, possibility of "losing" money spent on experts, etc.), should be a strong incentive for the plaintiff's attorney to always keep the possibility of settlement alive.

§ 8.16 Isolating Areas of Disagreement

Where possible, areas of disagreement should be isolated. For example, if liability is questionable, the parties should first attempt to agree on the case's full value, then negotiate a percentage of liability. Whenever possible, favorable agreements on a particular area should be memorialized (i.e., via a letter to, or from, the insurance claims representative).

§ 8.17 Being Respectful

It is important to work together. The plaintiff's attorney should not always attempt to convince the claims representative that s/he is right and the claims representative is wrong. Rather, the plaintiff's attorney should be reasonable and realistic. Additionally, the plaintiff's attorney should not make an enemy out of his or her adversary or the insurance company. Disagreements should be limited to evaluations of liability, damages, evidence, and case value. The plaintiff's attorney will ultimately need defense counsel to participate in, and encourage, settlement discussions; both sides will increase the possibility of settlement if the discussions remain civil. The plaintiff's attorney must always remember that s/he may well encounter the same claims representative and defense attorney in the future.

§ 8.18 Responding to "Lowball" Offers

Some insurance carriers respond to the plaintiff's attorney's demand with lowball offers. Rather than becoming frustrated, the plaintiff's attorney should attempt to change the claims representative's mind. The claims representative should be asked to explain the basis for his or her offer; the plaintiff's attorney should explain the basis for rejecting the offer, and why the case should be re-assessed at a higher value.

Practice Tip: In responding to a lowball offer, it is important not to retreat from the initial demand too quickly; this may lead a claims representative to believe that the plaintiff's attorney is fishing for a high offer but is willing to accept much less. It places the plaintiff's attorney in a weak bargaining position. It is far better for the plaintiff's attorney to keep the demand high and be careful not to bid against himself or herself.

In some cases, once negotiations have reached an impasse, the plaintiff's attorney may choose to go above the claims representative and speak with a supervisor or regional manager. The plaintiff's attorney should refrain from personally attacking the claims representative; instead, the supervisor should be told that an impasse has been reached because the claims representative may not have a full understanding of all the elements of the claim or possibly may not have the authority to offer more money. In cases where negotiations are going nowhere, there is no downside to speaking to a supervisor or manager.

§ 8.19 Laying Foundation for Bad Faith Claim

Where an insurer is clearly acting in bad faith, the plaintiff's attorney should send a letter to that effect; the letter, without any time restriction, should make clear that the plaintiff is willing to settle the matter within the insurance policy limits. It may lead to a change in their stance on a particular case; it will also lay a strong foundation for a claim against the insurer if there is ultimately a verdict which exceeds the insurance policy limits. See also §8.20 below.

Where liability is clear and the potential recovery far exceeds the insurance coverage, the insurer is obligated to accept a settlement demand within the policy limits. A jury must find that the insurer acted intentionally and in gross disregard of the insured's interest and that there was a deliberate or reckless decision made to disregard the insured's interest in the insurer's pursuit of a litigation strategy. Mere negligence does not support an excess liability verdict. The amount of damages is equal to the amount by which the judgment in the underlying tort action exceeds the insured's insurance policy. *Pavia v. State Farm Insurance Company*, 82 N.Y.2d 445, 183 A.D.2d 189 (1993). *See also New England Underwriters Mutual Insurance Company v. Healthcare Underwriters Mutual Insurance Company*, 295 F. 3d. 232 (2d Cir., 2002) (Second Circuit adopts multi-pronged test as set forth in *PJI §4:67* wherein clear liability is not threshold requirement for bad faith).

§ 8.20 Sending "Excess Verdict" Letter

Where the claims representative is not offering a satisfactory amount on a case which could certainly result in an excess verdict, a letter should be sent to the claims representative stating that the possibility for an excess verdict is great given the facts of the case (and the injures and economic losses sustained). The claims representative should be advised to place his or her insured on notice of same, along with the suggestion that the insured retain its own attorney to represent its interests. Insurance carriers and claims representatives become nervous when the possibility of an excess verdict exists; further, placing their insured on notice of the possibility of an excess verdict is not good for business. The bad faith letter can be combined with the excess verdict letter where applicable. See also §8.19 above.

§ 8.21 Refraining from Rejecting Offer Before Conveyed

The plaintiff's attorney should not "reject" an offer before it is made. For example, suppose the claims representative asks, "Are you going to consider the offer if it's less than six figures?" Even if the attorney knows that any offer less than six figures will certainly not settle the case, the response should be, "I will discuss all offers with my client. It is his or her ultimate decision whether or not to accept the offer." Otherwise, if the response is "No way," there will be no offer made, the gap will not have been narrowed, and there will be nothing for the plaintiff's attorney to use as a springboard. Once the insurance carrier makes an offer, the plaintiff's attorney can simply reject it (the next day) as extremely insufficient. At least the case, from the plaintiff's perspective, will have moved closer to settlement.

§ 8.22 Avoiding Traps that Appear Too Good to be True

The defense may offer to concede liability in exchange for something (e.g., capping damages at the insurance policy limits or stipulating that certain photographs will be admitted in evidence at trial). As a plaintiff, nothing is gained by accepting these offers, for they are typically presented in cases where liability is already clear-cut. In fact, where such offers are made, the defense is likely to concede liability just before trial anyhow (i.e., without gaining anything) so as not to lose credibility with the jury.

By agreeing to cap the damages at the insurance policy limits, the plaintiff loses negotiating leverage against the insurance company, for the possibility of an excess verdict no longer exists. As soon as the plaintiff's attorney agrees to cap damages at the insurance policy limits, the insurance company loses any incentive to negotiate. A counter-proposal that the plaintiff's attorney might want to make is to cap damages at the insurance policy limits and to arbitrate the claim.

PART D: SETTLING CASE
§ 8.23 Settling on Record

When a case settles in court (e.g., during jury selection or on trial), it is good practice to place the terms of the settlement on the record. Unless the settlement is on the record or there is a written stipulation (signed by the respective attorneys), there is the risk that the offer could be decreased or withdrawn (e.g., the offer was a "mistake"). *See CPLR §2104.*

When the plaintiff is present, s/he should allocute on the record, making sure s/he understands the terms of, and accepts, the settlement. The plaintiff's attorney should inquire:

Q: You understand an offer of $X has been made to settle the case involving your accident of…?

Q: And you understand that the disbursements on the file of approximately $Y get deducted from the settlement amount?

Q: And you further understand that the attorney's fee of approximately $Z then gets paid from the proceeds?

Q: You also understand that any liens on the file, presently known or unknown, are solely your responsibility?

Q: And you understand that all liens are paid from your share of the settlement?

Q: And you understand that you will be indemnifying and holding the defendants harmless from all liens, presently known or unknown?

Q: And you understand that by settling the case, after disbursements, attorneys' fees, and liens are paid, you will be receiving approximately $A as your net share of the settlement proceeds?

Q: You understand that by settling, you will be forever ending this case, and can never re-open it – no matter what happens in the future?

Q: You also understand that by settling you are giving up your right to have a jury decide the outcome?

> Q: And you realize that a jury could award you more, or less, money than you will receive from this settlement?
>
> Q: Is it your desire to settle the case at this time under the terms just discussed?
>
> Q: Has anyone coerced you to settle the case?
>
> Q: Has anyone promised you anything other than a net recovery of approximately $N to settle this case?
>
> Q: Have you been satisfied with your legal representation in this matter?
>
> Q: Have you taken any medication in the last 24 hours that may affect your ability to think or understand?

Once the plaintiff leaves the witness stand, the plaintiff's attorney should place the stipulation of discontinuance on the record, as follows:

> It is hereby stipulated, by and between the respective attorneys, that the above-entitled action be hereby discontinued with prejudice as against all defendants herein, inclusive of interest, costs, and disbursements. It is further agreed that the plaintiff will indemnify and hold the defendants harmless of any and all liens on the file, presently known or unknown. Further, the plaintiff will be exchanging a general release and stipulation of discontinuance and, pursuant to *CPLR §5003-a*, a check in the sum of $X is to be issued within 21 days (or 90 days, where the defendant is a government entity) thereafter.

Practice Tip: To protect the client, the plaintiff's attorney should obtain the defense counsel's consent to stipulate, where appropriate, that the settlement reflects compensation for pain and suffering only (i.e., as opposed to loss of earnings and/or reimbursement for medical expenditures). *See Internal Revenue Code §104(a)(2).* This insulates the plaintiff from income taxes, and protects the plaintiff against claims by healthcare insurers and/or lienors attempting to recoup monies advanced for medical bills. See §8.35 below.

§ 8.24 Settling with Only One of Multiple Defendants – General Obligations Law

The plaintiff's attorney must be *very* careful when contemplating settling with one defendant but not with another, particularly where plaintiff's comparative negligence is an issue. This can be illustrated with the example where there are 2 defendants (S = settling defendant; N = non-settling defendant). While the settlement lets S out of the case entirely, S's share remains in the case if N wishes. At trial, N cannot mention the fact that S settled (nor the amount of the settlement), but is likely to try the case against an empty chair and seek to place all or most of the liability on S. N can introduce S's share of fault into the trial so the jury can apportion fault. The sum to be subtracted from the jury's verdict is the actual settlement share paid by S or S's *pro rata* share of the verdict, whichever is greater.

In the absence of an apportionment for S, N is still entitled to have the actual amount of S's settlement applied in reduction of the verdict. The Court of Appeals has opted for the "settlement-first" method. Consider a jury verdict of $2.4M with the plaintiff found 92% negligent, N found 8% negligent, and S having settled for $1.6M. In such a case, the court first will reduce the verdict to $.8M (i.e., $2.4M - $1.6M), then will apportion the 8% to N. Thus, N is only responsible for $64,000 (benefiting from S's settlement even though N deliberately failed to inject S's fault into the case). *See Whalen v. Kawasaki Motors Corp.*, 92 N.Y.2d 288, 680 N.Y.S.2d 435 (1998); *General Obligations Law §15-108(a)*; *CPLR §4533-b*. Where the plaintiff is not held comparatively negligent, the verdict will simply be reduced by the settling defendant's settlement amount.

A non-settling defendant (N) seeking the protections of *§15-108*, must plead it. If plead early, it might be deemed to inject S's share of fault into the trial (which N purposely wants to avoid). Thus, N is permitted to raise the defense by moving to amend its answer (to include the defense) even *after* the verdict because there is no prejudice to the plaintiff. *See CPLR §3018(b), GOL §15-108(a).*

§ 8.25 Considering Issues Raised When There are Multiple Plaintiffs

[1] Multiple Plaintiffs – Insufficient Insurance Coverage

Where, for example, there are multiple plaintiffs (with different attorneys) and single insurance policy limits, there may be insufficient funds to cover all the claims. In such a case, all the plaintiffs can agree that the total settlement (e.g., tender of the insurance policy) be held in escrow, subject to an arbitration or mediation to determine the split.

[2] Multiple Plaintiffs as Leverage

Where the plaintiff's attorney represents multiple plaintiffs in the same case (e.g., two passengers in a motor vehicle accident case) and one of the plaintiff's injuries are worth more than the policy limits while the other plaintiff's injuries are worth less than the policy limits, the plaintiff's attorney may want to make a "total demand" rather than individualized demands. For example, suppose there is a 100/300 policy, the plaintiffs' attorney may demand $200,000 even though one plaintiff's case may be worth $200,000 while the other's is worth only $10,000 by itself. The possibility of an excess verdict in regard to the one plaintiff may lead to more money for the second plaintiff.

§ 8.26 Dealing with Client

Convincing the client to accept a reasonable offer can sometimes be challenging. Clients sometimes hear about extraordinary cases (e.g., hot coffee spilled at McDonald's) and believe that their cases are worth a million dollars. The plaintiff's attorney should discuss the following points with the plaintiff: the plaintiff's share (as opposed to the plaintiff's attorney's share) is tax-free, there will be no further expenses (e.g., $8,000 for a medical expert to testify), the money can be received now rather than in the future (i.e., the present value of money, opportunity costs), the certainty of settlement (versus risk of losing at trial), and the finality of settlement (i.e., no appeals). The plaintiff's attorney should never pressure the plaintiff to accept the money, though, as it is ultimately the client's decision; the plaintiff will not be happy if s/he feels as if s/he was pressured into settling. It is important, though, that the plaintiff makes an informed decision.

§ 8.27 Preparing Appropriate Paperwork
[1] General Release

Once the plaintiff's attorney and the claims representative agree on the settlement amount, the plaintiff's attorney should request that the claims representative fax over a confirmation letter. The plaintiff (at least 18 years of age) must then sign a general release (which states that in exchange for a sum of money, s/he is extinguishing any claim against those defendants being released). The settlement funds must be tendered within 21 days, or 90 days where the defendant is a government entity, from the date plaintiff tenders the executed general release and stipulation of discontinuance. *CPLR §5003-a.*

> **Practice Tip:** The plaintiff's attorney should ask the insurance claims representative and/or defense counsel for the names needed to be included on the release. Otherwise, the release may be rejected and time will have been wasted.

> **Warning:** In an uninsured or under-insured motorist case, the plaintiff must sign a release and trust, as opposed to the standard general release. The plaintiff's attorney should simply ask the UM/ SUM insurance carrier to fax him or her the appropriate release form required.

[2] Authorization to Endorse Settlement Check

The settlement check is made payable to the plaintiff and the plaintiff's attorney. At the time of the signing of the general release, the plaintiff should also sign an authorization allowing the plaintiff's attorney to endorse his or her name on the settlement check and to deposit the check into the attorney's escrow account. From there, the plaintiff's attorney will cut the checks. See chapter 11, §11.15 for a Settlement Worksheet.

> **Practice Tip:** The plaintiff's attorney should also have the plaintiff sign a list of the disbursements and liens on the file, as well as an indication as to what the client's net share of the settlement proceeds will be (i.e., after disbursements, attorney's fee, and any liens), to make sure the client fully understands the settlement.

[3] Stipulation of Discontinuance

A stipulation discontinuing the action with prejudice must be signed by the attorneys for all parties, assuming the case was settled after a lawsuit was commenced. Pursuant to *CPLR §2104*, the stipulation must be filed with the court (and a nominal fee paid) by the defendant.

> **Practice Tip:** If the case is to be discontinued against one (or some) but not all parties, the stipulation of discontinuance should state (in bold capital letters) that the action is to continue against the remaining defendants. Otherwise, the court may inadvertently discontinue the entire case.

[4] OCA Closing Statement

The plaintiff's attorney must file a closing statement with the Office of Court Administration once all the settlement funds are disbursed. A copy of the closing statement must be sent to the plaintiff, as well.

PART E: INFANT'S COMPROMISE

§ 8.28 Settling Infant's Case

Pursuant to Article 12 of the *CPLR*, settlements involving infants (i.e., those people under 18 years of age, pursuant to *CPLR §105-j*) or incompetents must meet with judicial approval known as an infant's compromise. An infant's compromise is required even when the case settles (or proceeds to arbitration) prior to the commencement of a lawsuit, even where the settlement is for the entire insurance policy. If the settlement meets with the judge's approval, an infant's compromise order is signed by the judge, directing the infant's portion of the proceeds to be placed in a bank account or annuity until the infant reaches at least 18 years of age.

> **Practice Tip:** In uninsured and under-insured motorist cases, an infant-claimant can proceed to arbitration without seeking court approval (unlike a third-party arbitration with a voluntary high-low). *See CPLR §1209.*

> **Practice Tip:** Where the infant is going to be receiving a fairly significant sum of money, it is beneficial to "structure the settlement" wherein the infant's portion of the settlement proceeds is placed in an annuity (i.e., as opposed to a bank account). The younger the infant, the more a structured settlement will help him or her. If the money is simply placed in a bank account, over time it will lose value. However, where the money is placed in an annuity (as part of the settlement), it will grow – tax-free – before the infant reaches the age of majority, often outpacing inflation and cost of living increases.

§ 8.29 Scheduling Infant's Compromise Hearing

The plaintiff's attorney must send the following to the court (i.e., Infant's Compromise Part or Ex-Parte Part):

- proposed infant's compromise order (which should include, among other things, the name and address of the bank where the infant has, or will, open an account, or pertinent structured settlement information);
- parent's affidavit (basically stating that the settlement meets with parental approval and the injury is not going to get any worse);
- attorney's affirmation (basically stating that the settlement meets with the attorney's approval and the injury is not going to get any worse);
- physician's affirmation (stating that, based on a recent examination, the injury is not going to get any worse); and
- an insurance company letter (confirming the settlement, waiving their appearance at the hearing, and stating that they know of no excess insurance coverage for the defendant).

Practice Tip: One of the only times where a plaintiff's attorney should *downplay* the plaintiff's case and injuries is in connection with an infant's compromise.

When the case is settled prior to the commencement of a lawsuit, a special proceeding for an infant's compromise must be commenced (captioned, "In the Matter of X, as parent and natural guardian of Y, an infant, Petitioner, for leave to compromise a claim against Z, Respondent"), and an index number must be purchased for the infant's compromise proceeding.

Practice Tip: If the settlement is for less than $25,000, the petition can be filed in a lower court (i.e., as opposed to Supreme Court) where the index number fees are less costly.

§ 8.30 Proceeding with Infant's Compromise Hearing

The infant's compromise hearing is informal and typically lasts only a few minutes. At the hearing, the judge will typically ask the infant's parent and the infant, if old enough, a few questions regarding the injuries having resolved. Typical questions include, "Did the child go back to the doctor in the last 3 months? Is the child able to perform his or her usual activities (gym, sports)? Does the child have any restrictions? Any pain? Did the scar go away? Has your lawyer explained to you the proposed settlement?" Where there is a scar, the judge will usually want to view it.

If the judge is satisfied, s/he will approve the settlement. Where the injuries are significant and the insurance policy is tendered, the judge may require the plaintiff's attorney to produce an affidavit (of no excess insurance coverage) from the defendant, and conduct an asset search showing that the defendant has no assets to pursue. The judge will ask the plaintiff's attorney for the name and address of the bank where the money will be deposited (as the infant's compromise order will instruct the bank not to release the money to the infant until s/he reaches the age of majority) or the structured settlement information.

§ 8.31 Proceeding Following Infant's Compromise Hearing
[1] Obtaining Certified Copy Infant's Compromise Order

A certified copy of the infant's compromise order may be obtained (for a nominal fee) – usually from the County Clerk's office.

[2] Sending Documentation to Insurance Carrier or Defense Counsel

The plaintiff's attorney should send the insurance carrier or defense counsel a copy of the signed infant's compromise order and a general release (signed by the parent on behalf of the infant), along with a letter requesting two checks. One check should be made payable to X, parent and natural guardian of Y, jointly with an officer of (bank name) in the sum of $Z (or, in the case of a structured settlement, this check will be directly paid to fund the structure); the other check should be made payable to the plaintiff's attorney for legal fees and disbursements (pursuant to the infant's compromise order).

[3] Sending Check to Plaintiff

The settlement check and a certified copy of the infant's compromise order (which must be presented to the bank or financial institution at the time of deposit) should be sent to the plaintiff. This should be sent via certified mail, return receipt requested.

PART F: CONSIDERING LIENS WHEN SETTLING CASE
§ 8.32 Workers' Compensation Liens
[1] Consent of Workers' Compensation Insurance Carrier to Settle

When injured in the course of employment, typically the workers' compensation carrier pays for the injured party's medical bills and lost wages. Written consent of the workers' compensation insurance carrier is then required in order to settle the third-party claim. *Workers' Comp. Law §25(a)*. Otherwise, the plaintiff will lose his or her right to future workers' compensation benefits (as well as subjecting himself or herself to a possible lawsuit). If the carrier refuses to consent to a settlement (which is rare), consent can be forced via the courts; a petition can be brought *nunc pro tunc*. Where a case is settled at the time of trial, the plaintiff has three months thereafter to obtain the workers' compensation carrier's written consent. *Workers' Comp. Law §29(5)*.

[2] Workers' Compensation Liens in Motor Vehicle Accident Cases

Pursuant to an exception under *Workers' Compensation Law §29*, workers' compensation coverage is primary over no-fault coverage (and thus the workers' compensation carrier pays before the no-fault carrier). Payments made by the workers' compensation carrier in lieu of no-fault benefits (i.e., generally the first $50,000) are not recoverable (i.e., "lien-able"), however. Payments in excess of basic economic loss (see chapter 2, §2.02), result in the workers' compensation carrier having a lien against the proceeds in the third-party negligence case. In the event of a lien, the procedure is the same as discussed below (regarding lien reduction and the *Kelly* calculation*)*.

[3] Workers' Compensation Liens in Non-Motor Vehicle Accident Cases

In the non-motor vehicle accident case setting, the workers' compensation insurance carrier, by statute, has a lien against the third-party action for any sum the workers' compensation carrier paid out as a result of the accident (including medical expenses and lost wages). The amount of the lien will be reduced, as discussed in the section below.

[4] Reducing Workers' Compensation Liens – Cost of Litigation Reduction

If the plaintiff is not entitled to any future workers' compensation benefits relating to the accident (i.e., s/he is back to work, etc.), the lien will, statutorily, be reduced by slightly more than 1/3 (as attorneys' fees and disbursements are taken into consideration). The actual, precise formula used to determine a cost of litigation (COL) reduction, is as follows:

- (attorney's fee + disbursements) / (gross settlement) = COL%
- COL% x workers' compensation lien = net workers' compensation lien

The plaintiff's attorney can still negotiate a further reduction (see §8.32[7] below).

[5] Reducing Workers' Compensation Liens – The Kelly Calculation

Where the plaintiff is entitled to *future* benefits from the workers' compensation carrier, a formula is set forth to determine the present value of future benefits as an offset against the lien.[12] *See Kelly v. State Ins. Fund*, 94 A.D.2d 609, 461 N.Y.S.2d 989 (1st Dep't 1983). Hence, if the plaintiff is entitled to future compensation, the workers' compensation lien is reduced *twice* (once for the cost of litigation reduction of the past lien, discussed above, and once for the future credit). A *Kelly* calculation ("equitable apportionment"), based on the projected settlement value, is necessary.[13] In essence, if the workers' compensation carrier is allowed to close out the case, the lien can be reduced by the present value of future payments (the workers' compensation carrier will no longer have to make). The workers' compensation carrier may be required to waive its lien altogether. If workers' compensation benefits continue after

---

12 According to the Third Department, the rules set forth in *Kelly* do not apply where there has been a permanent *partial* disability classification. *Burns v. Varriale*, 34 A.D.3d 59, 820 N.Y.S.2d 655 (3d Dep't 2006). This is sure to be the subject of future litigation. See §8.32[6] below.

13 *Kelly* Calculation: 1) (total WC lien to date + present value of future WC benefits) / (gross PI recovery x total attorneys' fees & disbursements) = WC carrier's share of attorney's fees & disbursements
2) Total paid lien - WC carrier's share of attorney's fees & disbursements = (if positive, lien amount owed; if negative, cash owed by WC carrier).
Note: PV of future WC benefits = PV of $1 per week for number of years expected to live (see life expectancy chart in *PJI*) at 6% x the weekly rate of payment received from WC each week.

the settlement (something that can be negotiated for), there will be no offset; in such a case only the cost of litigation lien reduction applies.

Practice Tip: Where the plaintiff is entitled to future workers' compensation benefits, the workers' compensation insurance carrier often waives its lien (i.e., past payments) in exchange for the plaintiff waiving its future payments.

Practice Tip: The workers' compensation carrier could (as a result of *Kelly*) be required to pay "fresh" money (i.e., money in addition to that being paid by the defendants) to the plaintiff in addition to a waiver of its lien. The ability to argue to the workers' compensation carrier that it actually *owes* money profoundly affects the plaintiff's negotiation position.

[6] Permanent *Partial* Disability Classification

The Third Department has held that where a claimant has been determined to be permanently *partially* disabled, the amount and duration of his or her future benefits are speculative in nature. Hence, s/he is only entitled to a "cost of litigation" reduction of the workers' compensation lien; that is, the sum of attorneys' fees and disbursements divided by the gross settlement amount. S/he is not entitled to the benefit of a *Kelly* reduction regarding future benefits. *Burns v. Varriale*, 34 A.D.3d 59, 820 N.Y.S.2d 655 (3d Dep't 2006). However, according to the court, such a claimant is nonetheless entitled to petition the Workers' Compensation Board for continued weekly benefits equal to the proportionate share of the attorneys' fees and disbursements, as further reimbursement of cost of litigation fees. If the plaintiff would have received further workers' compensation benefits but for the settlement and exhaustion of the carrier's holiday[14], the workers' compensation carrier will be required to pay claimant in a weekly sum calculated as follows:

- cost of litigation (i.e., attorneys' fees + disbursements) / gross settlement = COL%
- COL% (from above) x average weekly WC wage benefit being received by claimant

These payments then continue, assuming the plaintiff / claimant remained unable to work as a result of the accident, until the workers' compensation carrier's offset (or holiday) is exhausted. Thereafter, the plaintiff / claimant is (assuming s/he remained unable to work as a result of the accident) entitled to his or her entire weekly workers' compensation payment (i.e., as opposed to only receiving the "cost of litigation" reimbursement). *Burns* does not apply to any case where there has been a permanent

---

14 *Workers' Compensation Law §29(4)* provides a credit or offset, which is a holiday that the workers' compensation carrier receives from payment of future benefits to a claimant until the proceeds recovered by a plaintiff in a personal injury action are exhausted (i.e., the time it would take for the normal weekly workers' compensation checks to equal the plaintiff's share of the settlement proceeds). *See Kelly v. State Ins. Fund*, 94 A.D.2d 609, 461 N.Y.S.2d 989 (1st Dep't 1983).

total disability finding, death, or a scheduled loss (i.e., loss for a static rate for a fixed number of weeks).

[7] Negotiating Liens Beyond Statutory Reduction

All liens are negotiable. Where there is uncertainty with the outcome of the case, the plaintiff will generally have to discount the value of the case in proportion to the uncertainty. Hence, if there is a 50% chance of losing at trial, the settlement value of the case is essentially half of what it otherwise could have been. Thus, just as the plaintiff and plaintiff's attorney will have to settle for only 50% of the full value of the case, so too should the workers' compensation insurance carrier. If the case does not settle, the workers' compensation insurance carrier risks losing everything, just like the plaintiff and the plaintiff's attorney. Hence, the plaintiff's attorney can often negotiate workers' compensation liens beyond the statutory reduction. Where a greater reduction than the equitable apportionment of costs of litigation is negotiated, the plaintiff's attorney can receive a fee on the differential only upon approval of the Workers' Compensation Board. *WC Law §24. Matter of Fullman*, 180 Misc.2d 30, 687 N.Y.S.2d 554 (Surr. Ct. N.Y. Cty. 1999).

> **Practice Tip:** Where the plaintiff's employer is a third-party defendant and contributes to the settlement in part via a lien reduction, the plaintiff's attorney is entitled to an additional fee of 1/3 of the reduction amount (i.e., beyond the statutory reduction). *Brock v. Mack Trucks, Inc.*, 178 A.D.2d 701, 577 N.Y.S.2d 149 (3d Dep't 1991); *Estate of Castiglia*, 158 Misc.2d 611, 601 N.Y.S.2d 559 (Surr. Ct. Bronx Cty. 1993).

§ 8.33 Liens in Motor Vehicle Accident Cases

[1] Workers' Compensation Liens in Motor Vehicle Accident Cases
See §8.31 above.

[2] UM / SUM Recoveries

Neither the workers' compensation carrier nor the APIP (Additional Personal Injury Protection) carrier is entitled to a lien from a recovery in an uninsured motorist (UM) or supplementary uninsured / under-insured motorist (SUM) case, for the obligation to pay arises out of contract, not tort. *See 11 NYCRR §60-2.3(f) (Regulation 35-D)*. There is no viable medical subrogation right for SUM recoveries. *Shutter v. Phillips Display Components Co.*, 90 N.Y.2d. 703, 655 N.Y.S.2d 379 (1997) (subrogation rights are only exercisable against third-parties).

[3] No-Fault Liens

[a] Additional Personal Injury Protection (APIP)

No-fault payments made in *excess* of basic economic loss, which is generally $50,000 (unless OBEL was purchased to increase it to $75,000), will become a lien against the third-party claim. Such payments are known as additional personal injury protection (APIP). Hence, the plaintiff's attorney must be sure to contact the no-fault insurance carrier prior to settling the case, to obtain consent to the settlement (and attempt to negotiate a lien reduction).

> **Practice Tip:** Since APIP payments mean that there is an economic loss greater than basic economic loss, the plaintiff has the right to recover such payments (i.e., generally above the first $50,000) via the third-party negligence action (and therefore that should be factored into settlement negotiations or awarded at trial). No-fault insurance carriers usually do not negotiate the APIP liens because they can pursue the claimant for reimbursement (as discussed in section [c] below). See chapter 2, §2.02[2].

[b] Third-Party Lawsuit Against "Non-Covered Person"

The no-fault insurer also has a lien right regarding the recovery from the "non-covered person". A situation where one might see this is with a motor vehicle accident which occurs due to a road defect (with a municipal defendant). In the lawsuit against the non-covered person (e.g., the municipality), the plaintiff can recover all medical expenses and lost earnings via the third-party negligence case. In such a case, the no-fault insurer has a lien on the recovery to prevent the plaintiff from obtaining a double-recovery.

[c] Statute of Limitations

The no-fault insurer has three years to bring a lawsuit against the responsible third-party (i.e., the defendant) regarding its APIP subrogation rights. *Allstate v. Stein*, 1 N.Y.3d 416, 775 N.Y.S.2d 219 (2004). If it does not exercise its APIP subrogation rights within the three-year statute of limitations period, the rights are waived. Thus, if the plaintiff settles his or her case before the three years have passed and a general release is issued, the plaintiff is extinguishing his or her rights as well as the no-fault carrier's APIP subrogation rights, giving the no-fault carrier the right to sue the plaintiff.

§ 8.34 Healthcare Provider Liens

Plaintiffs are often in need of treatment and/or surgery, yet have no way of paying for it (e.g., no health insurance or, in a motor vehicle accident case, following the no-fault denial). Certain healthcare providers will agree to render treatment and/or perform surgery without being compensated until the conclusion of the lawsuit. Essentially, the physician requires the plaintiff and the plaintiff's attorney to sign a lien form that states that the physician will be paid at the conclusion of the case from the plaintiff's proceeds.

Practice Tip: The plaintiff's attorney, in signing such a lien form in a motor vehicle accident case, should write onto the form that the physician will continue to submit all bills to the no-fault insurance carrier in a timely fashion so as not to prejudice the plaintiff's rights (for reimbursement from the no-fault carrier) and that the physician will bill at the "no-fault rates". See chapter 2, § 2.10[2].

§ 8.35 Medicaid Liens

Indigent accident victims often have their medical bills (including surgery) paid for by Medicaid. The Medicaid program was established by Title XIX of the *Social Security Act*, codified at *42 USC §1396-1396v*. Medicaid, once aware of a lawsuit, will place the attorneys (and the plaintiff) on notice of a statutory lien which must be paid from the plaintiff's share of the settlement proceeds. Medicaid liens are only allowed for medical expenses paid relating to the injuries claimed in the lawsuit. Where a Medicaid recipient (e.g., plaintiff) dies, however, there is a lien on his or her estate for all Medicaid expended after the age of fifty-five (whether or not causally related to the accident). Such a lien is to be satisfied from the lawsuit proceeds.

Medicaid liens are assigned to the Department of Social Services (DSS), and are absolutely enforceable. However, the United States Supreme Court has held that only the portion of the settlement attributable to medical expenses paid by Medicaid are subject to reimbursement. The anti-lien provision of *42 U.S.C. §§1396(a)(18)* and *1396p* precludes encumbrance or attachment to the remainder of the settlement (e.g., to the pain and suffering or loss of earnings portions). *See Arkansas Department of Health and Human Resources v. Ahlborn,* 547 U.S. 268, 126 S. Ct. 1752, 164 L. Ed. 459 (2006). Furthermore, where, for example, the plaintiff settled for half of the full value of the case (e.g., on account of liability difficulties), Medicaid is only entitled to recover half of the monies expended for plaintiff's medical costs relating to the accident. *Id.*

Practice Tip: At the time of the settlement, the plaintiff's attorney should attempt to obtain a stipulation from defense counsel regarding how much of the settlement reflects repayment of medical expenses (paid by Medicaid), taking liability into account. The plaintiff's attorney should then have Medicaid stipulate to the allocation.

Further, imposition of a Medicaid lien must procedurally adhere to *New York Social Services Law §104-b* (which is very strict, and will render an improperly imposed lien a nullity, e.g., incorrect time frame or manner). The Medicaid recipient also has a duty to notify the Department of Social Services (DSS) whenever there is a lawsuit. Thus, a court could find that the plaintiff's failure to notify the DSS nullifies the DSS' failure to follow *Social Services Law §140-b*. Where the funds have already passed to the claimant / plaintiff, the DSS cannot assert a lien for the first time. Additionally, if the plaintiff is less than twenty-one years of age, Medicaid cannot pursue the proceeds of the lawsuit, unless at the time the Medicaid services were rendered, the injured party had money and assets in excess of reasonable living requirements.

Medicaid liens, while negotiable, do *not* have an automatic statutory offset of 1/3 of the lien amount (i.e., unlike workers' compensation liens; see §8.32[4] above). Additionally, following a settlement, the plaintiff may well lose his or her Medicaid benefits.

> **Practice Tip:** In cases where the City of New York is a defendant, the City may offer a "low cash settlement" with a waiver of its Medicaid lien (which may be very large). At the time of settlement (even if the City is not contributing), the plaintiff's attorney should ask the City attorney to agree to a non-assertion of any Medicaid and/or public assistance liens; sometimes they will agree in order to provide resolution.

§ 8.36 Supplemental Security Income (SSI)

Supplemental Security Income (SSI) is a welfare program for the poor, aged, blind, and/or disabled. See http://policy.ssa.gov/poms.nsf. SSI does not have a lien on a personal injury case, but an SSI recipient may not retain in excess of $2,000 (a couple may not retain in excess of $5,000) in available resources, as well as a vehicle (valued at $4,500 or less) and a home residence. Thus, a client will lose eligibility for SSI and Medicaid (i.e., if on SSI, one automatically receives Medicaid) as a result of a settlement. As with a Medicaid recipient, the client cannot keep both the proceeds and the SSI. Therefore, the plaintiff's attorney should have the client execute an acknowledgment of this. Only the *client* has the duty to notify SSI of the receipt of the funds.

If the client then transfers his or her resources (i.e., gift out), s/he must wait up to 36 months for future SSI eligibility. *See 42 USC 1396p.* The period of ineligibility is computed by dividing the gross settlement amount by the benefit rate (e.g., $600 / month) with the maximum being 36 months (i.e., if the calculated number is greater than 36, it automatically becomes 36).

> **Practice Tip:** If the lawsuit recovery is transferred (or spent on a sheltered item such as a home) within the same (calendar) month, the argument can be made that it is a transfer of income and would not result in a wait for SSI benefits. *See SSI regs (42 CFR §416.1210-1218).* There have not yet been any cases regarding this issue.

Practice Tip: If the recipient is less than 65 years of age, s/he can keep the benefits without any wait if the assets are placed in a supplemental needs trust.

§ 8.37 Medicare Liens

Medicare is a Social Security health insurance program. People 65 years of age or greater who are entitled to receive Social Security are entitled to receive Medicare, as are disabled people who have received Social Security Disability benefits for 25 months and people with end-stage renal disease who require dialysis or a kidney transplant. *42 USC §1395, 42 USC §406*. Medicare has the right to reimbursement for medical expenditures related to a plaintiff's accident, pursuant to *Public Law 108-173* – signed into law in December 2003. Further, Medicare is not required to send notice; thus, the obligation is on the recipient / plaintiff and his or her attorney to be proactive. Additionally, the Medicare Secondary Provider (MSP) regulations require attorneys to satisfy Medicare's interest prior to distributing any settlement proceeds. Medicare has the first right of recovery on any liability claim for reimbursement of conditional payments. In cases where Medicare's interest is not satisfied, all parties that received settlement funds are subject to Medicare collection efforts. Further, Medicare must be paid within sixty days of receipt of the proceeds from the third-party; otherwise, interest may be assessed.

§ 8.38 ERISA Liens

Sometimes health insurance companies assert ERISA (Employees Retirement Income Security Act of 1974) liens (*29 USC §1001*), which have been held valid by the U.S. Supreme Court. *Sereboff v. Mid Atlantic Medical Services, Inc.*, 547 U.S. 28, 126 S. Ct. 1869, 164 L.Ed. 612 (2006). To qualify as an ERISA plan, the it must be:

- a plan, fund, or program;
- established or maintained by an employer or employee organization, or both;
- for the purpose of providing medical benefits;
- to participants or their beneficiaries.

See 29 USC §1002. ERISA does not apply to state government plans, foreign plans, or to self-pay insurance contracts (i.e., where the employer purchases group health coverage but does not administer or control any of the benefits). Where an ERISA lien is asserted, the plaintiff's attorney should request a copy of the policy to determine whether all of the ERISA requirements (as set forth above) were met (making the lien valid).

Prior to *Sereboff*, in *Great-West Life & Annuity Ins. Co. v. Knudson*, 534 U.S. 204, 122 S. Ct. 708 (2002), the U.S. Supreme Court denied the right of healthcare carriers to recover monies paid to insured's from third-party cases in federal court under ERISA where the money had been placed in a special needs trust – and were, hence, not identifiable funds within the plaintiff's possession and control.

§ 8.39 Private Medical Insurance Liens

While private healthcare providers often attempt to assert a contractual (i.e., as opposed to statutory) lien on the case, they often have merely an unenforceable subrogation right. Pursuant to *CPLR §4545(c)* (the collateral source rule), if the plaintiff is awarded money at trial for past medical expenses, the court is to subtract from the recovery any amounts already paid from another source (e.g., private healthcare insurance). Upon a verdict, the plaintiff is not entitled to a "double recovery", and the collateral source provider is not entitled to reimbursement. Thus, if the healthcare provider is not entitled to reimbursement following a jury verdict, it should not be entitled to reimbursement following a settlement. *Humbach v. Goldstein*, 229 A.D.2d 64, 653 N.Y.S.2d 950 (2d Dep't 1997); *Holloran v. Don's 47 West 44 St. Restaurant Corp.*, 255 A.D.2d 206, 680 N.Y.S.2d 227 (1st Dep't 1998); *Berry v. St. Peter's Hosp. of NY*, 250 A.D.2d 63, 678 N.Y.S.2d 674 (3d Dep't 1998).[15] See chapter 10, §10.21[5][e] below. Medicaid, Medicare, and workers' compensation are presently exempted from the collateral source rule. As those entities are entitled to recoup their outlays, the plaintiff is allowed to collect same from the defendant in the third-party action without offset.

> **Practice Tip:** The plaintiff's attorney should delineate the settlement (i.e., in the general release) as for "pain and suffering only"; as a *quid pro quo*, the defendants will require that they be "held harmless" by the plaintiff for any liens or contractual rights (i.e., in the general release).

Where there is a valid "contractual lien", which is not the norm, there should be some concern; usually, though, there is merely an unenforceable subrogation right. The actual insurance policy language must be examined.

> **Practice Tip:** Where there is a valid contractual lien, it is subject to negotiation (as are all liens). That is, if liability is 50/50, the health insurance carrier should take fifty cents on the dollar (just like the plaintiff and the plaintiff's attorney), being mindful that there may be no recovery in the event of a verdict.

§ 8.40 Social Security Disability

Social Security Disability (SSD) benefits are based on the plaintiff's pre-disability income. There is no lien for SSD benefits because the proceeds a plaintiff receives from a negligence award are not taxable and are not considered wages or earned income for SSD purposes. SSD benefits received by a plaintiff, however, can be used by the defendant as an offset against lost earnings claimed in the action.

---

15 The Fourth Department holds a differing view. *See Oakes v. Patel & Health Now New York, Inc.*, 23 A.D.3d 1023, 803 N.Y.S.2d 455 (4th Dep't 2005).

CHAPTER 9

JURY SELECTION

PART A: OVERVIEW

§ 9.01 Overview – Jury Selection

Jury selection plays a vital role in negligence cases. For starters, this is the time when settlement offers are generally maximized. Insurance companies know they have reached the end. They cannot delay any longer, and their offer must be increased – particularly in a plaintiff-friendly venue, where the fear of a large, runaway verdict is closer to becoming a reality. Settlement aside, trials are often won or lost at jury selection. That is, choosing the right jurors, or failing to challenge the wrong jurors, can be the difference in the case.

PART B: JURY SELECTION PROCEDURE

§ 9.02 Settlement Conference Prior to Jury Selection

Prior to the commencement of jury selection, the attorneys appear in the trial assignment part, or the trial judge's courtroom (depending on the court), for the purpose of settlement. *See 22 NYCRR §202.33(b)*. If there is no resolution, the judge may direct them to select a jury.

§ 9.03 Role of Judge at Jury Selection

Civil jury selection is generally left to the attorneys. While the judge has discretion to preside over part or all of jury selection (*see 22 NYCRR §202.33[e]*), a judge is usually not present at the proceedings. If the attorneys need a ruling, they can seek one from the judge. On application of any party, pursuant to *CPLR §4107*, a judge shall be present at the examination of the jurors. The judge may establish time limits for the questioning of prospective jurors and will generally direct the method to be used for jury selection, such as "White's Method", "Struck Method", or, in rare cases, the "Strike and Replace Method". *See 22 NYCRR §202.33(c) and (d)*.

§ 9.04 Conducting *Voir Dire*

[1] Seating Jurors and Reviewing Juror Questionnaires

The prospective jurors are seated differently depending upon which jury selection method is being utilized. Once the prospective jurors are seated, the attorneys are able to review the juror questionnaires (prior to questioning) which ask general questions such as length of time living in the particular county, highest level of education, occupation, hobbies, prior jury service, and family background. See §9.07[1] and §9.08[1] below.

[2] Questioning Jurors

During jury selection, each attorney may state the general contentions of his or her client(s), and identify the parties, attorneys and witnesses likely to be called. The plaintiff's attorney proceeds first, followed by defense counsel, in the order of the caption. The attorneys, however, are not permitted to read from the pleadings in the case or to inform the potential jurors of the *amount* of money at issue. The attorneys are prohibited from discussing legal concepts such as burden of proof, which are the province of the court. Where an unusual delay or lengthy trial is expected, counsel may advise the prospective jurors. *22 NYCRR §202.33.* See chapter 11, §11.11 for an outline of topics for jury selection.

[3] Discussing Damages at Jury Selection

As stated above, counsel is prohibited from discussing the *amount* of money at issue (*22 NYCRR §202.33*). However, this does not preclude counsel from discussing and exploring jurors' ideas on damages issues. See §§9.11, 9.16 below.

[4] Objections During Jury Selection

If counsel wishes to object to anything said or done by any other counsel during jury selection, the objecting counsel is to *unobtrusively* request that all counsel step outside of the jurors' presence. If a determined effort to resolve the problem amongst themselves fails, all counsel are to immediately report to the presiding judge for a ruling. *22 NYCRR §202.33.*

§ 9.05 Number of Jurors and Alternates to be Selected

Generally, six jurors plus two alternates will be selected; the court may allow a greater number of alternates if a lengthy trial is expected, or for any appropriate reason. *See CPLR §§4105* and *4106.* Counsel may consent to the use of "non-designated" jurors (i.e., for efficiency purposes), in which event no distinction is to be made during jury selection between jurors and alternates (i.e., 8 jurors are selected without knowing which two will be the alternates); in such a case, the number of peremptory challenges permitted is the sum of the peremptory challenges that would have been available to challenge both jurors and alternates. *See 22 NYCRR §202.33.*

§ 9.06 Grounds to Challenge Jurors

[1] Consenting to Excuse Jurors

Counsel may stipulate to excuse a juror. *CPLR §4108.* Where counsel do not agree, a challenge for cause will likely be made and ruled upon by the judge.

Practice Tip: Sometimes counsel stipulate to excuse two jurors – one perceived to be "pro-plaintiff" and one perceived to be "pro-defendant" – at the same time. This will allow counsel to preserve their peremptory challenges.

[2] Challenging Jurors *For Cause*

[a] Challenges to the Favor

Jurors can be automatically challenged "for cause", meaning the attorney challenging them does not lose a peremptory challenge. There are two types of challenges for cause: challenges to the favor and challenges for "principal cause". Pursuant to *CPLR §4110(a),* each of the following constitute grounds for a challenge to the favor:

- Juror is in the employ of a party to the action.
- Juror is a shareholder of a corporate defendant.
- Juror is a shareholder, director, officer, employee, or in any manner interested in any insurance company issuing policies for protection against liability for personal injury or property damage.

The fact that a juror is a resident of, or liable to pay taxes in, a city, village, town, or county which is a party to the action does not constitute a ground for challenge to the favor. *CPLR §4110(a).*

Practice Tip: Where the attorney can establish that a juror cannot be impartial, the juror may be excused for cause. If opposing counsel disagrees, a ruling from the court must be sought. *See CPLR §4108.* If the judge does not find the juror to be biased, the attorney must use a peremptory challenge if s/he wants to excuse the juror.

[b] Challenges for "Principal Cause"

Jurors will be disqualified from sitting as jurors if related within the sixth degree by consanguity or affinity to a party. The party related to the juror must raise the objection before the case is opened; any other party must raise the objection no later than six months after the verdict. *CPLR §4110(b).*

[c] Challenging Entire Jury Panel

The entire array of jurors can be challenged for cause. The parties are entitled to have a jury selected from a fair cross-section of the community. *N.Y. Jud. Law §800.*

[3] Using Peremptory Challenges

[a] Grounds for Peremptory Challenges

No reason needs to be given to excuse a juror via a peremptory challenge. However, a peremptory challenge cannot be used to discriminate against a juror based on race or gender. *Batson v. Kentucky*, 476 U.S. 79, 106 S. Ct. 1712, 90 L. Ed. 2d 69 (1986). Peremptory challenges may not be used to systematically exclude members of a "cognizable group" – such as race, gender, or religion – from the jury; doing so amounts to "group bias" or the "presumption that certain jurors are biased merely because they are members of a cognizable group." *Id. See also People v. Langston*, 167 Misc.2d 400, 641 N.Y.S.2d 513 (Sup. Ct. Queens Cty. 1996).

[b] Number of Peremptory Challenges Available

The plaintiff(s) have a combined total of three peremptory challenges plus one peremptory challenge for every two alternate jurors. The defendant(s), other than any third-party defendant(s), also have a *combined* total of three peremptory challenges plus one challenge for every two alternate jurors. Prior to jury selection, the court may, in its discretion, grant an equal number of additional challenges to both sides as may be appropriate. Where a side has two or more parties, the court, in its discretion, may allocate that side's total number of peremptory challenges among those parties in any manner which the court deems appropriate. *CPLR §4109*. Peremptory challenges are to be exercised outside of the presence of the panel of prospective jurors. *22 NYCRR §202.33.*

[c] Requesting *Batson* Hearing

Where the use of peremptory challenges is disputed on the basis of discrimination against a cognizable group, a motion for a *Batson* hearing must be made. The court must conduct a hearing to determine whether the challenges are based on discrimination against a cognizable group or whether there is a legitimate race-neutral reason for excusing specific jurors. *People v. Hernandez*, 75 N.Y.2d 350, 553 N.Y.S.2d 85 (1990), *aff'd sub nom. Hernandez v. New York*, 500 U.S. 352, 111 S. Ct. 1859 (1991).

Practice Tip: In the context of a *Batson* hearing, the notes taken by counsel during jury selection are subject to review by opposing counsel and the judge.

The moving party must establish a *prima facie* case by showing:
- that the persons excluded are members of a cognizable group;
- a strong likelihood that such persons are being challenged to remove members of a cognizable group; and
- facts and other relevant circumstances that raise the inference that the party discriminated based on group bias.

See People v. Jenkins, 75 N.Y.2d 550, 555 N.Y.S.2d 10 (1990).

Following presentation of the moving party's evidence, the judge must determine whether a reasonable inference arises that the peremptory challenges were exercised in a purposefully discriminatory way. *People v. Bolling*, 79 N.Y.2d 317, 582 N.Y.S.2d 950 (1992). If the court finds that a *prima facie* showing has been made, the other side has an opportunity to show a legitimate neutral basis for the challenges related to the particular case. *People v. Hernandez*, 75 N.Y.2d 350, 553 N.Y.S.2d 85 (1990), *aff'd sub nom. Hernandez v. New York*, 500 U.S. 352, 111 S. Ct. 1859 (1991). While the reasons proffered need not rise to the level of a challenge "for cause", they must be *bona fide. People v. Bolling*, 79 N.Y.2d 317, 582 N.Y.S.2d 950 (1992).

Practice Tip: Where the peremptorily challenged juror(s) are no longer available following a successful *Batson* challenge, the court must quash the remaining panel and start jury selection from a new panel. Hence, the *Batson* challenge may be made before the challenged juror(s) are dismissed.

PART C: JURY SELECTION METHODS

§ 9.07 White's Method

[1] Seating and Questioning Jurors Under White's Method

After prospective jurors complete a brief questionnaire (regarding their backgrounds), generally a panel of 25 jurors are told to report to a particular room. Once there, the jurors' cards (with their names) are placed into a pill cart. One of the attorneys spins the cart so the cards are thoroughly mixed. The attorneys randomly select six cards from the cart; with each pick, a prospective juror's name is called and s/he is asked to sit in one of the six seats (in the order of the pick) directly in front of the attorneys (generally in the jury box). The attorneys place the selected cards across a wooden board, one through six. As they are seated, the prospective jurors hand their questionnaires to counsel for review. The questioning of the seated prospective jurors is initially conducted by the plaintiff's attorney followed by counsel for the remaining parties, in the order in which the parties' names appear in the caption. This holds true for each round of questioning. *22 NYCRR §202.33(g).*

[2] Challenges for Cause Under White's Method

Challenges for cause can be exercised regarding a prospective juror's inability to be fair. *CPLR §4110.* Such challenges must be made prior to the exercise of peremptory challenges, within each round. Further, a challenge for cause may be made as soon as the reason for it becomes apparent. *22 NYCRR §202.33(g).*

[3] Peremptory Challenges Under White's Method

In exercising peremptory challenges, prospective jurors may be "struck" for any reason other than race or gender. *See Batson v. Kentucky*, 476 U.S. 79, 106 S. Ct. 1712, 90 L. Ed. 69 (1986). Following questioning and challenges for cause, peremptory challenges (each side has three total) are to be exercised one at a time, as follows: In the first round, in caption order, each attorney may exercise one peremptory challenge by removing (or turning over) a card with a prospective juror's name from the board which is passed between counsel. Where an attorney waives the making of a peremptory challenge, s/he may not exercise any further peremptory challenges within that round. An attorney may exercise an additional, single peremptory challenge within the round only after all other attorneys have either exercised or waived their first peremptory challenges. The attorney last able to exercise a peremptory challenge in a round may exercise one or more peremptory challenges. *22 NYCRR §202.33(g).*

In subsequent rounds, the first exercise of peremptory challenges alternates from side to side. That is, in the first round, the plaintiff proceeds first; in the second round, the defendant proceeds first. Where a side consists of multiple parties (e.g., two defendants), initiation of peremptory challenges within that side rotates among the parties within that side. Before the board is passed to the other side, it must be passed to all remaining within the side (in caption order), beginning with the first party in the rotation for that round. *22 NYCRR §202.33(g).*

[4] Peremptory Challenges Under Modified White's Method

Some courts utilize "Modified White's Method" whereby, in the first round of peremptory challenges, the plaintiff must make *all* of his or her peremptory challenges for the round at once (i.e., anywhere from zero to three); then, the defendant(s) make *all* of their peremptory challenges at once (also anywhere from zero to three in total); that way, the board is only passed once in each round.

> **Warning:** The plaintiff's attorney should attempt to avoid the use of "Modified White's Method", for it is clearly a disadvantage to the plaintiff. Under "Modified White's Method", the plaintiff's attorney is at risk of depleting his or her peremptory challenges before defense counsel's first turn arises.

[5] Informing Challenged Jurors They Have Been Excused

At the end of each round, the challenged jurors are removed from the room and sent back to the Central Jury Part. It is traditionally the plaintiff's attorney's duty to inform the challenged jurors that they have been excused, hand them their juror questionnaires and juror cards, and send them back to the Central Jury Part. The seated jurors (i.e., one through six) who remain unchallenged are then removed from the room (preventing their future contamination) and are sent (or escorted by the attorneys) to the jury clerk (along with their cards and the top copy of their questionnaires) to be sworn. The challenged jurors' seats are replaced (by choosing additional cards from the pill cart), and a new round then begins in an effort to secure jurors for the seats vacated by the challenged jurors. *See 22 NYCRR §202.33(g).*

[6] Selecting Alternate Jurors Under White's Method

Once the six jurors are selected, the selection of alternate jurors (usually two) commences. Alternate jurors are selected in the same way as the initial six jurors, with the order of peremptory challenges continuing from the previous round. The total number of peremptory challenges of alternates may be exercised against any alternate, regardless of seat. Pursuant to *CPLR §4109*, each side is allowed one peremptory challenge for every two alternates.

Practice Tip: Some courts allow one peremptory challenge for each side; other courts allow each side one peremptory challenge per seat when selecting alternates. This is something that should be discussed amongst counsel prior to the commencement of jury selection; counsel sometimes, amongst themselves, agree to use a modification of the court's rules.

§ 9.08 Struck Method

[1] Seating and Questioning Jurors Under Struck Method

Under the Struck Method, 25 prospective jurors are randomly seated and assigned numbers (one through twenty-five). The attorneys (or sometimes the judge or judicial hearing officer) begin by making general inquiries to the prospective jurors (as a group) to determine whether any prospective jurors have knowledge of the subject matter, the parties, the attorneys, or possible witnesses. Counsel may exercise challenges for cause at this time.

After general questioning, the plaintiff's attorney begins questioning the full panel of prospective jurors. Questioning then continues with the other attorney(s), in the order in which the parties' names appear in the caption. *22 NYCRR §202.33.*

[2] Challenges for Cause Under Struck Method

By the end of the questioning (if not sooner), counsel must exercise all challenges for cause. Following challenges for cause, counsel must make sure there are ample prospective jurors remaining on the panel (so that if all peremptory challenges are used there will still be enough for a jury, including alternates). If not, additional prospective jurors must be added; counsel for each party then has the opportunity to question the replacements. Once the number of prospective jurors (who are no longer subject to challenges for cause) is sufficient to ensure that a complete jury (including alternates) will be selected, peremptory challenges are to be made. *22 NYCRR §202.33(g).*

[3] Peremptory Challenges Under Struck Method

In exercising peremptory challenges, prospective jurors may be "struck" for any reason other than race or gender. *See Batson v. Kentucky*, 476 U.S. 79, 106 S. Ct. 1712, 90 L. Ed. 69 (1986). Peremptory challenges are made one at a time by counsel for each party, beginning with the plaintiff's attorney. Counsel alternately strikes a single name from a list or ballot passed back and forth between counsel until all challenges are used or waived. The peremptory challenges are exercised by counsel in the order in which the parties' names appear in the caption. Once an attorney waives a challenge, s/he may not exercise any further peremptory challenges. Any objections (including a *Batson* objection wherein an attorney feels that there has been a race or gender-based challenge) are to be resolved by the court before any of the struck jurors are dismissed. Following peremptory challenges, the jurors (including alternates when non-designated alternates are used) are then selected (in the order in which they have been seated) from the prospective jurors remaining on the panel. *22 NYCRR §202.33(g)*.

[4] Selecting Alternate Jurors Under Struck Method

Generally, two alternates are to be selected. In the event a lengthy trial is expected, the attorneys may agree to select three alternates. Where the use of non-designated alternates (i.e., the alternates are not specifically designated as alternates) is consented to, eight (six plus two alternates) jurors are selected from the initial panel.

However, if designated alternates are to be used, they are to be selected *after* the selection of the six jurors. The selection takes place in the same manner as is used for selecting the original six, except that the initial panel is to be comprised of ten or less prospective alternate jurors. The total number of peremptory challenges for alternates may be exercised against any alternate regardless of seat. *22 NYCRR §202.33(g)*. Pursuant to *CPLR §4109*, each side is allowed one peremptory challenge for every two alternates.

PART D: MEETING JURY SELECTION GOALS[16]

§ 9.09 Seeking Prototype Jurors

The plaintiff's attorney's main goal of the jury selection process is to end up with a jury comprised of plaintiff-friendly jurors. This means, of course, weeding out those who may be biased in favor of the defense. For example, if the plaintiff is a tenant suing a landlord for negligence, the plaintiff's attorney will likely prefer a tenant (and disfavor a landlord) to be on the jury. Similarly, the plaintiff's attorney will typically prefer prior (or present) personal injury plaintiffs to be on the jury; likewise, jurors who are, or once were, defendants in personal injury actions will typically be disfavored by the plaintiff's attorney.

Further, the plaintiff's attorney will usually favor jurors who do *not* own real property or a motor vehicle. Jurors who pay insurance premiums (on real property or a motor vehicle) often believe that a plaintiff's verdict may result in increased premiums. Hence, more affluent counties are defense-oriented while less affluent counties are plaintiff-oriented.

Defense attorneys generally favor jurors who are affluent, well-educated, and/or precise / detail-oriented (e.g., accountants) whereas plaintiffs generally favor jurors who are charitable and/or perform volunteer work for charitable agencies, as well as social workers, counselors, and care givers; sympathetic jurors are typically the best jurors for a plaintiff. On the other hand, plaintiffs will generally disfavor jurors who are practical, "tough it out" types, as they are often insensitive to hardships and trauma, believe in working through pain, rarely visit their doctors, and often downplay difficult experiences that might otherwise be traumatic to the average person. Similarly,

---

16 *See "Voir Dire* in Medical Negligence Cases: A Plaintiff's Perspective," *New York Law Journal*, October 24, 2004, Rubinowitz, Ben and Evan Torgan.; "Dealing With Monetary Damages From *Voir Dire* to Summation," *New York Law Journal*, November 29, 2001, Rubinowitz, Ben and Evan Torgan.

plaintiffs might generally disfavor naive (i.e., carefree, never been injured, do not worry about dangers / precautionary measures) jurors, for they have had generally positive experiences and view the world as safe. There are a variety of reasons to choose or strike particular prospective jurors; the plaintiff's attorney should have a plan, but ultimately must use his or her instincts.

§ 9.10 Interjecting Theme

The plaintiff's attorney should always have a theme for trial which should start at jury selection. Themes such as "responsibility" should be sufficiently borne out through the jury selection process.

§ 9.11 Exploring Jurors' Thoughts and Opinions Via Non-Leading Questions

Non-leading questions (e.g., who, what, where, when, why, and how) help to learn about the potential jurors and to explore their thoughts and opinions. For example, "What do you think about a person's right to bring a lawsuit for money damages?"

> **Practice Tip:** The plaintiff's attorney must be cognizant, though, that use of non-leading questions may well elicit information that will cause defense counsel to strike plaintiff-friendly jurors (either for cause or by use of peremptories). Hence, the plaintiff's attorney may not want to ask too much of a juror s/he believes to be plaintiff-friendly from the outset.

§ 9.12 Conditioning Jury Via Leading Questions

Leading questions help to condition the jury as to the attorney's theory of the case, to make a point, or to have an unfavorable juror to admit possible bias. An example of this is, "Do you agree that if someone is injured through the fault of another, the party who caused the injury should pay for it?"

The plaintiff's attorney may wish to condition the jury as to some of the important phrases (from the *Pattern Jury Instructions*) they will hear from the judge at trial. To accomplish this artfully, so as to fend off defense counsels' objections, the plaintiff's attorney may have to ask one question on each side of the fence.

> **Example:**
> Q: Does anyone have a problem with a property owner earning money by renting an apartment?
> Q: Would you agree, however, that a for-profit landlord has an obligation to keep the premises *reasonably safe*?

The "buzz words" (e.g., "reasonably safe") from the jury instructions should be conditioned upon the jury through the use of leading questions. The plaintiff's attorney must keep in mind that the words *negligence* and *substantial factor* are the ones which the jury will generally need to find (as they usually appear on the verdict sheet); hence, added importance should be associated with those terms. These types of leading questions are simply a way for the plaintiff's attorney to "teach" the potential jurors how s/he want them to digest the judge's instruction at the end of the case.

In a case where credibility is at issue, the attorney may want to ask, "Do you think that just because a witness swears to tell the truth, that he will automatically tell the truth?" In a case where the credibility of experts is at issue, the attorney may want to ask, "Do you think simply because someone has a medical degree and is called 'doctor' s/he must have a reputation for honesty?" The answers to the leading questions should be followed-up with non-leading questions such as "Why do you feel that way?" or "How do you feel about that?" in order to explore the prospective jurors' thoughts.

§ 9.13 Preserving Peremptory Challenges

The true art of jury selection is in the attorney's ability to *preserve peremptory challenges* of unfavorable jurors via the skilled use of challenges for cause and/or consent. A skilled attorney will turn what otherwise would have been a peremptory challenge into a challenge for cause. Further, a skilled attorney who has no peremptory challenges remaining and is faced with an unfavorable juror, will thoroughly question the juror until a challenge for cause is warranted. This should be accomplished through the use of leading questions.

Example:

Q: You told us that you were once named as a defendant in a lawsuit?

Q: I assume that it wasn't a very pleasant experience?

Q: In fact, the litigation process can be a real pain, right?

Q: You had to talk to lawyers who represented you, right?

Q: And attend a deposition?

Q: And answer questions from the opposing lawyer?

Q: This took time from your family and work?

Q: It was a nuisance, right?

Q: And, I don't blame you for it, but you must have some very interesting opinions about lawsuits like this?

Q: And I assume some of those opinions are negative, right?

Q: However, you'd agree that anyone who comes into a court of law is entitled to a fair trial?

Q: And that people are entitled to a jury who can decide the case on the evidence, and not based on personal opinions unrelated to the case at hand?

Q: And I can tell by talking to you that if you even thought there was slight possibility that you may let your experience of being sued affect your decision-making, that you'd let us know?

Q: Would you agree that there is certainly a possibility that having been a defendant in a lawsuit, that you may ever-so-slightly identify with the defendant in this case?

Q: And based on your sense of fairness, if that were the case, you'd want to excuse yourself from service on this case?

Q: Knowing that you were a defendant, and that you have certain negative feelings about cases like this, would you agree that based on what you've told us, that strictly from a fairness perspective, that it would be inappropriate for you to sit on this case?

While it is easier to perform this type of questioning outside the presence of the rest of the panel, it is preferable to accomplish this in front of the entire panel. The advantage to conducting this *voir dire* in front of the entire panel is that the defense attorney will be forced to concede the "cause" challenge or otherwise will be perceived by the panel as attempting to seat a clearly biased juror.

Practice Tip: It is generally easier to elicit an affirmative response to the (leading) question that the potential juror cannot be "impartial", as opposed to "fair".

§ 9.14 Rehabilitating Prospective Jurors

Where a clearly pro-plaintiff response is elicited by one of the prospective jurors, the plaintiff's attorney should attempt to "rehabilitate" the prospective juror (i.e., at the conclusion of defense counsel's questioning). Otherwise, the defense may be able to use a challenge for cause on that juror. The plaintiff's attorney should attempt to force the defense to use a peremptory or, if none left, keep the pro-plaintiff juror.

Practice Tip: The prospective juror should be asked leading questions to the point where s/he promises that s/he can listen to the evidence and render a fair verdict based solely on the facts of the case and the law as given by the judge. Oddly, the plaintiff's attorney should attempt to have "pro-plaintiff" jurors state that they will be fair to the defense (and *vice versa*).

§ 9.15 Discussing Negative Aspects of Plaintiff's Case

The jury panel should be questioned on the negative aspects of the plaintiff's case. They should not be saved for trial. For example, suppose the plaintiff's illegal immigration status will be disclosed during the trial where plaintiff's motion *in limine* was denied. By being aboveboard, the plaintiff's attorney may be able to excuse jurors for cause, while also elevating his or her credibility and desensitizing the panel to the problem.

Example:

Q: I'll tell you that my client is an undocumented alien. It is our position that his status in the country has nothing to do with the facts of this case, the negligence of the defendant, and the injuries sustained by Mr. Smith (the plaintiff). How do you feel about that?

Practice Tip: In the example above, it is important to finish with a non-leading question. The juror's narrative response will help determine whether to press after him or her for cause, or whether to keep him or her with the assurance that the negative will not be held against the plaintiff.

If the plaintiff's attorney feels that the juror can disregard the negative aspect of the plaintiff's case, the potential juror's commitment on the issue should be sought.

Example:

Q: Can I have your assurance that, if you are chosen as a juror, you will not allow that fact to govern your decision?

On the flip side, certain positive aspects of the plaintiff's case may best be left for trial. If defense counsel does not bring out a negative aspect regarding the defendant (e.g., defendant was convicted of DWI for the subject accident), the plaintiff's attorney should wait to make the announcement in opening statements. However, if the defense attempts to diffuse the issue during jury selection, the plaintiff's attorney should discuss those facts before exercising challenges so as not to leave the jury with the defense attorney's version of the issue.

§ 9.16 Discussing Damages

The plaintiff's attorney's ultimate goal is to recover as much money as possible. Hence, it is imperative that the issue of damages is discussed with the panel of jurors.

Example:

Q: The only remedy for which the law provides when someone has been injured through the negligence of another is monetary compensation. If someone were to say, "this case is about money," that would be true. There is no way for us to go back in time and undo the events of the past. Mr. Smith (the plaintiff) would like nothing more than to come to court today and have you render a verdict that somehow changes the past, and makes the defendant act reasonably and avoid this accident. Obviously, that can't happen.

The potential jurors whose biases prevent an award of fair and adequate compensation must be discovered and challenged. Using non-leading questions (e.g, "How do you feel about people's right to bring a lawsuit for money damages?") can assist the plaintiff's attorney in determining prospective jurors' true feelings and biases.

Example:

Q: I am going to discuss an area which is much more difficult to quantify than lost earnings or medical costs. That is an award for somebody's pain and suffering. Do you agree with our civil justice system which provides that injured people are not only entitled to be compensated for their medical costs, or loss of earnings, but also for their pain and suffering? How do you feel about that? Can I have your assurance that if I prove that aspect of the case, you will make an award for that if my client is entitled to it?

Inquiry should also be made of the potential jurors regarding their ability to award *substantial* damages.

Example:

Q: Would you have any hesitation at all in awarding Mr. Jones a substantial sum of money if you believe he is entitled to it based upon the evidence in the case and the law as instructed by the judge? Can you assure me of that?

Q: If you add up all the individual components of damages – past medical expenses, future medical expenses, past pain and suffering, future pain and suffering, past loss of earnings, and future loss of earnings – and the total is a *huge* number, will you have any hesitation in awarding that amount? Can you assure me of that?

§ 9.17 Discussing Sympathy

The plaintiff's attorney may anticipate his or her adversary addressing the issue of sympathy at jury selection. As such, the plaintiff's attorney may, or may not, wish to address it first; it depends on the practitioner's preference.

Example:

Q: If this case were about sympathy, surely my client wins. He's been through hell. But, you know what, he's had his support group of family and friends to comfort him and help him through this. He's not here seeking sympathy. Can we agree that if your verdict was based on sympathy, that would be wrong?

Having established a position of fairness, the plaintiff's attorney can then address concerns with the prospective jurors.

Example:

Q: What Mr. Smith (the plaintiff) does seek is justice and fairness. And while it would be wrong to render a verdict based on sympathy, it would be just as wrong to render a verdict based on forgiveness. How do you feel about that?

PART E: GENERAL PRESENTATION TIPS FOR JURY SELECTION

§ 9.18 Various Tips for Jury Selection

[1] Be Well-Prepared

The plaintiff's attorney should be familiar with the entire contents of the legal file prior to selecting a jury. If not, jurors will sense it (e.g., when defense counsel asks the plaintiff's attorney the name of a particular treating physician, etc.) and minimize the significance (and, hence, the value) of the case. Additionally, in many jurisdictions the trial begins immediately after jury selection is concluded (as opposed to other jurisdictions which allow a week or so gap between jury selection and the commencement of trial).

[2] Maintain Credibility

The plaintiff's attorney should not state anything s/he is not sure will be proved at trial. It is important to be well-liked and trusted by the jurors.

[3] Be Respectful to Jurors

Jurors should not be spoken "down to". Additionally, best attempts should be made to properly pronounce jurors' (last) names; if mispronounced, an apology should be given (and it should not happen again).

[4] Listen Carefully to Jurors' Responses

The plaintiff's attorney should not be so engaged in his or her questions that s/he fails to listen to the jurors' responses. For example, a juror who speaks of a "minor ankle surgery" is not someone the plaintiff's attorney will want on the jury. Similarly, where a prospective juror states that s/he would find for the plaintiff "if you prove it" or "if it's not frivolous", follow-up questions should be asked in an effort to have the juror excused "for cause".

[5] Personalize Plaintiff

The plaintiff should always be referred to by his or her name, not "the plaintiff".

[6] Importance of Alternates

Alternates are more important than many attorneys believe. First, even if not needed, the alternates talk and share their thoughts with the other jurors (e.g., at lunch, during breaks), notwithstanding the judge's instructions not to discuss the case. Second, there is a chance that at least one alternate will be needed to replace a non-alternate.

[7] Responding to Jurors Requesting to be Excused

If a prospective juror offers an excuse as to why s/he may have difficulty sitting as a juror (e.g., vacation plans next week, have to pick up child from school, etc.), the plaintiff's attorney must quickly assess the situation. If the plaintiff's attorney has a strong desire to keep this juror, s/he may wish to tell the juror, "The judge has strict rules. We can't just let you out for that. Some days the judge lets us out early so you might not be affected," or "We (i.e., all the lawyers) will discuss it with the judge and get back to you." On the other hand, if the plaintiff's attorney dislikes the juror, s/he may attempt to gain the quick consent of the defense attorney(s) to excuse the juror.

[8] Be Aware of Apathetic Jurors

Typically, the plaintiff's attorney does not want jurors who appear annoyed to be there or who simply seem uninterested (e.g., reading a book during jury selection).

[9] Poisoning the Well

If one of the prospective jurors, or one of the opposing attorneys, makes an incendiary remark in front of the entire panel, an application can be made to the judge requesting a new panel. Thus, where the plaintiff's attorney is very unhappy with the panel (and/or running low on peremptories) and has a negative feeling about the rest of the panel (i.e., in the back of the room), s/he may wish to give his or her adversary free reign (i.e., not voicing any objections, etc.); then, an application can be made to the judge to excuse the entire panel (e.g., "Judge, s/he shouldn't have asked those questions and s/he knew it."). The plaintiff's attorney should be careful, however, not to allow the defense attorney to go too far, as the judge may decide to excuse only one juror while leaving the rest of the panel intact.

CHAPTER 10

TRIAL

PART A: OVERVIEW

§ 10.01 Overview – Trial

Knowing how to properly try a negligence case is essential. The value of most cases is maximized at, or near, trial. If the plaintiff's attorney does not know how to properly try a case, s/he will undoubtedly attempt to settle prematurely – for far less than the true value. Additionally, a strong evidentiary background allows the attorney to properly evaluate, negotiate, and prepare a case from intake through trial. Further, the more cases the attorney tries, the more likely s/he is to gain respect from the insurance carriers; this will translate into higher offers on future cases.

The venue of a case will generally determine whether the trial is to be bifurcated or unified. In a bifurcated trial (e.g., Second Department venues), the issue of liability is tried first; if the plaintiff prevails (i.e., any defendant is held at least 1% responsible), the issue of damages is tried (often, but not always, with the same jury). In a unified trial (e.g., First Department venues), both liability and damages are tried together with the same jury. *See CPLR §§ 603, 4011. Uniform Rule 202.42* "encourages" judges to order bifurcation.

PART B: PRELIMINARY ISSUES

§ 10.02 Arrival at Trial Judge's Part

The attorneys are assigned to a trial judge; in pure IAS (Individual Assignment System) jurisdictions, however, the judge who presided over discovery will also be the trial judge. Upon arrival at the trial judge's courtroom, the attorney for the party who has filed the note of issue (almost always the plaintiff's attorney) must provide the assigned judge's clerk with a copy of the marked pleadings (including the summons and complaint and answer[s], along with a copy of the bill[s] of particulars and notice[s] to admit, if any) clearly indicating which statements are admitted and which controverted by the responsive pleading. *CPLR §4012.* The plaintiff's attorney should also hand the clerk a business card, and ask him or her to have someone retrieve the subpoenaed records (from the subpoenaed records room).

§ 10.03 Settlement Conference

Prior to the commencement of the trial, the judge will usually hold a settlement conference in order to explore whether there is any hope to avoid the trial. A high percentage of cases sent to a trial judge settle prior to verdict (i.e., either at the settlement conference, during trial, or after the trial but prior to verdict). Some judges make a strong push for a settlement while other judges simply feel their role is to preside over the trial.

During the settlement conference, the judge will begin by asking the attorneys to give an overview of the case. The plaintiff's attorney typically proceeds first, providing an overview of liability and damages. The defense attorney(s) will then have an opportunity to refute the plaintiff's attorney's claims.

> **Practice Tip:** Some discretion must be used so as not to divulge nuances of trial strategy. Sometimes the attorney may wish to request to speak to the judge privately.

> **Practice Tip:** The more prepared the plaintiff's attorney is to proceed with the trial (i.e., witnesses available, knows facts thoroughly, etc.), the more s/he stands to gain settlement-wise at the conference.

If the parties are unable to settle the case, the judge will want to discuss the upcoming scheduling. The parties inform the judge as to the approximate number of witnesses and the expected length of the trial, while the judge alerts the parties as to any days off (e.g., Friday is conference day in that judge's part). Finally, the judge will inform the parties as to when the Charge Conference will take place. See §10.12 below.

§ 10.04 Motions *in Limine*

[1] Motions *in Limine* – In General

Immediately prior to the start of the trial, the judge will ask the parties whether there are any motions *in limine.* The plaintiff's attorney should be prepared to make and oppose such motions, well in advance of the trial. In preparing to oppose motions *in limine,* the plaintiff's attorney should begin by looking at the affirmative defenses raised in the defendant's answer. Further, the plaintiff's attorney must consider the entire case to determine what evidence the defense may attempt to bar the jury from hearing or seeing. The plaintiff's attorney must, similarly, be prepared to make his or her own motions *in limine.*

Examples of motions *in limine* include asking:
- that a party be precluded from utilizing photographs which were not exchanged, or which fail to fairly and accurately depict the scene or damage to the vehicles, or which are highly prejudicial;
- that the defendant be precluded from injecting an issue (e.g., alcohol or seatbelt defense) into the trial;

- that an expert be precluded as a result of an untimely expert witness disclosure;
- that the plaintiff be precluded from mentioning a statute alleged to have been violated (e.g., as the statute is inapplicable); and
- that the plaintiff be precluded from offering evidence relating to aggravation of a prior existing condition (e.g., on the grounds that such was never plead in the complaint or in a bill of particulars).

Practice Tip: It is important that adverse rulings are on the record so that an objection (as well as an exception, although unnecessary) can be taken to preserve the right to an appeal. *See CPLR §5501(3).*

[2] Motion *in Limine* to Preclude Statements in Medical Records Re: Liability

The ambulance call report, emergency room records, and other medical records often contain descriptions of the accident. These statements may well be inadmissible, as discussed below.

[a] Diagnosis or Treatment

An entry in a hospital record, or ambulance call report, comes within *CPLR §4518*'s business records rule (i.e., exception to hearsay) only if it is relevant to diagnosis or treatment of the patient's ailment. Otherwise, the entry cannot be said to have been "made in the regular course of the 'business' of the hospital and for the purpose of assisting it in carrying on that 'business'". *Williams v. Alexander*, 309 N.Y. 283, 129 N.E.2d 417 (1955). "It might, for instance, assist the doctors if they were to know that the injured man had been struck by an automobile. However, whether the patient was hit by car A or car B, by car A under its own power or propelled forward by car B, or whether the injuries were caused by the negligence of the defendant or another, cannot possibly bear on diagnosis or aid in determining treatment. That being so, entries of this sort, *purportedly to give particulars of the accident,* which serve no medical purpose, may not be regarded as having been made in the ordinary course of the hospital's business." *Id.* at 288 (citing *Scott v. James Gibbons Co.*, 192 Md. 319, 330, 64 A.2d 117 [1949]).

Similarly, in *Passino v. DeRosa,* 199 A.D.2d 1017, 606 N.Y.S.2d 107 (4th Dep't 1993), there was a discrepancy in the hospital records (fell on icy driveway) versus trial testimony (tripped on raised portion of the walkway). The court held that the information in the hospital records concerning the precise cause of the fall was not relevant to the plaintiff's diagnosis and treatment and should <u>not</u> have been admitted. Further, in *Echevarria v. City of New York*, 166 A.D.2d 409, 560 N.Y.S.2d 473 (2d Dep't 1990), the court held that a statement in the hospital records stating that the plaintiff fell at home (as opposed to plaintiff's testimony that the police officers struck him with their night sticks) was inadmissible hearsay, as the statement attributed to the plaintiff was not germane to the diagnosis and treatment.

[b] Admission by Plaintiff

In order for a statement attributable to the plaintiff to be admissible, there must be a showing that the plaintiff was the source of the information. *Sanchez v. Manhattan & Bronx Surface Transit Operating Auth.*, 170 A.D.2d 402, 566 N.Y.S.2d 287 (1st Dep't 1991). Where the report itself does not suggest that the information was provided by the plaintiff, the statement in the hospital record is inadmissible. *Id. See also Ginsberg v. North Shore Hosp.*, 213 A.D.2d 592, 624 N.Y.S.2d 257 (2d Dep't 1995); *Del Toro v. Carroll*, 33 A.D.2d 160, 306 N.Y.S.2d 95 (1st Dep't 1969). Where the origin of the statements is *unclear*, the proponent of the admission of the hospital records fails to establish that they contained any admission. *Musaid v. Mercy Hosp.*, 249 A.D.2d 958, 672 N.Y.S.2d 573 (4th Dep't 1998). Where the plaintiff makes the purported statement through an interpreter, the recorder can only testify as to what the interpreter said and therefore is inadmissible hearsay. *Quispe v. Lemle & Wolff, Inc.*, 266 A.D.2d 95 (1st Dep't 1995).

To establish the foundation for the admission of the statement, the proponent must produce the witness who recorded the statement. *Gunn v. City of New York*, 104 A.D.2d 848, 480 N.Y.S.2d 365 (2d Dep't 1984). Further, the recorder of the information must have an unequivocal recollection of the statement and its source. *Musaid v. Mercy Hosp.*, 249 A.D.2d 958, 672 N.Y.S.2d 573 (4th Dep't 1998). Statements in the hospital record attributed to plaintiff are inadmissible where the nurse who recorded them cannot say with *certainty* whether they came from the plaintiff. *Castro v. Alden Leeds, Inc.*, 144 A.D.2d 613, 535 N.Y.S.2d 73 (2d Dep't 1988). In *Gunn, supra*, the notation in the hospital admission form stated that the plaintiff slipped on ice while walking down the street, whereas the plaintiff's testimony was that she slipped while descending from a bus. The purported statement could not be received as an admission where the individual who prepared the report was *unable to say* that the information was based on statements made by plaintiff. Parenthetically, the entry also was not admissible as a business record because it was not germane to diagnosis and treatment.

> **Warning:** A hearsay entry in a hospital record may be admissible, even if not germane to diagnosis or treatment, if the entry is inconsistent with plaintiff's claim, provided that there is evidence to connect the party to the entry. *Berrios v. TEG Management*, 35 A.D.3d 775, 826 N.Y.S.2d 740 (2d Dep't 2006).

[3] Motion *in Limine* Re: Alcohol on Breath

Admissions in records (e.g., hospital records) regarding alcohol use on the day of the accident are subject to the same scrutiny as other admissions (as discussed above). Furthermore, it is error to allow the defendant to introduce and comment on an ambulance report containing notations regarding alcohol on the plaintiff's breath. *Rodriguez v. Triborough Bridge & Tunnel Auth.*, 276 A.D.2d 769, 716 N.Y.S.2d 24 (2d Dep't 2000). *See also Amaro v. City of New York*, 40 N.Y.2d 30, 386 N.Y.S.2d 19 (1976) (physician precluded from testifying that he detected odor of alcohol on plaintiff's breath).

[4] Motion *In Limine* Re: Plaintiff's Criminal Convictions

A witness may be "examined with respect to specific immoral, vicious or criminal acts which have a bearing on the witness' credibility." *Badr v. Hogan*, 75 N.Y.2d 629, 634, 555 N.Y.S.2d 249, 251 (1990). *See also M. v. NYCTA*, 4 Misc.3d 829, 781 N.Y.S.2d 865 (Sup. Ct., Richmond County, 2004) (relating to drugs). *See CPLR §4513.*

> **Practice Tip:** The plaintiff's attorney must be aware of the plaintiff's prior criminal convictions and be prepared to argue to keep them out of the trial. However, so as not to "tip off" the defense (i.e., they may be unaware), the plaintiff's attorney may prefer to wait to see whether there is any attempt by defense counsel to inject the issue into the trial.

Records of prior treatment for substance abuse are inadmissible. *Mental Hygiene Law §33.13(c)(1)* and *§22.05(b)*.

PART C: PHASES OF TRIAL

§ 10.05 Opening Statements

[1] Opening Statements – In General

Opening statements allow each side to speak directly to the jury, with the parties stating what they believe the evidence presented during the trial will show. The opening remarks are generally conceived as the most important part of the trial. The plaintiff's attorney must attempt to gain the jury's interest, making a "big bang" first impression. Studies have shown that a high percentage of jurors do not change their minds after opening remarks. The plaintiff's attorney proceeds first, as the plaintiff has the burden of proof.

> **Practice Tip:** It is essential that the jury is not told anything which is untrue, for credibility is crucial. For example, where the plaintiff had a pre-existing injury, the jury should be told during plaintiff's opening, enhancing plaintiff's credibility. Further, if something negative about the plaintiff is known, but it is not known whether the defendant's attorney is aware, the jury should be told that the defendant may talk about something unrelated to the case which will be addressed by plaintiff later. It is important to be able to state, during closing arguments, that everything promised in opening remarks was brought out.

Generally, an attorney should not object much (if at all) during opening remarks. Objections often give the jury the appearance that the attorney has something to hide. The most common objection during an opening is that the adversary is setting forth "argument" (i.e., that which is allowed only in closing) rather than simply stating what s/he reasonably expects the evidence to show. For example, if the defense attorney begins to say "In my opinion", "I believe", "You would assume", "I'm sure", or anything similar, such "argument" is not appropriate and should be stopped.

Practice Tip: In the event an objection is sustained, the attorney can simply resume by stating, "The evidence will show…".

During opening remarks, it is important to make eye contact with the jurors. The attorney should not read his or her opening, but rather should utilize an outline. Further, simple, easy-to-understand words should be used, as opposed to legal jargon. The attorney's goal should be to have the jury believe and trust him or her. The attorney should never attack his or her adversary, for the jury may like the adversary. The plaintiff's attorney should prepare the jury for the defendant's arguments by providing them with a logical response to the defendant's anticipated position. Negative admissible material should be disclosed and dealt with in the most favorable terms. See chapter 11, §11.12 for an opening remarks outline.

[2] Opening Statements – Damages

In the opening statements of a damages trial (or a unified trial), the jury should be given a fairly detailed outline of what to expect, including the ambulance arriving at the scene, EMS and emergency room treatment, hospital stays, diagnosis, treatment, surgery, prognosis, loss of enjoyment of life, economic losses, and the identity of the witnesses expected to be called. The jury should be told what they will have to determine (e.g, past pain and suffering, future pain and suffering, life expectancy, past economic losses, future economic losses, etc.). The plaintiff's attorney should be sure not to make any outlandish claims which cannot be proven.

Practice Tip: The plaintiff's attorney may want to prepare the jury for some large numbers (e.g., "You are going to be surprised at some of the numbers you're going to hear, but when you hear the basis for the numbers, you won't be surprised."). Actual numbers are only allowed in summation. *CPLR §4016(b)*.

[3] Opening Statements – Defense

The defendant's opening may consist of some or all of the following points and/or arguments: plaintiff's lack of credibility, defendant's lack of negligence, open and obvious condition (i.e., in premises liability case), comparative negligence, assumption of risk, pre-existing injuries, failure to meet "serious injury" threshold (i.e., in motor vehicle accident), good recovery, successful surgery (i.e., no further pain and suffering post-surgery), plaintiff's age (e.g., spine degenerates over time, or young people recover easily), and plaintiff's occupation (e.g., manual laborer and, therefore, more susceptible).

§ 10.06 Order of Proof

It is often difficult to have witnesses aligned in perfect order. Often, the plaintiff's attorney will have to call witnesses as they become available.

Practice Tip: Where possible, the plaintiff's attorney may wish to have all non-party fact witnesses (i.e., not experts) testify prior to the plaintiff. This is because the plaintiff is allowed in the courtroom for the entire trial, unlike non-party witnesses (who will be excluded, upon either attorney's request to the judge). Thus, the plaintiff will have the benefit of hearing all other lay witness' testimony prior to testifying, often yielding an advantage.

In a trial involving expert testimony (e.g., engineer, physician, economist, etc.), typically the plaintiff will testify before the experts, in order to establish a factual basis (i.e., foundation) for the experts to then testify.

Practice Tip: In the event there are major economic losses claimed, the economist is usually the preferred final plaintiff's witness, ending the plaintiff's case with a "bang".

Warning: The plaintiff's attorney should be aware that calling the plaintiff or an expert (e.g., physician) to the witness stand in the afternoon will often allow the adversary all night to prepare for cross-examination.

§ 10.07 Direct Examination

Below is a list of some things for the plaintiff's attorney to keep in mind during direct examination:

- The required elements must be met with respect to each cause of action.
- The witness should be the center of attention, and the attorney should not detract from him or her.
- The witness' credibility (determined by background, content, and demeanor) is very important, and should be developed.
- Testimony should generally be presented chronologically. Sometimes, however, the plaintiff's attorney may want to present the most dramatic or important testimony early in the direct examination (when the jury is most alert).
- The jury should have a complete description of the scene before hearing about the action.
- At the important part of the testimony, the plaintiff's attorney should slow-down the action – like a slow-motion film, frame by frame (i.e., assuming there is a capable witness on the stand).
- Witnesses should not be asked leading questions on direct examination, for it is improper and generally disfavored by the jury.

THE LAWYERS' GUIDE TO PERSONAL INJURY LAW

- Open-ended questions should generally be used on direct examination, for they allow a witness to tell the story in his or her own words. For example, "What did you see / hear / do next? What happened next? Then what happened?"

- When a witness gives a particularly good answer, the answer should be used as part of the next question. For example, "After the defendant said 'I'm sorry, it was my fault,' what happened next?"

- In the event an answer was not clear, the witness should be asked to explain. For example, "Dr. Jones, I didn't understand the last term. Exactly what is a herniated disc?", or "I'm sorry. I didn't follow you there. Where were you standing when you actually saw the collision?"

- Weaknesses should be volunteered on direct examination, for they come across much better on direct examination than they do on cross-examination.

§ 10.08 Cross-Examination

[1] Cross-Examination Pointers

Below is a list of pointers for the plaintiff's attorney to keep in mind during cross-examination:

- A determination should be made as to the importance, the credibility (i.e., leave well enough alone?), and the mileage of the witness in determining how to proceed with cross-examination. The stronger the plaintiff's case is, the less risk the plaintiff's attorney will have to take.

- Only a few basic points (e.g., three points) need to be established to support the plaintiff's case.

- The strongest points should be made at the beginning and the end of cross-examination.

- Direct-examination should not be repeated (for this is rarely successful).

- The subject matter should be varied, for indirection will make it difficult for the witness to realize the purpose of the line of questioning.

- The answers to the questions should generally be known before they are asked (e.g., already asked at EBT). Cross-examination should not be a fishing expedition.

- The plaintiff's attorney should keep control of the witness by asking precisely-phrased questions which do not allow the witness to explain. If the witness blurts something out anyway, the questioning attorney should move to strike as non-responsive and ask the judge to instruct the jury to disregard it.

- Open-ended questions should never be asked on cross-examination (e.g., why / how questions are usually disastrous).
- That *one* question too many (i.e., that last question to drive home a point) should not be asked because the response may not be the desired response. Rather, during summation, the last question and answer can be rhetorically posed.
- Short, clear questions should be asked.
- A confident, take-charge attitude should be projected.
- The attorney should be prepared to be a good actor (i.e., put on a poker face when an undesired answer is received).
- The witness should be discredited in regard to motive, interest, and/or bias.
- The testimony should be discredited in regard to memory, perception and communication, as well as prior inconsistent statements or conduct.

[2] Impeaching Witness

A witness may be impeached by a prior inconsistent statement or prior testimony. *See CPLR §§4514, 4517.* Often, the most points on cross-examination are scored by directly impeaching the witness. The general procedure for impeachment is as follows:

- Recommit the witness to the fact s/he asserted on direct examination (in a matter-of-fact way that does not arouse suspicion);
- Direct the witness to the date, time, place and circumstances of the prior inconsistent statement (e.g., EBT);
- Show the witness the prior inconsistent writing (this step is not necessary where impeaching EBT testimony); and
- Read the prior inconsistent statement to the witness and ask him or her to admit making it.

Practice Tip: If attempting to build up the credibility of the prior inconsistent statement, the attorney should establish that the statement was made at a time and under circumstances that ensure its reliability. If, however, the theory is that neither statement is true, the statement should not be built up.

The witness should be recommitted to a single fact, then impeached. This process should be repeated for each significant fact the witness can be impeached on.

Example:

Q: Mr. Witness, you saw . . ., is that right?

Q: There's no question in your mind you saw . . ., is there?

Q: Mr. Witness, you gave a deposition in this case last year, didn't you? (At that time, the judge can be asked to instruct the jury, i.e., as to the evidentiary value of the deposition.)

Q: And at that time, your lawyer, a court reporter, you, and I were all present, isn't that true?

Q: And you were asked questions about the accident, weren't you?

Q: Before you answered those questions, you were sworn by the court reporter, weren't you?

Q: You told the truth, didn't you?

Q: After you finished testifying, you had a chance to read your testimony to make sure it was accurate, didn't you?

Q: After reading it to make sure it was correct, you signed it, didn't you?

Q: You gave deposition testimony only x months after the date of the accident? So it was pretty fresh in your mind? (This step can be skipped if the questioner does not want to show that the earlier statement was more accurate.)

Q: Mr. Witness, during the deposition you were asked the following questions and gave the following answers, didn't you? (Read from transcript, after stating the page and line number.)

Q: You gave those answers, didn't you?

§ 10.09 Reading Deposition Testimony into Trial Record

CPLR §3117(a)(2) allows a party's deposition to be used "for any purpose" by an *adverse* party. Therefore, the deposition of a party (i.e., not a non-party witness) may be used as evidence-in-chief, as well as for impeachment by any adverse party.

Practice Tip: Pursuant to *GML §50-h*, a 50-h hearing transcript may be used as evidence-in-chief by *any* party (as opposed to the limitation under the *CPLR* which only allows an adverse party to use an EBT transcript as evidence-in-chief). However, *see Barnes v. City of New York*, 44 A.D.3d 39, 840 N.Y.S.2d 582 (1st Dep't 2007) (plaintiff's avoidance of appearing at trial held to frustrate defendant's fundamental right to cross-examination). See chapter 7, §7.04.

The plaintiff's attorney will almost always either call the defendant as a witness or read excerpts from the defendant's deposition transcript(s) in the plaintiff's case-in-chief. By reading selected questions and answers from the defendants' deposition transcript(s), those portions become evidence and aid the plaintiff's attorney in making out a *prima facie* case. Further, the plaintiff may want a certain charge to the jury (e.g., *res ipsa loquitur*; therefore, the plaintiff's attorney may read the portion of the deposition where the defendant stated that the instrumentality was under its exclusive control). Unless testimony is elicited during the trial or read into the record (i.e., from a deposition), it cannot be utilized in closing argument.

> **Practice Tip:** Immediately prior to reading from a defendant's deposition transcript, the plaintiff's attorney must provide a copy for the judge and state, "Your Honor, I intend to read from the deposition of . . . and I ask that you advise the jury accordingly." The judge will then read certain instructions to the jury regarding the use of EBT testimony at trial. Before the plaintiff's attorney reads certain excerpts (i.e., questions and answers), s/he must first state the page and line number s/he is reading from. Alternatively, someone can be brought in to role play (i.e., read the witness' answers) from the witness stand in order to make it more memorable for the jury.

Since, pursuant to the "usual stipulations", objections to deposition questions are preserved for trial (i.e., other than objections to the *form* of the question), the opposing attorney(s) may object to deposition questions after they are read to the jury. If an objection is sustained, the attorney must skip the answer and continue reading the next question s/he would like to read. Further, if any of the deposition testimony is read out of context (e.g., the next two lines would make the testimony clear), the adversary can object and ask the judge for the next two lines to be read; in the event the judge denies the request, the adversary can, on "cross", read the entire excerpt or simply the two additional lines.

§ 10.10 Motion to Dismiss for Failure to Establish *Prima Facie* Case

In the plaintiff's case-in-chief, the plaintiff must make out a *prima facie* case. This means that the plaintiff's attorney must know what *PJI* charges s/he will seek, and must establish some level of proof with respect to each element (unless admitted in the answer or pursuant to a notice to admit, or via a stipulation). For example, if ownership is not admitted, it must be established by reading from the defendant's deposition transcript or by introducing a certified copy of the deed into evidence, etc. Otherwise, a motion to dismiss for failure to make out a *prima facie* case may well be granted at the conclusion of the plaintiff's case (i.e., as soon as plaintiff rests). Often, the defense attorney will make a *pro forma* motion to dismiss at the conclusion of plaintiff's case-in-chief. *CPLR §4401.*

§ 10.11 Motion for Directed Verdict

At the conclusion of all the evidence (i.e., after the defense rests), once the jury is retired, the court will ask if there are any motions at this time. Motions must be made in order to preserve appellate rights. For example, the defense may move to dismiss the case as a matter of law, while the plaintiff's attorney may move for a directed verdict with respect to one or more causes of action or issues. *CPLR §4401.* The granting of a motion for a directed verdict in favor of the plaintiff on the issue of liability would then leave the jury with only the damages issues.

§ 10.12 Charge Conference

[1] Charge Conference – In General

A charge conference is usually held towards the end of the trial, in the judge's chambers. At the charge conference, the attorneys exchange their respective Requests to Charge with one another and the court. *See CPLR §4110-b*. The Request to Charge is typically a one-page memo listing the *Pattern Jury Instruction* sections (by section number and title), in numerical order, which the party is seeking to have the judge read to the jury (following summations). The plaintiff's attorney should also keep in mind that a request to modify the wording of the *PJI* charge (i.e., tailored to the specific case) can be made, as well as requests for charges emanating from the Insurance Law or other specific statutes (e.g., Vehicle & Traffic Law).

It is imperative that the plaintiff's attorney attempt to anticipate the defense attorneys' arguments, as well as which charges defense counsel will seek. Otherwise, the plaintiff's attorney will be caught "off guard" at this crucial phase of the trial. Ultimately, objections to charges (either allowed or disallowed) should be made on the record (to preserve them for appeal) and the objecting attorney should take exception. Thus, at the end of the charge conference, the court reporter generally is called into chambers for this reason.

[2] Missing Witness Charge

A missing witness charge is a powerful charge that allows the jury to infer, from a party's failure to call a material witness at trial, that the witness' testimony would not have supported that party's position and would not have contradicted the evidence of the opposing party. To qualify for the charge, the party seeking the charge must:

- request the charge prior to the close of all the evidence;
- establish that the missing witness was under the opposing party's control; and
- establish that the missing witness was expected to provide non-cumulative testimony on a specific, material issue in dispute.

Buttice v. Dyer, 1 A.D.3d 552, 767 N.Y.S.2d 653 (2d Dep't 2003).

A missing witness charge should not given against the plaintiff for failing to call the treating physician where his or her testimony would be cumulative to the testimony given by other expert(s). *Dowling v. 257 Assocs.*, 235 A.D.2d 293, 652 N.Y.S.2d 736 (1st Dep't 1997). Where the treating physician is no longer under the plaintiff's control, the missing witness charge is inappropriate. *Pagan v. Ramirez*, 80 A.D.2d 848, 444 N.Y.S.2d 472 (2d Dep't 1981). Where the defendant fails to call the examining physician (i.e., IME doctor) as a witness at trial, the missing witness charge is appropriate. *Leahy v. Allen*, 221 A.D.2d 88, 644 N.Y.S.2d 388 (3d Dep't 1996); *Grey v. United Leasing Inc.*, 91 A.D.2d 932, 457 N.Y.S.2d 823 (1st Dep't 1983).

§ 10.13 Verdict Sheet

At the end of the charge conference, the judge will discuss the verdict sheet with the attorneys. Again, there may be objections and exceptions placed on the record, in order to preserve the issue(s) for appeal. *See Suria v. Shiffman*, 67 N.Y.2d 87, 499 N.Y.S.3d 913 (1986) (failure to object to problem with verdict sheet precluded successful appeal). The verdict sheet must be printed as soon as possible, for it is required prior to summation (so the attorneys can address the questions in the summation). Each verdict sheet should be marked as an exhibit, as there may be several before the final modification. The verdict sheet is extremely important, for it comprises each question to be asked of the jury.

A typical verdict sheet (on the issue of liability) may have the following questions:

- Was the defendant negligent?
- Was the defendant's negligence a substantial factor in causing the accident?
- Was the plaintiff negligent?
- Was the plaintiff's negligence a substantial factor in causing the accident?
- Plaintiff was _____% negligent and the defendant was _____% negligent. (Percentages must total 100%)
- Itemization of the amount of money, if any, to compensate the plaintiff for each component of damages (i.e., past pain and suffering, future pain and suffering, past loss of earnings, future loss of earnings, past medical expenses, future medical expenses, derivative losses, etc.).

§ 10.14 Summation

[1] Summation – In General

Summation is generally perceived as the second most important part of the trial, next to opening statements. The attorneys, for the first time, are allowed to argue their positions to the jury. The attorneys can essentially say whatever they want (unlike opening) as long as it is somewhat related to the evidence presented. The defendant's summation is first, and the plaintiff's is last (for the plaintiff has the burden of proof). See chapter 11, §11.14 for a summation outline.

Practice Tip: It is essential that the basic summation arguments are organized and planned *before* trial. The plan must be implemented in jury selection, and continued throughout opening, direct examination, presentation of experts, cross-examination, and summation. As the trial progresses, and evidence is presented, the plaintiff's attorney should continuously update his or her "summation notes" (i.e., at the end of each day).

Practice Tip: The plaintiff's attorney should be forceful in summation, utilizing terms such as "the evidence clearly shows", as opposed to "I think" or "I believe".

[2] Summation – Pointers

Listed below are some pointers that can be utilized in summation:

- Be well-prepared, and minimize the use of written notes.
- Use a theme, argue the theory of the case, and argue the facts of the case.
- Arguments should be prioritized, pushing the strongest points.
- Use the exhibits (admitted in evidence), including photographs, by showing (or reading) them to the jury.
- Weave the judge's (soon-to-be-read) instructions into the argument (e.g. "The court will instruct you…").
- Make use of rhetorical questions (e.g., "You may be saying to yourself…").
- Make use of analogies and stories.
- Minimize the amount of time spent on your opponent's summation because it will equivocate yours. Only refute his or her most outrageous, easily refutable arguments. Do not answer the defendant's strong points which are difficult to refute; jurors forget many things, so they certainly should not be reminded. Do not be abusive or overly critical of your opponent.
- Try to be concise, enhancing the chance it will be understood.
- Refrain from the use of humor, for it may undermine or trivialize the case.
- Thank the jury for its service.

[3] Summation – Concluding Summation

[a] Asking for Specific Dollar Amounts

Pursuant to *CPLR §4016(b)*, a party is allowed to make reference, during summation (i.e., where damages are at issue), to a specific dollar amount the attorney believes to be appropriate compensation for the elements of damages sought to be recovered in the action. The jury should be asked for specific amounts on each item (preferably using blackboard):

- past pain and suffering   +
- future pain and suffering +
- past loss of earnings   +
- future loss of earnings   =
- TOTAL   ____

[b] Whole Man Theory

An example of an approach one can take during summation is the "Whole Man Theory", which points out that an injury to part of one's body affects much more than that isolated area. "Anything less than justice is injustice. The plaintiff is entitled to a full recovery which is $150,000. If you give the plaintiff $140,000, s/he is not getting $140,000 of justice, s/he is getting $10,000 of injustice. When you talk of justice, you cannot talk of partial justice and when you talk of pain, you cannot talk of partial pain. An injury to part of a man (or woman) is an injury to all of him (or her) – and his (or her) family. A seemingly small thing can affect you greatly."

[c] Finish on Emotional Moment

Where possible, the plaintiff's attorney should attempt to finish on an emotional moment. For example, " It is not enough that Mr. Smith was burned beyond recognition. Now they're trying to take his name too – just to save some money."

[d] Review Verdict Sheet with Jury

The verdict sheet should be read and explained to the jury, and they should be told how they are expected to answer each of the questions.

§ 10.15 Charging Jury

Charging the jury typically takes approximately 30 minutes. Once the judge concludes the charges, the attorneys will be asked if there are any additions or any further exceptions regarding the jury charges. If so, a sidebar takes place. The attorneys will be able to place their exceptions on the record either at the sidebar or in chambers (while the jury is still in the jury box). Once deliberations begin, it is too late for further exceptions regarding the jury charges. An opportunity to make objection(s) outside of the presence of the jury must be provided. *CPLR §4110-b. See also CPLR §5501(a)(3).*

§ 10.16 Post-Verdict Motions

The plaintiff's attorney must be prepared for a defendant's verdict. In the event of such, once the jury leaves, the plaintiff's attorney should ask the judge to set aside the verdict as "contrary to the weight of the evidence" and order a new trial, or to grant judgment to the plaintiff as a matter of law. *CPLR §4404(a).* Assuming the motion is denied, the plaintiff's attorney should then ask the judge for permission to renew the motion on paper. Pursuant to *CPLR §§4404, 4405*, the losing party has fifteen days to make a written motion seeking to have the court set aside the verdict (and direct a verdict or grant a new trial).

> **Practice Tip:** The plaintiff's attorney should also immediately send the plaintiff a letter advising of the right to appeal, indicating the time constraints and the significant cost of same.

PART D: EVIDENCE

§ 10.17 Objections

The following is a list of objections that can be made during an adversary's questioning of a witness:

- relevance
- hearsay
- leading (i.e., on direct)

- prejudice outweighs probative value
- beyond the scope
- lack of foundation
- materiality
- privileged
- Best Evidence Rule
- Parol Evidence Rule (e.g., oral testimony regarding a writing e.g., a contract)
- lack of authentication
- calls for a narrative response
- calls for a conclusion (i.e., of a non-expert)
- calls for an opinion (i.e., of a non-expert)
- asked and answered
- assuming facts not in evidence
- misstates the evidence or misquotes the witness
- confusing / misleading / speculative
- compound question
- argumentative
- cumulative.

§ 10.18 Hearsay Exceptions
[1] Hearsay Exceptions – In General
It is important to be aware of the exceptions to the hearsay rule, as listed below:

- admissions (i.e., *anything* said, or silence) by a party opponent
- former testimony
- statements against interest
- present sense impression
- excited utterance
- state of mind
- statements for the purpose of medical treatment / diagnosis
- past recollection recorded (and insufficient recollection to testify fully and accurately)
- business records
- public records and reports
- learned treatises.

Practice Tip: Where the words are not being offered for the truth of the matter asserted, they are not hearsay (and, hence, not inadmissible on hearsay grounds).

[2] Admitting Conversation into Evidence

To properly admit a conversation into evidence, the following elements must be established:

- when the conversation occurred;
- where the conversation occurred;
- who was present; and
- who said what to whom.

With respect to telephone conversations, further elements are necessary.

[3] Refreshing Present Recollection

To refresh a witness' present recollection, the following elements must be established:

- witness knows the facts, but has a memory lapse on the stand;
- witness knows his or her report or other writing, etc. will refresh his or her memory;
- witness is given (and reads, etc.) the pertinent part of his or her report or other writing;
- witness states his or her memory has been refreshed; and
- witness now testifies as to what s/he knows without the further aid of the report or other writing.

§ 10.19 Entering Exhibits into Evidence

[1] Stipulation Between Parties

The easiest way to enter exhibits into evidence is by consent of the adversary (before trial if possible). This allows the parties to admit certain evidence as joint exhibits, and avoids the need to provide a foundation.

[2] General Procedure to Admit Evidence

In the event the adversary will not stipulate, a specific procedure will have to be followed. The procedure will differ depending on the type of evidence being offered. The following steps should be employed:

- Step 1: Mark Exhibit: "Reporter, please mark this (e.g., Plaintiff's Exhibit 1 for Identification)." Then, the exhibit should be handed to the court reporter (or the court officer who then hands the exhibit to the court reporter). The court reporter will then place an exhibit sticker on it and return it to the questioning attorney. This step is not necessary if pre-marking is allowed (and done).
- Step 2: Show Exhibit to Opposing Counsel (and allow counsel to look at / read it).
- Step 3: Show Exhibit to Witness: Hand the witness the exhibit, then walk back to the podium to ask the necessary foundation questions.

- Step 4: Lay Foundation for Exhibit: This step varies depending on the type of exhibit (see subsection [3] below).

- Step 5: Offer into Evidence: "Your Honor, I'd like to offer this in evidence." When an offer is made, the judge will ask if there are any objections. The opposing attorney can then take the exhibit and question the witness regarding foundation questions (and then object to same being admitted in evidence). After the judge admits the evidence, it can be retrieved from the witness.

- Step 6: Publish to Jury: "Your Honor, may I show (or read) Plaintiff's Exhibit 1 in Evidence to the jury at this time?" With the judge's permission, photographs or documents may then be shown and/or read to the jury. The exhibit should be handed (by the attorney or court officer) to the first juror. Once all the jurors have seen it, the attorney should retrieve it. The reading of an exhibit (to the jury) can be done by either counsel or the witness. Counsel may state, "Ladies and Gentlemen, Plaintiff's Exhibit 1 in Evidence reads as follows…", or "Mr. Witness, please read Plaintiff's Exhibit 1 in Evidence to the jury."

Warning: Opposing counsel may ask the judge for an evidentiary hearing (i.e., a preliminary offer of proof) outside the presence of the jury. In such a case, the foundation must be laid outside the presence of the jury so as to satisfy the judge. Thereafter, the attorney must proceed with the normal procedure of admitting the evidence in front of the jury (when they return). The exhibit should not be offered into evidence until the jury is present.

---

[3] Foundation Questions
[a] Photographs
- How long have you lived at …?
- Are you familiar with how the exterior stairs at … looked on the date of the accident?
- Steps 1-3 above (in §10.19[2]).
- I show you what has been marked as Plaintiff's Exhibit 1 for Identification and ask you to examine it. <u>Do you recognize what is depicted in the photo?</u>
- <u>What does the photo show?</u>
- Does Plaintiff's Exhibit 1 for Identification <u>fairly and accurately portray / depict the scene as it appeared on the date of accident?</u>
- Steps 5-6 above (in §10.19[2]).

[b] Tangible Objects
The following elements are required for tangible objects (discernible ones, i.e., no chain of custody problems):

- exhibit is relevant;
- exhibit can be identified visually (or through other senses);
- witness recognizes the exhibit;
- witness knows what the exhibit looked like on the relevant date; and
- exhibit is in the same, or substantially the same, condition as when the witness saw it on the relevant date.

The essential foundation questions are as follows:

- Please describe the (ladder).
- Steps 1-3 above (in §10.19[2]).
- I show you Plaintiff's Exhibit 1 for Identification and ask you to examine it. When was the first time you saw this exhibit?
- How are you able to recognize this as being the same (ladder)?
- Is Plaintiff's Exhibit 1 for Identification in the same or substantially the same condition as when you first saw it on the date of the accident?
- Is there anything different about this exhibit today compared to when you first saw it?
- Steps 5-6 above (in §10.19[2]).

[c] Stipulations

Stipulations are usually written. They should be marked as exhibits, but are usually not admitted in evidence. One of the attorneys should state, "Your Honor, may we read a stipulation which has been marked Plaintiff's Exhibit 1 for Identification to the jury at this time?" "Ladies and Gentlemen of the jury, this stipulation, or agreement, between the parties states as follows: . . . At the bottom are the signatures of both attorneys."

[d] Certified Hospital Records or Weather Records

Certified copies of certain records are self-authenticating. Therefore, no witness is necessary to qualify the exhibit for admission in evidence. Such records need only be offered (in evidence) and published (i.e., shown to jury). For example, "Your Honor, we offer for admission in evidence, Plaintiff's Exhibit 1 for Identification. It is a certified copy of the Jacobi Hospital records." Permission may then be requested of the judge to allow publication to the jury. Certified hospital records are admissible under *CPLR §4518(b)*. See also §10.20[2] below. Further, certified weather records are admissible pursuant to *CPLR §4528.*

[e] Business Records

Business records can be admitted into evidence without the need to call a foundation witness if the requirements of *CPLR §3120* and *CPLR §3122* are met. See §10.20[5] below for further details. Business records are also admissible pursuant to *CPLR §4518* (which requires a foundation witness). The following elements are necessary:

- record is relevant;

- record is a "memo, report, record or data compilation in any form";
- witness is the custodian or other qualified witness;
- record was made from information transmitted by a person with knowledge of the facts; and
- Record was kept in the ordinary course of regularly conducted business activity.

The essential foundation questions are as follows:

- Mr. Witness, please state your occupation (e.g., "records keeper").
- What does your job involve (e.g., "maintaining company records")?
- Steps 1-3 above (in §10.19[2]).
- Mr. Witness, I am showing you what has been marked as Plaintiff's Exhibit 1 for Identification. Do you recognize it?
- Was that record made by a person with knowledge of, or made from information transmitted by a person with knowledge of, the acts and events appearing on it?
- Was that record made at, or near, the time of the acts and events appearing on it?
- Is it the regular practice of ABC Corp. to make such a record?
- Was that record kept in the ordinary course of regularly conducted business activity?
- Steps 5-6 above (in §10.19[2]).

Practice Tip: If the record is an important part of the case, the credibility of the witness and the record should be enhanced by developing both fully (such as the witness' background and the entire procedure behind the production of the record).

Often what is contained in the business record is also hearsay. For example, a witness' statement on a police report poses a double hearsay problem. Therefore, there is the need to find an appropriate exception to the hearsay rule (i.e., in addition to the business records exception). Below is a list of common exceptions to the hearsay rule which are found within business records:

- admissions by a party (including silence)
- statements against interest
- present sense impression
- excited utterance
- state of mind (expansion of present sense impression)
- statements for the purposes of medical diagnosis / treatment.

See §10.18 above.

[f] Tangible Objects (with chain of custody problems)

Tangible objects with chain of custody problems refer to objects which cannot be uniquely identified by, or through, the senses (e.g., paint chips in a lead paint poisoning case). For these types of objects, chain of custody must be established in one of the following ways:

- by showing that the exhibit has been in one or more person's continuous, exclusive, and secure possession at all times; or
- by showing that the exhibit was in a uniquely marked, sealed, tamper-proof container at all times.

[g] Diagrams and Models

In laying the foundation for these types of exhibits, the following elements are required:

- diagram / model is relevant;
- witness is familiar with the scene represented by same;
- witness is familiar with the scene on the relevant date (and time);
- diagram / model is useful in helping the witness explain his or her testimony (or it aids the jury in understanding his or her testimony); and
- diagram / model is reasonably accurate or to scale.

[h] Drawings by Witness

The elements necessary in laying the foundation for drawings by a witness are the same as for diagrams and models (above).

Practice Tip: In making such drawings, the use of artist's paper (rather than a blackboard) is preferred in order to preserve the exhibit for appeal.

Practice Tip: It is generally better practice to use a diagram and have the witness prepared to qualify it, rather than having the witness draw something.

[i] Summary Charts

Summary charts may be prepared by a witness who, for example, sits in court while the evidence is being presented. Each fact appearing on the chart must then be related to the exhibit or the witness that established the particular fact. This is usually done on the chart itself. At the appropriate time, the witness can be called to demonstrate the evidentiary sources of the facts, as well as any resulting mathematical computations s/he performed. When so qualified, the chart is admissible if it will aid the jury in understanding the evidence.

[j] Demonstrations by Witness

Demonstrations by witnesses include the display of body parts (e.g., scar, deformity) or physical acts (e.g., lack of range of motion). In doing so, the attorney should (after obtaining the judge's permission) have the witness step down, stand before the jury box, and display or demonstrate. The two elements necessary to lay the foundation for such a demonstration are as follows:

- demonstration is relevant; and
- probative value outweighs the prejudicial effect.

When displaying or demonstrating to the jury, the attorney should state, "Your Honor, may the record reflect that Mr. Plaintiff has pointed to a white scar approximately two inches long running horizontally over his left eye".

Practice Tip: Injuries can often be better displayed by photographs than in person, as they often heal over time. Additionally, photographs allow for the injuries to be enlarged, as well as the best possible lighting.

[k] Signed Documents

In regard to a document signed by the party against whom it is being used, the attorney can do any of the following:

- call the witness who saw the party sign the document;
- call the witness who is familiar with the party's signature and can identify it;
- call the signing party as an adverse witness to admit the signature as his or her own; or
- call a handwriting expert.

The following elements are necessary in laying the foundation:

- the document is relevant;
- the document has a signature (or is handwritten); and
- the document is in the same condition now as it was when executed.

With respect to a signed document, there may also be a need to overcome a hearsay problem (e.g., admission, business record, etc.).

[l] Letters

The elements necessary to lay the proper foundation for a letter sent to the plaintiff by another party are as follows:

- the letter is relevant;
- the witness received the letter;
- the witness recognizes the signature as the other party's; and
- the letter is in same condition as when first received.

The second and third elements (as listed above) can be established by separate witnesses.

The elements necessary to lay the proper foundation for a letter sent by the plaintiff to another party are as follows:

- the letter is relevant;
- the witness dictated the letter, addressed to a party;
- the witness saw the typed original and a copy of the letter;

- the witness signed the original letter;
- the original letter was placed in a properly addressed and postmarked envelope, bearing a return address;
- the envelope was deposited in a U.S. mail depository.
- the photocopy of the original is a true and accurate copy of the original; and
- the original letter and envelope were never returned to the sender.

[m] Copies (of originals)

The elements necessary to lay the proper foundation with respect to copies (of originals) are as follows:

- the copy is relevant;
- the original once existed (executed);
- the copy is a true and accurate copy; and
- the original was unintentionally lost (and a thorough search for the original in every possible location failed to produce it).

[n] Pleadings and Discovery

Papers filed with the court have already been authenticated as coming from a particular party. Verified pleadings ("judicial admissions") and non-verified pleadings ("evidentiary admissions") are both admissible.

[o] Bill or Invoice for Services or Repairs

Pursuant to *CPLR §4533-a*, an itemized bill or invoice receipted or marked paid for services or repairs of $2,000 or less is admissible.

[4] Pointers Regarding Use of Exhibits at Trial

- Exhibits are best utilized at the end of a witness' testimony, so as not to distract the jury from his or her testimony.
- Where a witness has to mark, or read parts of, an exhibit, the questioning attorney should remain by the witness stand and make sure the record reflects what the witness is doing to an exhibit (e.g., "Your Honor, may the record reflect…".)
- After an exhibit is admitted (e.g., blown up photograph), the questioning attorney may request the judge's permission for the witness to leave the stand and continue his or her testimony by the exhibit. In such an instance, the witness should be given a pointer. The questioning attorney should refer to the exhibit by name (e.g., Plaintiff's Exhibit 1 in Evidence), and should let the record reflect what the witness points to.
- At the conclusion of the plaintiff's case-in-chief, before resting, the plaintiff's attorney may wish to re-offer all exhibits in evidence or confirm (with the judge) that s/he correctly recorded the admission of exhibits (i.e., the judge will then run down his or her list of exhibits and report what his or her ruling was on each one).

PART E: DAMAGES EVIDENCE

§ 10.20 Entering Medical Records and Films in Evidence

Often, the most difficult trial task for the plaintiff's attorney is having medical records and diagnostic films admitted in evidence. Without following the appropriate procedures, the plaintiff's attorney may be precluded from offering medical evidence (i.e., hospital / medical records, x-rays, MRIs, etc.), leading to the dismissal of the plaintiff's case. There are several ways to have medical records and diagnostic films admitted in evidence, as discussed below.

[1] Stipulation

The simplest way to have medical records and diagnostic films admitted in evidence is to obtain a stipulation (from the adversary) in advance of the trial. This avoids the need for subpoenas, additional witnesses, and affidavits. Such stipulations, though, are not commonplace. Often, defense attorneys will not stipulate without other "strings attached", if at all.

Warning: The plaintiff's attorney should avoid stipulating to allow medical records in evidence prior to the plaintiff's testimony. Doing so enables defense counsel to read (all of the unhelpful entries, e.g., "feeling much better", etc.) from the medical records while cross-examining the plaintiff.

---

[2] Certified Hospital Records

Pursuant to *CPLR §4518-c* and *CPLR §2306*, certified hospital records are automatically admitted in evidence – without the need for a witness. Thus, the plaintiff's attorney need only subpoena the certified hospital records (in a timely fashion), make sure the subpoenaed records arrive at the court (which means periodically checking the court's subpoenaed records room and following up with the hospital), and ultimately offer the records in evidence at trial. Thus, even diagnostic films (e.g., x-rays) which are part of the certified hospital records can be admitted automatically (i.e., without the need for a witness or affidavit); x-rays are "documents" and therefore admissible as part of the hospital record. *See Hoffman v. City of New York*, 141 Misc.2d 893, 535 N.Y.S.2d 342 (Sup. Ct. Kings Cty. 1988); *Lanpont v. Savvas Cab Corp., Inc.*, 244 A.D.2d 208, 664 N.Y.S.2d 285 (1st Dep't 1997). See also §10.19[3][d] above.

[3] Radiology Affirmation

By serving a Notice of Intention along with a radiology affirmation, x-rays, MRIs, and EMGs can be admitted pursuant to *CPLR §4532-a*, without the need for a witness. In essence, the notice states that the films are available (i.e., at the attorney's office or in the court) for viewing by the defendant in advance of the trial. Hence, in the event there is any objection to the films being admitted in evidence, the defendant will have time to raise it prior to trial. The films must be imprinted with the requisite information (patient's name, medical record number, and the date) which must also be included on the affirmation. Further, the affirmation must be signed by the radiologist under whose supervision the films were taken (or the physician-director of the facility). The notice and affidavit must be served (i.e., upon the adversary) at least ten days prior to trial. Once the films are admitted in evidence, the testifying physician can then read, and explain, them to the jury. *Hoffman v. City of New York*, 141 Misc.2d 893, 535 N.Y.S.2d 342 (Sup. Ct. Kings Cty. 1988). Where the films are not yet admitted in evidence, the judge still may allow the testimony, subject to connection (i.e., later during the trial).

> **Practice Tip:** In order to properly accomplish the admission of films under *CPLR §4532-a*, the plaintiff's attorney should subpoena the films as well as the radiologist; a cover letter should be attached to the subpoena stating that the radiologist can avoid testifying by simply signing (and promptly returning) the enclosed affirmation and ensuring that the films are promptly sent to the court's subpoenaed records room (or the plaintiff's attorney's office).

[4] Serving Copy of Films on Defendant

Pursuant to *CPLR §4532-a(1)* and *(2)(a)*, films may be placed into evidence without the need for foundation simply by copying and delivering a copy of the films to the defendant's attorney's office (with a cover letter identifying each film). This obviates the need for a *CPLR §4532-a* radiology affirmation, but is much more costly.

[5] Business Records

[a] Admitting Business Records Via Records Keeper

Medical records can also be admitted in evidence under the business records exception to the hearsay rule (pursuant to *CPLR §4518-a*). This can be achieved by having a records keeper from the doctor's office (e.g., nurse) or the MRI facility (i.e., regarding the actual films), properly establish the records as a business record (i.e., made contemporaneous with the examination and maintained in the ordinary course of business). The records keeper should be subpoenaed to ensure his or her presence. While the testimony of a records keeper is not as dynamic as that of a physician, it cuts off any cross-examination.

> **Practice Tip:** Some judges will allow foundation witness testimony in the form of an affidavit, via telephone, or via a non-party witness deposition. Overall, judges will usually encourage stipulating to the admission of business records.

[b] Admitting Business Records Without Records Keeper

Medical records can be admitted into evidence without producing a foundation witness in court via the use of *CPLR §3122-a* and *CPLR §3120(3)*. Pursuant to *CPLR §3120(3)*, a subpoena *duces tecum* (along with an authorization signed by the patient) can be served on a non-party (such as a medical provider) for records. A copy must be served on the adversary and, within five days of compliance therewith (in whole or in part), the party who served the subpoena must give each adversary notice that the items produced are available for inspection. Then, pursuant to *CPLR §3122-a*, the aforementioned business records, are admissible at trial without the need to call a foundation witness, so long as the records are accompanied by a sworn certification signed by a custodian of the records stating that:

- the person signing the affidavit is a custodian of the records or has the authority to make the certification;
- the records or copies are an accurate version of the documents in their possession;
- the records or copies produced represent all of the documents described in the subpoena *duces tecum*; and
- the records or copies were made in the ordinary course of business.

[6] MRI / X-Ray Reports and Other Narrative Reports

There is an important distinction between a physician's office records made contemporaneously with the examination (which, as discussed, are clearly admissible) and a physician's opinion contained in a report (which is more problematic). *See Wilson v. Bodian*, 130 A.D.2d 221, 519 N.Y.S.2d 126 (2d Dep't 1987) (narrative report prepared for purpose of litigation inadmissible). A report (e.g., MRI report, x-ray report, narrative report) is not a "medical record" and will not be allowed in evidence as a business record. *See Wagman v. Bradshaw*, 292 A.D.2d 84, 739 N.Y.S.2d 421 (2d Dep't 2002) (admission into evidence of MRI report prepared by non-testifying healthcare provider would violate the hearsay rule). This applies to all diagnostic test reports contained in the treating physician's records. Notwithstanding *Wagman*, a physician may still testify based upon medical records (i.e., as opposed to reports) not in evidence under the professional reliability rule. *See People v. Sugden*, 35 N.Y.2d 453 (1974) (expert may rely on out-of-court material so long as "it is the kind accepted in the profession as reliable in forming a professional opinion."); *see also Cohen v. Haddad*, 664 N.Y.S.2d 621 (2d Dep't 1997) (records of other physicians contained in each doctor's records generally admissible). Further, a *treating* physician can testify regarding diagnostic tests not in evidence, so long as based on *personal* knowledge (i.e., looked at the films and relied on them in treatment and diagnosis of plaintiff). *See Lee v. Huang*, 291 A.D.2d 549, 738 N.Y.S.2d 371 (2d Dep't 2002).

Practice Tip: A non-treating physician-expert witness cannot testify regarding diagnostic tests not in evidence. Thus, the plaintiff's attorney must first have the films admitted in evidence (e.g., through *CPLR §4532-a* affirmation); then, the expert can interpret them in court.

Practice Tip: Pursuant to the Best Evidence Rule, if circumstances excuse the non-production of an x-ray film, the proponent of that evidence may establish its contents via secondary evidence (e.g., a radiology report). *See Schozer v. William Penn Life Ins.*, 84 N.Y.2d 639, 620 N.Y.S.2d 797 (1994).

[7] Treating Physician's Testimony

The plaintiff's treating physician may be asked to testify (for a fee) on behalf of the plaintiff. Calling a treating physician (e.g., surgeon) to give testimony has its benefits. There are few evidentiary hurdles, as the treating physician is testifying based upon personal knowledge (as opposed to a review of the records). Further, the treating physician, not being a "hired gun", often makes a very credible medical witness.

> **Warning:** Calling the treating physician (e.g., the surgeon) to testify, as opposed to a medical expert who examines the plaintiff and the records, can have a downside in that the treating physician will generally be inclined to testify that s/he did such a wonderful job that the plaintiff's injuries are fully healed.

Sometimes, the treating physician refuses to voluntarily come to court. In such an instance, the plaintiff's attorney may wish to subpoena the physician to testify. A subpoenaed physician, not being compensated to testify, is unlikely to offer much assistance to the plaintiff in terms of opinions (i.e., causation and prognosis). Thus, the plaintiff's attorney may simply want to use the subpoenaed physician as a "fact witness" to lay the foundation for the plaintiff's expert to testify. Alternatively, once the treating physician agrees to appear pursuant to the subpoena, the plaintiff's attorney can negotiate a fee with him or her, ensuring cooperation and helpfulness.

When faced with a treating physician who refuses to testify notwithstanding a subpoena, the physician will generally, at a minimum, agree to send a records keeper (to lay the foundation to allow the medical records in evidence) instead. The records keeper can then also testify that the treating physician was subpoenaed but could not attend (e.g., is in surgery), which can help avoid a "missing witness" charge (see §10.12[2] above). This is usually a good compromise, avoiding a "hostile" medical witness. See §10.21[3] below, regarding questioning of a medical witness.

§ 10.21 Expert Witnesses

[1] Experts – In General

Prior to trial, pursuant to *CPLR §3101(d)*, certain information regarding all experts expected to be called at trial must be disclosed. This information includes:

- the identity of the expert;
- the subject matter on which the expert is expected to testify;
- the substance of the facts and opinions to which the expert is expected to testify;
- the qualifications of the expert; and
- a summary of the grounds for the expert's opinion.

When expert testimony attempts to go beyond the scope of the *§3101(d)* disclosure, the expert may be precluded from giving that additional testimony.

[2] Experts – Timely Disclosure

The *CPLR* provides no specific time-frame within which the expert disclosure must be made. *See Vigilant Ins. Co. v. Barnes*, 199 A.D.2d 257 (2d Dep't 1993) (preclusion of experts not disclosed until three weeks before trial held not to be an abuse of discretion). It does state, however, that "where a party for good cause shown retains an expert in an insufficient period of time before the commencement of trial to give appropriate notice thereof, the party shall not thereupon be precluded from introducing the expert's testimony at trial solely on the grounds of noncompliance with this paragraph." *CPLR §3101(d)(1)(i)*. *See McDermott v. Alvey*, 198 A.D.2d 95, 603 N.Y.S.2d 162 (1st Dep't 1993) (plaintiff's economist allowed to testify despite eve of trial since there was "no proof of intentional or willful failure to disclose . . . and an absence of prejudice" to defendants); *see also Karoon v. New York City Transit Auth.*, 286 A.D.2d 648, 730 N.Y.S.2d 331 (1st Dep't 2001) (expert permitted to testify at trial, notwithstanding late notice, where opposing party not prejudiced). However, absent a local court rule or a time-frame set forth in a preliminary (or compliance) conference order, to be safe a party should serve its expert disclosures at least 30 days before trial. A party must show "good cause" for retaining an expert too close to the start of trial. *CPLR §3101(d)(1)(i); see also Quinn v. Aircraft* Constr. Inc., 203 A.D.2d 444, 610 N.Y.S.2d 598 (2d Dep't 1994) (expert's testimony precluded because plaintiff failed to show "good cause" for expert's retention only a few days before trial).

> **Practice Tip:** The argument can be made that 20 days before trial is a reasonable deadline, as similar sections of the *CPLR* have this requirement. *CPLR §3107* (20 days notice required for depositions), *CPLR §3122(a)* (20 days to respond to subpoenas *duces tecum), CPLR §3123(a)* (20 days to respond to notice to admit)*, CPLR §3133(a)* (20 days to provide responses to interrogatories).

[3] Disclosure of Treating Physician Testimony

A plaintiff is not required to give notice pursuant to *CPLR §3101(d)* in order to elicit testimony from a treating physician because the *§3101(d)* disclosure requirement "applies only to experts retained to give testimony at trial and not to treating physicians." *Mantuano v. Mehale*, 258 A.D.2d 566, 685 N.Y.S.2d 467 (2d Dep't 1999) (treating physician allowed to testify regarding causation)*; see also Rokitka v. Barrett*, 303 A.D.2d 983, 757 N.Y.S.2d 391 (4th Dep't 2003) (treating physician allowed to testify regarding need for future treatment); s*ee also Breen v. Entertainment Corp.*, 2 A.D.3d 298, 769 N.Y.S.2d 270 (1st Dep't 2003) *see also Butler v. Grimes*, 833 N.Y.S.2d 398 (2d Dep't 2007) (plaintiff's treating physician permitted to testify regarding future surgery and its cost, notwithstanding a lack of prior notice pursuant to *CPLR §3101[d]*)*; see also Hughes v. Webb*, 40 A.D.3d 1035, 837 N.Y.S.2d 698 (2d Dep't 2007) (error to preclude treating physician to opine on permanency).

[4] Direct Examination of Experts – In General

On direct examination, the expert's qualifications as an expert must be established. Otherwise, the expert will be precluded. A qualifications checklist for an expert witness (on direct) is as follows:

- occupation
- education
- training
- licensing
- professional associations
- other background
- previously qualified as an expert
- experience in specialty.

The plaintiff's attorney must establish facts in evidence upon which the expert (e.g., physician, economist) will be testifying, as well as establishing a basis for the expert's conclusions.

[5] Direct and Cross-Examination of Medical Experts

On direct examination, the plaintiff's attorney should establish the physician's qualifications, then proceed with questions regarding the examination(s) of the plaintiff, diagnosis, treatment, causation, prognosis, future treatment, cost of (past and future) treatment / care, and pain. See chapter 11 §11.13 for an outline regarding direct examination of a medical expert.

The defendant's medical expert will offer an opinion that the plaintiff's injuries were not causally related to the accident, were pre-existing, or (at the very least) have resolved. The plaintiff's attorney generally wants to show bias (and attack the examination), including that the physician was retained by the defense attorney's office, the physician knew that s/he would have to furnish a report for the defense, the physician knew the plaintiff would receive a copy of the report, the physician only examined the plaintiff once, the examination lasted only ten minutes, and the physician was sent information by the defense attorney prior to the exam (e.g., bill of particulars, medical records, etc.).

Warning: Where the plaintiff does not call a treating physician as a witness, but rather utilizes a non-treating expert, many of the above points will apply to the physician witnesses on both sides. Hence, this particular line of questioning is more effective where the plaintiff calls a treating physician as his or her medical witness.

In showing bias, the plaintiff's attorney should ask the expert whether defense examinations are part of his or her practice, whether these examinations are the bulk of his or her medical practice, the number of these examinations s/he conducts per week (or per year), how much the expert is paid for each examination and report, how often the expert testifies in court (the number of times per year), how much the expert is paid to testify (including the present case), the total amount earned per year to testify, and whether the testimony is primarily given on behalf of the defense. After some quick mathematical computations, the plaintiff's attorney will be able to derive just how much money the expert earns annually in this part of his or her practice. This information has the potential to destroy the expert's credibility.

A further safe line of questioning is to have the physician confirm all of his or her positive findings (per the physician's report) and confirm all the positive findings of the other physicians, by reading directly from those records which are in evidence. It is important for the plaintiff's attorney to look at the defendant's medical expert's report (which will list all that was relied upon), as it will open many doors for extensive cross-examination.

[6] Economist

[a] Utilizing Economist at Trial

In a case with large economic losses, the plaintiff should have an economist testify (in conjunction with a vocational rehabilitation expert, as discussed below). As with all expert testimony, the plaintiff's attorney must timely serve an expert disclosure pursuant to *CPLR §3101(d)*. The defense attorney will likely reject the *§3101(d)* disclosure of the economist as inadequate unless the defense expert is able to replicate the numbers from the disclosure. The defense rarely brings in an economist, out of fear that the defense economist's numbers will be used as a "floor".

> **Practice Tip:** Even undocumented illegal aliens are entitled to compensation for loss of earnings. *Balbuena v. IDR Realty, LLC*, 6 N.Y.3d 338, 812 N.Y.S.2d 416 (2006) (so long as employment not secured by tendering false work documents, economic recovery permitted).

[b] Preparation of Economist

As the economist will need a foundation for all of his or her conclusions, s/he must review the plaintiff's EBT testimony, the bill(s) of particulars, the plaintiff's W-2s and tax returns, the plaintiff's pension information, health benefits, annuities, the vocational rehabilitation expert's findings, pertinent medical findings, etc. Further, the economist must know not to reduce future loss of income to present value, not to reduce loss of earnings for collateral source payments, and not to subtract income tax deductions. Preparing the economist for cross-examination is crucial, as well.

> **Practice Tip:** Prior to the economist testifying, the plaintiff's attorney should have certain documents – upon which the economist relied in forming his or her opinion (e.g., W-2s, 1099s, tax returns, union contracts, benefits and pension records, medical bills, future medical expenses / life care plan, etc.) – admitted in evidence. If unable to do so before the economist testifies, the court should still allow the testimony "subject to connection" (i.e., later in the trial).

[c] Direct Examination of Economist

In qualifying an economist as an expert, the plaintiff's attorney should go through all the elements or his or her CV (e.g., degrees, papers, present employment, numerous times accepted as an expert witness in the past, etc.). It is important that the jury hears about all of the expert's qualifications. Hence, the plaintiff's attorney should not allow the defense to merely stipulate that the economist is qualified as an expert.

Practice Tip: The economist should testify in a "question and answer" format, rather than a lecture (which puts pressure on the economist to remember and makes him or her appear to be an advocate).

Practice Tip: The plaintiff's attorney should have the economist use an easel pad (rather than a blackboard) so it can be marked as an exhibit and taken to the jury room (as opposed to being erased). It is always helpful for the plaintiff to end with the numbers, on a high note.

Through direct examination of the economist, the following assumptions (which are made in arriving at the conclusions) must be elicited:

- The date when the economic losses began (e.g., date of accident).
- The length of time the economic losses will persist – up to retirement (which depends on the individual's expected work-life in the particular field of employment; some such tables can be found in the back of the *PJI*) and after retirement (e.g., retirement benefits).
- The plaintiff's pre-accident earnings capacity.
- The plaintiff's present earnings capacity (based on specific types of jobs, which requires a vocational rehabilitation expert, as discussed in §[6] below).
- How the plaintiff's earnings would have grown over time (based on a U.S. government index regarding average hourly earnings; the expert should testify that statistical tables are put together by the government, and are reliable tables in the industry, in order to have the judge allow such testimony).

The economist must then state his or her conclusions, to a reasonable degree of economic certainty, regarding total economic losses as a result of the accident.

Practice Tip: In giving his or her conclusion, the economist should provide alternatives. Otherwise, s/he will be viewed as an advocate rather than an expert.

Practice Tip: The plaintiff's attorney should ask the economist, on direct examination, to explain why the number used for the plaintiff's (most distant) future earnings capacity is so large, allowing the economist to explain inflation, cost of living increases, etc. This will take the sting out of the defense attorney's attack on the numbers being grossly inflated and/or overstated

[d] Life Care Plan

In cases with serious injuries and/or where the plaintiff has been unable to return to work, the plaintiff's attorney may wish to retain an expert (often a medical doctor specializing in physical medicine and rehabilitation) to prepare a life care plan detailing the plaintiff's future medical expenses. The economist can be used to tally the totals. This can serve as the basis for a large economic component of damages.

[e] Article 50-B Judgments

The economist should be familiar with *CPLR §4111*, as well as *Article 50-B* of the *CPLR*. Pursuant to *CPLR §4111*, the jury verdict shall specify the items of damages and shall further specify the number of years over which each component of *future* damages (e.g., loss of earnings, pain and suffering, future medical expenses) are intended to provide compensation. Pursuant to *CPLR §5041*, unless otherwise agreed by the parties, the plaintiff's share (i.e., as opposed to the plaintiff's attorney's share and costs) of *future* damages awarded in excess of $250,000 are to be paid in an annuity over 10 years or the number of years encompassed in the future damages award (as determined by the triers of fact), whichever is less, at a 4% annual rate of return. The first $250,000 (present value) of the plaintiff's share of future damages awarded, plus costs and the full amount of the attorneys' fees (including those based on future damages awarded) are due in a lump sum. The attorney's fees for future damages awarded are based on the present value of such damages.

[f] Collateral Source Hearing

Where the plaintiff seeks to recover for the cost of medical care, loss of earnings, or other economic loss, the defendant can seek a post-trial hearing for the court to consider evidence that any such past or future cost or expense was, or will be, replaced or indemnified, in whole or in part, from any collateral source such as insurance (except life insurance), social security (except benefits provided under Title XVIII of the Social Security Act, i.e., Medicare and Medicaid), workers' compensation or employee benefit programs (except such collateral sources entitled by law to liens against any recovery of the plaintiff). If the court finds, with reasonable certainty, that any such cost or expense was, or will be, replaced or indemnified by any collateral source, it is required to reduce the amount of the award by the amount of such finding *minus* the cost of the premiums paid two years prior to the action and *minus* the projected future cost to the plaintiff of maintaining such benefits. In order to find that any future cost will, with reasonable certainty, be replaced or indemnified by the collateral source, the court must find that the plaintiff is legally entitled to the continued receipt of such collateral source, subject only to payment of premiums. *CPLR §4545(c)*.

Practice Tip: As Medicare, Medicaid, and workers' compensation are exempt from the collateral source rule, the plaintiff is entitled to collect money from the defendant(s) in the third-party case **without** offset; this is so because the plaintiff will be required to reimburse the aforementioned entities at the conclusion of the case.

---

[7] Vocational Rehabilitation Expert

In determining earnings capacity after the accident versus before the accident, a vocational rehabilitation expert (i.e., a job counselor) should be used; an economist cannot testify to such. The vocational rehabilitation expert can determine (through an interview of the plaintiff, testing of the plaintiff, and utilization of books relied on in the industry) what the plaintiff can do with his or her skills, and what types of jobs those skills can be transferred to. A vocational rehabilitation expert may conclude, for example, that the plaintiff can no longer earn $50,000 per year and, with his or her injuries, can only be employed in a field where s/he would earn $20,000 per year. *See Bell v. Shopwell, Inc.*, 119 A.D.2d 715, 501 N.Y.S.2d 129 (2d Dep't 1986) (plaintiff has duty to mitigate loss of earnings by reasonably seeking vocational rehabilitation.

[8] Seatbelt Experts and the "Seatbelt Defense"

[a] Seatbelt Defense – In General

On the issue of damages in a motor vehicle accident trial, the defendants will sometimes utilize the seatbelt defense in an effort to mitigate damages. *See PJI §§2:87, 2:87.1,* and *2:87.2.*

> **Practice Tip:** The plaintiff's attorney must anticipate this defense. In doing so, s/he should determine whether such defense was plead as an affirmative defense in the defendant's answer. If not, a motion *in limine* should be made at the outset of the trial to preclude any such testimony and/or questioning. *See VTL §1229-c(8).*

> **Practice Tip:** In a bifurcated trial, evidence of plaintiff's failure to wear a seatbelt should be excluded if offered during the liability phase. The issue is relevant only on the issue of damages. *Speier v. Barker*, 35 N.Y.2d 444, 363 N.Y.S.2d 916 (1974); *VTL §1229-c(8)* (which has superseded *Speier* by enacting an absolute bar).

VTL §1229-c(3) requires the use of a seatbelt by an operator and any front-seat passenger 16 years of age or older. In addition to the statutory duty, each passenger has a duty to use reasonable care for his or her own safety which may include wearing an available seatbelt. *Stewart v. Taylor*, 193 A.D.2d 1078, 598 N.Y.S.2d 627 (4th Dep't 1993). A seatbelt must be available (and working) before the defendant can raise the defense. *DiMauro v. Metropolitan Suburban Bus Auth.*, 105 A.D.2d 236, 483 N.Y.S.2d 383 (2d Dep't 1984). Evidence that the plaintiff failed to wear a seatbelt is only admissible if the defendant is prepared to offer competent evidence demonstrating that any of the plaintiff's injuries were caused by the failure to wear a seatbelt. *Siegfried v. Siegfried*, 123 A.D.2d 621, 507 N.Y.S.2d 20 (2d Dep't 1986). Similarly, in a wrongful death action, evidence that the decedent failed to use an available seatbelt can only be used where there is competent evidence that the decedent would have survived had s/he worn the seatbelt. *Baginski v. New York Tel. Co.*, 130 A.D.2d 362, 515 N.Y.S.2d 23 (1st Dep't 1987).

[b] *Frye* Motion to Preclude Expert Testimony

The plaintiff's attorney may well want to make a *Frye* motion to preclude the expert testimony on the seatbelt issue. Pursuant to *Frye*, scientific expert testimony must be based on well-recognized scientific principles sufficiently established to have gained general acceptance in the field in which it belongs. *Frye v. United States*, 54 App. D.C. 46, 293 F. 1013 (1923).

> **Practice Tip:** It is important to look closely at the defendant's expert disclosures to determine whether the techniques they have used to make their findings meet the above criteria. If not, a motion for a hearing on the issue should be made. At the very least, a hearing will provide the plaintiff's attorney with sneak preview of the defense experts' testimony. If all goes well, the expert(s) will be precluded.

In *Daubert v. Merrell Dow Pharmaceuticals, Inc.*, 509 U.S. 579 (1993), the U.S. Supreme Court enunciated a four-prong test for admissibility of scientific testimony. The court held that such testimony proffered should be:

- based upon testable hypothesis;
- that has been tested at some specified error rate;
- which is then peer reviewed (the techniques, not the results) leading to publication; and
- which ultimately gained general acceptance in the relevant scientific community.

See also Kuhmo Tire Company, Ltd. v. Carmichael, 119 S. Ct. 1167 (1999). The *Frye* standard (as opposed to *Daubert*) is presently being followed by the New York State courts. *Parker v. Mobil Oil Corp.*, 7 N.Y.3d 434, 824 N.Y.S.2d 583 (2006).

[c] Presenting Seatbelt Defense

In presenting the seatbelt defense, the defense attorney will usually call a biomechanical engineer and a medical expert as witnesses. A biomechanical engineer (i.e., as opposed to an accident reconstructionist) is necessary to testify as to ultimate findings with respect to medical issues. If it seems likely that the defendant is going to call a seatbelt expert to testify, the plaintiff may wish to call one first. If, however, it seems unlikely that the defense is going to call a seatbelt expert to testify, the plaintiff should not rebut a defense that is not proffered; without an expert, the defendant will not be entitled to the jury instruction regarding the seatbelt defense.

> **Practice Tip:** Where the seatbelt defense is allowed, there are various ways to attack it. First, the defense expert's output is only as reliable as the input given to him. Where s/he did not have much of the relevant information and, the testimony is unreliable. Additionally, there is often an issue as to whether the seatbelt simply malfunctioned. Further, certain injuries are either caused *as a result of* the seatbelt use (e.g., pelvic injuries, abdominal injuries, etc.) or would not have been prevented (and may have been worse) by wearing a seatbelt (e.g., crushing collision to side of car where plaintiff is seated).

CHAPTER 11

OUTLINES / CHECKLISTS

PART A: OVERVIEW

§ 11.01 Overview – Outlines / Checklists

This chapter provides easy-to-use outlines / checklists for the most important phases of the litigation, including preliminary conferences, examinations before trial, jury selection, and trial. These outlines / checklists should be used as a guide, and should be amended and/or supplemented depending on the facts of the particular case.

PART B: OUTLINES / CHECKLISTS
   (Continued On Next Page)

§ 11.02 Preliminary Conference Checklist – Motor Vehicle Accident

1. All insurance information, including excess and umbrella coverage for driver, owner, driver's employer (if in course of employment), leasing / car rental company (if applicable).

2. All photographs and/or pictures depicting the scene of the accident, including, but not limited to, roadway markings, traffic control devices, skid markings, and roadway dividers.

3. All photographs depicting the damage to the vehicle(s) involved.

4. Copy of all estimates, invoices, repair bills, and canceled checks regarding property damage to the vehicle(s) involved.

5. Copy of defendant(s)' MV-104. *See Rodriguez v. Middle Atlantic Auto Leasing, Inc.*, 78 A.D.2d 629, 432 N.Y.S.2d 709 (1st Dep't 1980).

6. Copy of the police accident report (MV104-A), if having difficulty obtaining.

7. Names and addresses of all witnesses to the accident, regarding the property damage to the vehicle(s), and to the plaintiff's physical condition.

8. Name and address of the towing company, if applicable.

9. Name and address of the auto body repair shop.

10. Copy of the lease agreement, as well as name of the leasing company, if applicable.

11. Copy of the car rental agreement, as well as name of car rental company, if applicable.

12. Defendant's cell phone records on the date of accident, if applicable.

13. Surveillance film depicting the accident, if any (e.g., city bus).

14. Driver's trip sheet, if applicable.

15. Name and address of medallion owner, if applicable.

16. Permission to inspect vehicle (if applicable) on date certain, prior to EBTs.

17. Response to outstanding notices for discovery and inspection / combined demands.

§ 11.03 Preliminary Conference Checklist – Premises Liability

1. All contracts, including leases, affecting the premises on the date of the accident.

2. All contracts between defendants in effect on the date of the accident.

3. All accident reports.

4. Name and address of managing agent on the date of the accident.

5. All contracts between owner and managing agent in effect on the date of the accident.

6. All maintenance (e.g., cleaning, repairing, snow removal) contracts affecting the premises on the date of the accident.

7. All contracts, plans, blueprints, drawings, specifications, applications for permits, permits, certificates of occupancy regarding the construction of the premises (at location of accident).

8. All construction, alteration and repair records regarding the premises (at location of accident).

9. All accident reports and correspondence regarding prior similar accidents. *See Klatz v. Armor Elevator Co., Inc.*, 93 A.D.2d 633, 634, 462 N.Y.S.2d 677, 680 (2d Dep't 1983); *Coan v. Long Island Railroad*, 246 A.D.2d 569, 668 N.Y.S.2d 44, 45 (2d Dep't 1998).

10. All records regarding prior injury lawsuits against defendant(s), including caption(s), and index number(s), five years prior to the date of the accident through the date of the accident. *See Ielovich v. Taylor Mach. Works, Inc.*, 128 A.D.2d 676, 513 N.Y.S.2d 175 (2d Dep't 1987).

11. All records and logs of complaints regarding the condition of the premises at or about the accident location for five years prior to the date of the accident through the date of the accident.

12. All records and logs of repair requests regarding the premises at or about the accident location for five years prior to the date of the accident through the date of the accident.

13. All records regarding inspection of premises for five years prior to the date of the accident through the date of the accident.

14. All minutes of meetings (e.g., corporate, job, co-op, etc.) for three years prior to the date of the accident through the date of the accident.

15. Surveillance films of the accident, if any.

16. Pursuant to *CPLR §3120*, permission to enter the premises and conduct testing for the purposes of discovery, inspection, taking photographs and testing on date certain, prior to EBTs.

17. Response to outstanding notices for discovery and inspection / combined demands.

<u>Relevant Cases:</u>

Shapiro v. Fine, 95 A.D.2d 714, 464 N.Y.S.2d 126 (1st Dep't 1983) (production of 53 of 55 requested documents required).

Boone v. Supermarket General Corp., 109 A.D.2d 771, 486 N.Y.S.2d 284 (2d Dep't 1985) (disclosure of all slip and fall accidents that occurred in defendant's supermarket five years prior to date of accident allowed).

See Taylor v. John Doe, 167 A.D.2d 984 (4th Dep't 1984) (requests for prior similar accidents from date of construction through date of accident held proper).

Petty v. Riverbay Corp., 92 A.D.2d 525, 459 N.Y.S.2d 441, 442 (1st Dep't 1983) (production of documents required for building where assault took place, as well as two adjacent buildings).

Dukes v. 800 Grand Concourse Owners, Inc., 198 A.D.2d 13, 14, 603 N.Y.S.2d 138, 139 (1st Dep't 1993) (proof of prior leakage in other units in building admissible).

§ 11.04 Preliminary Conference Checklist – Construction Accident

1.   All leases and subleases relating to the subject premises on the date of the accident.

2.   All contracts, subcontracts, and agreements relating to work performed by, or for, any defendant relating to the premises on the date of the accident.

3.   All photographs, films and videotapes (including progress photographs, films and videotapes) of the premises.

4.   All written reports and memoranda relating to the progress of the project.

5.   All minutes of job meetings.

6.   Any document signed by, or on behalf of, the plaintiff relating to the project.

7.   All plans, specifications, blue prints, and drawings relating to the project.

8.   All inventories of safety equipment owned, leased or available for use by the defendant or its employees on the project.

9.   All financing agreements relating to the subject property on the date of the accident.

10. All payroll records relating to work performed at the premises.

11. All surveillance films depicting the accident, if any.

12. The entire contents of the job file.

13. All accident reports.

14. Pursuant to *CPLR §3120*, the right to enter the premises and conduct testing for the purposes of discovery, inspection, taking photographs, and testing on a date certain, prior to EBTs.

15. Response to outstanding notices for discovery and inspection / combined demands.

16. Documents requested for Premises Liability case (see §11.03 above), if applicable.

§ 11.05 Motor Vehicle EBT Outline

Background:

  Name / address / DOB

  Review docs / photos prior to testifying – have w/ you

  Discuss testimony w/ anyone – who – what entail

  Residential history – how long live @ current address – who live with

  Level of education

  Employment history – duties / position

    employed D/A – hours / supervisor's name – still work there

    working D/A – course of employment (add'l D)

Background D/A:

  Valid NYS driver's license – type – restrictions – glasses (reading / distance / both)

    last eye exam – difficulties w/ vision

  Valid registration

  Type of car – year, make, and model

    2 door / 4 door

    automatic / standard shift

    power steering / power brakes

  Own car – permissive use – how often used – primary driver – listed on ins. – other drivers

    purchase new / used

      how many miles D/A

      how many miles when purchased

      ever change brakes / tires

  Last inspected – by who

  Last serviced – by who

  Any problem w/ steering / brakes

  Frequency drive car

  Anything mechanically out of ordinary D/A

  Plate #

  Medication / alcohol D/A – any supposed to take but didn't – dosage / Dr's care

Pre-accident:

  Day of week

  Where coming from / going to – reason – (doing anything for work)

    time supposed to be there – supposed to meet anyone there

    plans for later that day

  Time woke D/A

    Weather – roads wet / dry

    rain: wipers / headlights / high beams

    sunlight: direction, sunglasses, visor, glare

    visibility: fog

    light (sun / artificial) / dark / lights on road / cars

  Route – to accident location

    time leave – amount of time elapsed before accident

    stops

passengers – relationship

length of time on X St. prior to accident

intended route if accident not occurred

Traffic conditions – l, m, h – cars in front / behind / in opp. direction

Lane config – # travel lanes / # parking lanes/directions / pvmt mkgs / dividers / shoulder

entered road to place of accident – any change

road – flat / incline or decline

straight / curved

Max speed – speed limit

Cars in front / behind / to side – describe

Cell phone (#) / smoke / eat / drink / radio / talking / texting / windows open

signal – traffic control devices – obstructions

familiarity w/ road

Accident:

Describe how accident occurred

Specifics from PJI – depending on type of case

Prior to impact:

Apply brakes – describe – l, m, h

for how long prior to impact

rate of speed when first applied brakes

distance from other car

distance from intersection

ever take foot off brake prior to impact

Skidding – which direction – marks

Turn steering wheel – either car

Horn / Brakes screeching

Say anything – passenger say anything

Vehicle in front come to a stop (MSJ – rear end)

Directional

Impact:

Describe – light, medium, heavy

Speed @ time of impact

Pos'n of each car at impact – lanes – at or near intersecting road

Pos'n of each car after came to rest

Points of impact

at impact, foot on brake / gas / neither

cars continue to move after impact

After impact:

Vehicle come to stop – where – still in contact – direction of each car

Airbags deploy – lose consciousness – bleeding – ambulance

Moved (off road) – either car – how – where – towed – how leave scene

Damage – parts of car – other car

repaired – where – how much – written estimates – book value

Conversations at scene w/ P – content – discuss accident – conv w/ P since D/A

Conversations w/ passenger(s) / others

Police at scene – who called – cars moved prior to arrival – conversations – citations
Witnesses to accident – names – describe – male / female – why believe witnessed it
Tickets / citations at scene
Photos of damage to either car / of scene

Other:

MV-104 before speak to attorney
Course of employment
Plaintiff's condition – seat belted – ambulance
Defendant / others injured – receive treatment

§ 11.06 Premises Liability EBT Outline

Background: Education, degrees, licences, training

Employment: History, position, supervisor(s) – subordinates, duties, days / hours

Ownership: Premises (d/a), any accident-causing instrumentalities

Maintenance: Premises (d/a), procedures, written / verbal instructions, outside service contracts

Possession: Premises (d/a), leases, contracts

Control: Premises (d/a) - clean, shovel snow, etc., managing agent

Special Use:

Inspections: Premises – over the years – prior to d/a; records

Creation: Construction, alteration, repair, hiring contractor, records

Actual Notice: Prior complaints, repair requests, accidents, claims / lawsuits, prior accident reports, government violations, records (or lack thereof), minutes

Constructive Notice: Prior inspections, prior visits to dangerous area, failure to follow standard procedures d/a and just prior thereto

Res Ipsa: Exclusive control

Statutory Violations:

Specific Law of Case:

Defect(s): Identify and describe

Accident: Eyewitness, personal knowledge, witnesses, photographs, conversations (w/ plaintiff, co-workers, etc.), weather, accident report(s)

§ 11.07 Construction Accident EBT Outline

Labor Law §240:

Plaintiff was employed on a construction project

Defendant owner / tenant-in-possession

    Premises not 1 or 2-family dwelling (or owner substantially involved in project OR premises being renovated for commercial rental)

Defendant (general) contractor had right to control work, authority to supervise and control site and/or plaintiff's activities, stop any unsafe work practices

Agent of owner / GC had authority to supervise / control activity which caused injury, stop any unsafe work practices

Work performed on building or structure

Work was erection, demolition, repair, alteration, painting, cleaning, or pointing

    Work was not routine maintenance

Injury was elevation-related - worker needed to be at elevated height to perform job

No safety devices / inadequate safety devices provided

    OR device not properly erected, constructed, placed as to give adequate protection

Scaffolding / staging > 20 feet high - safety rails required

Scaffolding / staging > 20 feet high - be so fasted as to prevent swaying from building / structure

Scaffolding / staging to be constructed to bear 4x maximum weight required to be placed thereon

Proximate cause - violation of statute (*§240*) was proximate cause of injuries sustained

Plaintiff not recalcitrant worker

Plaintiff not sole proximate cause of accident

Labor Law §241(6):

Plaintiff employed on construction project

Non-delegable duty on all owners, contractors, and their agents (can delegate work, but not responsibility) - no exemption for owners of one or two-family dwellings

Work = construction, demolition, or excavation

Unsafe condition at work site

Specific (not general) violation(s) of the NYS Industrial Code

Proximate Cause between the violation and the plaintiff's injuries

Plaintiff not recalcitrant worker / sole proximate cause (comparative negligence inapplicable)

Labor Law §241 (1) - (5):
Plaintiff employed on construction project

Defendant = owner / tenant-in-possession, contractor, or agent

> Premises not 1 or 2-family dwelling (or owner substantially involved in project OR premises being renovated for commercial rental)

Work = construction, demolition, or excavation

Establish violation of *§241(1),(2),(2),(4), or (5)*

Fall through open space within building where permanent floors are planned to be installed

Proximate Cause

Plaintiff not recalcitrant worker / sole proximate cause

Labor Law §241-a:
Plaintiff worker in / at elevator shaftway, hatchway, or stairwell of building in course of construction or demolition

Non-delegable duty on owners / contractors

Violation of *§241-a*

Work being performed in elevator shaftway, hatchway, or stairwell

> breach: failure to provide sound planking at least 2" thick over opening at heights < 2 stories above or 1 story below workers to protect them from falling hazards

Proximate Cause

Labor Law §200:
Plaintiff was a worker at a construction / work site

Elements of common-law negligence

Control: must show defendant exercised supervisory control over the work place (means and methods of plaintiff's work)

> OR dangerous condition at work site pre-existed project

> OR defendant created dangerous condition

§ 11.08 Motor Vehicle Accident EBT Preparation Outline

<u>Rules of Testifying</u>:
    Purpose of EBT
    Think before speak – take time – not a race
    Do not volunteer information – concise responses – the fewer words, the better
    Do not guess
    Do not answer questions do not understand / difficult questions
    Do not answer unfair questions / objections
    Verbal responses
    Be polite / dress properly / no notes
    Do not deflect attention to attorney

<u>Motor Vehicle</u> – <u>Liability</u>:
    PJI – specific elements attempting to prove in this case
    describe accident
    time, speed, distance
    maximum rate of speed
    car properly functioning
    not tailgating
    skidding
    car leave road
    glasses
    when first saw other car; constant observation
    where looking immediately prior to accident
    areas of impact
    cars moved prior to police arriving
    attempted to avoid collision (horns, brakes, etc.)
    why failed to avoid collision
    paying attention v. distractions (cell phone, eating, conversations, music, etc.)
    conversations (admissions) – driver, witnesses, police, ambulance, hospital,
        family, friends, spouse, etc.
    medical records (description of accident)
    photos – fair and accurate
    witnesses (and witness statements)
    accident report, MV-104
    experts' reports / findings

<u>Motor Vehicle</u> – <u>Damages</u>:
    "serious injury" – usual and customary daily activities – <u>90</u> in 180 – personal / work
        / school / leisure / sexual)
    amount of damage to car
    areas of impact (and causally related to injuries)

force of impact – cars move as result of impact

body make contact with inside of car – part(s) of body / car

seatbelt – wearing – describe – medical records (mention of seatbelt / no seatbelt)

airbags deploy

cars towed

ambulance / hospital

pain and suffering – past and future – do not minimize – describe

how often in pain – as sit here – increased or decreased over time

medications – prescriptions – pharmacy – over the counter

activities before v after accident

how employment affected – length out of work – light duty – leave job

trips outside state

memberships to gyms

weight increase since d/a

ambulance, hospital

treatment – names, addresses of healthcare providers (hospitals, doctors, therapy, diagnostic testing)

how referred – dates of visits

diagnostic tests and results

therapy – type, length, frequency

devices – canes, crutches, walkers, wheelchairs, casts, boots

still treating – reason for stopping (MMI, home exercises, etc.)

scheduled appointments for doctor in future

surgery – future surgery – surgery recommended

confinement – hospital, bed, home – length and dates

present complaints - pain, ROM

scarring, deformity

decreased range of motion, etc.

economic losses – loss of income, property damage, out of pocket expenses

collateral source

priors and subsequents – injuries to same body parts

bill of particulars

medicals

Other Concerns:

venue

citizenship status

prior convictions

travel to EBT, drs' appointments

review documents

§ 11.09 Premises Liability EBT Preparation Outline

<u>Rules of Testifying</u>:

    Purpose of EBT

    Think before speak – take time – not a race

    Do not volunteer information – concise responses – the fewer words, the better

    Do not guess

    Do not answer questions do not understand / difficult questions

    Do not answer unfair questions / objections

    Verbal responses

    Be polite / dress properly / no notes

    Do not deflect attention to attorney

<u>Premises Liability – Liability</u>:

    PJI – defendant created / had notice (actual / constructive)

    describe defect

    when first noticed / knew (comparative negligence)

    why failed to notice before accident (walked there prior to accident? regular patron of store?)

    why failed to have accident on prior occasion? what was different d/a?

    someone walking i/f/o you? blocking view?

    describe accident

    where coming from / going to

    where looking immediately prior to accident

    precise positioning (e.g., of feet, hands, eyes) leading up to / at time of accident

    no misstep

    no debris

    lighting

    type of shoes

    carrying anything (which hand, etc.?)

    glasses

    weather conditions

    alcohol, drugs, meds

    comparative negligence / assumption of risk / culpable conduct

    not distracted e.g., talking, looking elsewhere

    return to scene

    photos – fair and accurate – place "x" on spot

    witnesses

    conversations (admissions) – defendant, witnesses, ambulance, police, hospital, friends, spouse, etc.

    medical records (description of accident, alcohol, etc.)

    experts' reports / findings

    accident reports

Premises Liability – Damages:

  ambulance / hospital

  pain and suffering – past and future – do not minimize – describe

  how often in pain – as sit here – increased or decreased over time

  medications – prescriptions – pharmacy – over the counter

  activities before v after accident

      how get to EBT

      how get to doctors' appointments

      miles on car d/a and now

  how employment affected – length out of work – light duty – leave job

  trips outside state

  memberships to gyms

  weight increase since d/a

  treatment – names, addresses of healthcare providers (hospitals, doctors, therapy,
      diagnostic testing)

  how referred – dates of visits

  diagnostic tests and results

  therapy – type, length, frequency

  devices – canes, crutches, walkers, wheelchairs, casts, boots

  still treating – reason for stopping (MMI, home exercises, etc.)

  scheduled appointments for doctor in future

  surgery – future surgery – surgery recommended

  scarring, deformity

  decreased range of motion, etc.

  priors and subsequents – to same body parts

  bill of particulars; medicals

  present complaints - pain, ROM

  economic losses – loss of income, property damage, out of pocket expenses

      why unable to work,

      attempts to work, apply for jobs

      any physician instruct not to work

      seek any other type of employment, seek vocational rehab professional

      educational background, other skills

      apply for disability, how supporting self

Other Concerns:

  venue

  citizenship status

  prior convictions

  review documents

  travel to EBT today, drs' appointments

  WCB hearing testimony (if applicable)

§ 11.10 Construction Accident EBT Preparation Outline

Rules of Testifying:

  Purpose of EBT

  Think before speak - take time - not a race

  Do not volunteer information - concise responses - the fewer words, the better

  Do not guess

  Do not answer questions do not understand / difficult questions

  Do not answer unfair questions / objections

  Verbal responses

  Be polite / dress properly / no notes

  Do not deflect attention to attorney

Liability:

1. Type, and condition, of ladder / scaffolding

  defective, inadequately secured, or otherwise failed to protect plaintiff

  old, wobbly, worn, shaky, loose rungs, or loose rivets

  no rubber feet or missing rubber feet

  lacked locking spreader

  lacked side rails for gripping

  lacked non-slip treads

  A-frame, step ladder, extension ladder

  Max height of ladder; height at time of accident

2. Ladder Unsecured

  no ties, tie downs, not tied back

  nobody to hold ladder (e.g., co-worker)

  not secured at top or bottom

  not chocked or wedged to anything stable

  collapsed, slipped, tipped, or otherwise failed to perform its function

  ladder moved, was not steady; shook and moved; shook and tipped

  no slip-resistant feet

3. No Misuse of ladder / equipment

  didn't knowingly choose to use defective / inadequate equipment

  no overreaching

  not standing on top rung

  no over-leaning / leaning

  not standing / walking on/up side of ladder (rather, middle)

  no application of lateral force

  not improperly placed by plaintiff (i.e., sideways, on top of debris, unlevel ground, etc.)

  no misstep

  no debris

level surface

no intentional misuse (e.g., taller ladder available, but not used)

locked locking mechanism

no failure to tie safety line

no use of ladder w/o opening it / no leaning of closed A-frame ladder against wall

4. No safety equipment available / Not Recalcitrant Worker

no failure to use available equipment

no intentional disregard for safety instructions

no tie backs

nobody to hold ladder

no nets / life nets

no safety line

no safety belt or harness

no better ladders / no taller ladders available (and unnecessary anyhow)

only device provided

directed to use ladder / scaffold by employer, etc. (not directed to use any other device)

no choice / no alternative - even if waited

couldn't request new equipment - even from off site

5. Ladder slipped / tipped / collapsed FIRST

ladder moved before accident - tipped (b/c defective, malfunctioned), then caused to fall

NOT plaintiff began to fall, then ladder failed; rather, ladder failed, then plaintiff fell

6. Positioning

height of ladder

height of plaintiff's feet at time of fall

height of (AC unit) working on

height of plaintiff

direction ladder facing

space around ladder

ladder open wide (fully opened)

where plaintiff's feet and hands were - # rungs from top/ bottom

how walked up / down (which foot first, sequence, which rung, etc.)

two feet on each rung?

anything in hands

hand on ladder rails?

who positioned ladder?

level surface?

which direction tip / slide to?

where fell, where landed, where ladder landed

7. Plaintiff Not Sole Proximate Cause of Accident
   not working from top rung
   not jump from ladder
   not knowingly using defective equip, knowing could request / obtain proper equipment
   not free from defect; not previously steady (implying P sole prox cause)
   P knows what caused it to fail (e.g., unsecure, unsteady, rods loose, etc.)

8. Protected Activity
   "Erection, demolition, repair, altering, painting, cleaning, pointing of bldg / structure"
   construction (not repair, not maintenance)
   performing protected activity at time of accident
   equipment failed while performing protected activity

9. Accident Descriptions
   no witnesses
   accident Reports
   notes / Logs re accident
   amb call report
   ER, hospital records
   drs' records
   conversations re: accident - w/ who? What said? W stmts?
   hearsay - not source - never spoke to W? - NOT "I don't remember"

10. Prior Usage by Plaintiff
    never used before?
    prior trips up / down - wobbly; all like that
    prior days? Same ladder? # of times?
    complaints?
    not free from defect; not previously steady (implying P sole prox cause)

11. Gravity-related
    needed to be at height to perform work
    fell from ladder / scaffold

12. Inspect ladder before use
    how so? After set up? How so?
    how appear?

13. Safety Meetings / Job Meetings
    any? Describe?
    complaints?
    fail to follow instructions?

14. Describe Accident
    fell off ladder
    "scaffold collapsed and I fell"
    "ladder tipped and I fell"

15. Defendants had Authority to Direct / Control Plaintiff's Work
    GC - super at site daily - inspected work and gave advice (examples?)
    sub-contractor - contractor hired plaintiff's employer - super at site 2x/wk -
    inspected work and gave advice (examples?)
    authority to change work / stop work
    full-time employees on site
    responsible to oversee site
    bi-weekly progress meetings
    authority to supervise contractors and stop unsafe work practices
    employees directed plaintiff
16. Labor Law 200 COA v each defendant
    direct / control work - manner and methods of P's work - D provide equipment?
    instructions? D have control of positioning of equipment?
    notice (actual or constructive) / complaints re ladder / scaffolding
    prior accidents w/ ladder / scaffolding
    D created condition
    defective condition pre-exist project?
17. Position of ladder / scaffolding and plaintiff AFTER accident
    position when entered room
18. All elements v all Defendants - all COAs
    vios of Industrial Code
19. Permission to Enter and Work
20. Other:
    accident reports (C-2, C-3, etc.)
    describe defect
    when first noticed / knew (comparative negligence)?
    why failed to notice before accident?
    why failed to have accident on prior occasion? What was different d/a?
    someone walking i/f/o you? Blocking view?
    describe accident
    where coming from / going to
    where looking immediately prior to accident
    precise positioning (e.g., of feet, hands, eyes) leading up to / at time of accident
    lighting
    wearing (type of shoes, goggles / glasses, gloves)
    carrying anything (which hand, etc.?), holding onto anything?
    what wearing (gloves, goggles, hard hat, etc.)
    glasses
    weather conditions
    alcohol, drugs, meds
    not distracted e.g., talking, looking elsewhere
    return to scene

    photos

    witnesses

    conversations (admissions) - defendant, witnesses, ambulance, police, hospital, friends, spouse, etc.

    medical records (description of accident, alcohol, etc.)

    experts' reports / findings

    WCB hearing testimony

Damages - Labor Law:

    ambulance / hospital

    pain and suffering - past and future - do not minimize - describe

    how often in pain - as sit here - increased or decreased over time

    medications - prescriptions -pharmacy - over the counter

    activities before v after accident

    how employment affected - length out of work - light duty - leave job

    trips outside state

    memberships to gyms

    weight increase since d/a

    treatment - names, addresses of healthcare providers (hospitals, doctors, therapy, diagnostic testing)

    how referred - dates of visits

    diagnostic tests and results

    therapy - type, length, frequency

    devices - canes, walkers, casts, boots

    still treating - reason for stopping (MMI, home exercises, etc.)

    scheduled appointments for doctor in future

    surgery - future surgery - surgery recommended

    present complaints - pain, ROM

    scarring, deformity

    decreased range of motion, etc.

    economic losses - loss of income, property damage, out-of-pocket expenses

    education

    languages

    vocational training, seek alternative jobs

    priors and subsequents - to same body parts

    review BP

    medicals

Other Concerns:

    venue

    citizenship status

    prior convictions

    travel to EBT, drs' appointments

    review docs

§ 11.11 Jury Selection Outline

D/A: Caption:

non-lead – attitudes – f/u w/ why
lead – condition

<u>General / Liability:</u>
    1. Intro
        names of counsel and clients
        capsule: trip and fall accident on sidewalk as a result of Ds' failure to use
            reas care (or, negligence) resulting in extremely serious injury
        theme
        not time to try case – pick 8 impartial
        civil case – BOP – liability/damages
        only time to talk . . .
        feel free to talk – explosive
        think about Qs
        don't mean to pry – apologize in advance
        __ years for trial – justice/fairness
        know parties / attorneys
    2. Gen'l Qs
        homeowner / car owner
        married / kids / work / work-spouse / prior jury duty
        educational background
        volunteer work / charitable
    3. Prior suits
        family member
    4. Legal background in family
    5. Employed by / own stock in insurance company
    6. *PJI*-specific questions
    7. Other

    (Continued on Next Page)

<u>Damages:</u>
1. Only remedy courts allow is for $ – P would like nothing more than to back in time and have Ds act reasonably and avoid accident

Only remedy is monetary comp – agree that if injured thru D's negl, entitled to comp for p and s
> how feel?
> assurance that if prove that aspect of case, you'll make award for that if feel P entitled
> OK to come to court to resolve dispute
> only day in court – balance scales of justice (w/$)

2. Plaintiff's injuries
> ever have
> family/friends
> dominant-side injury – ever have

3. Add up individual components of damages after case and = A LOT
> any hesitation awarding
> assure me
> glass ceiling?
> fair and compensatory damages
> have to determine how much p and s (past and future), med expenses (past and future)
> going to hear about u and c before / after – part of damage award

4. List of Drs:

5. Want self as juror
> award fair and compensatory damages

§ 11.12 Opening Remarks Outline

I. Introduction
   A. Re-introduce self
   B. Theme
   C. Still not evidence, but more (than allowed to tell at jury selection)
   D. Already admitted (e.g., ownership) – therefore, don't have to prove
   What I tell you is subject to change (depending on Judge, witnesses, defense)
   E. Purpose at opening: Jigsaw puzzle – (going to give you the pieces as move throughout – may not be in order; one piece at time – now giving you the box – if give you enough pieces so that you can see the picture, i.e., not every piece, you'll find for plaintiff).

II. Parties
   A. Plaintiff
   B. Defendant

III. Scene
   A. Describe scene / defect(s) (e.g., providing verbal picture of negligence)
   B. Only access (e.g., combating claim for comparative negligence)

IV. How it Happened

V. Basis of Liability
   A. Notice of condition
      prior incidents
      prior notice / conversations
      constructive notice
   B. Creation of Condition
   C. *PJI* words (apply to the evidence)
      not reasonably safe
      foreseeable danger of injury
      conduct unreasonable in proportion to danger
      substantial factor in causing plaintiff's injury
   D. Exclusive Control (*Res Ipsa*)
      owned
      responsible for repairs (EBT)
      refused tenant's offers to fix

VI. Defense Contentions

   (Cont'd on next page)

VII. Damages (in unified trial or damages-only trial)
    A. Ambulance
    B. ER, hospital
    C. Diagnostic testing
    D. Treatment
    E. Surgery
    F. Physical therapy
    G. Residuals / prognosis
    H. Pain and suffering
    I. Economic losses (loss of income, medical expenses, life care, out-of-pocket expenses, fringe benefits – annuity, pension, health insurance)

VIII. Conclusion
    A. Use common sense
    B. Ask for evidence
    C. Evidence will show defendant liable

§ 11.13 Direct Examination of Medical Expert Outline

[a] Qualifications
- licensed – when – where
- education and training – undergraduate - medical school - internship (and where), residency (and where)
- specialty – training – specialty boards (Board Certified – tell jury what means)
- hospital staff memberships - past and present
- teaching positions
- publications and lectures
- medical society memberships
- other honors
- previously testified as expert
- experience
- describe practice – number of patients
- experience with x-rays, MRIs, etc. (important for discussing / reading from same)

[b] Examination of Plaintiff
- Did there come a time you examined Mr. Smith (i.e., plaintiff)?
- Did you take a history? Can you share it with us? (e.g., physician can state that plaintiff was involved in motor vehicle accident, went to hospital, saw Dr. X, then Y . . .)
- Did Mr. Smith have any history of prior . . . injury?
- Were Dr. X's report part of the history? What did they say? Explain (here, the witness can explain, in detail, findings of other physicians.)
- \Did you conduct physical examination? What did it consist of? Complaints? Positive findings? Objective tests?

[c] Diagnosis
- Did you reach a diagnosis with a reasonable degree of medical certainty? What was it?

The physician should then be asked to explain the plaintiff's injuries in detail.

[d] Treatment

The questioning of the physician-witness should then go through all of the plaintiff's treatment (including physical therapy), subsequent testing (e.g., MRIs), and surgeries (if any). The physician should show (and explain to) the jury the positive objective findings (e.g., fracture on x-ray). Further, after admitting the surgery report in evidence, the physician should be asked to read and explain each sentence of the report.

[e] Causation

The physician-witness must be asked to opine on the issue of causation, as follows:

- Did you reach an opinion with a reasonable degree of medical certainty as to what caused the injuries? What is it?
- What is the significance of Mr. Smith being asymptomatic before the accident versus symptomatic after?

[f] Prognosis

The physician-witness must be asked to opine on the plaintiff's prognosis, as follows:

- What was Mr. Smith's present condition based on your last examination of him?
- Did you form an opinion with a reasonable degree of medical certainty as to whether injury is a permanent one? What's your opinion?
- Did you form any other opinions with a reasonable degree of medical certainty as to Mr. Smith's prognosis? (e.g., future surgery, etc.)
- What types of activities would those injuries make it difficult for Mr. Smith to perform (e.g., physician can corroborate the plaintiff's testimony)?

[g] Future Treatment

- Did you form an opinion with a reasonable degree of medical certainty as to whether Mr. Smith will require future treatment? What type?

[h] Pain

Questions should be asked regarding the amount of pain associated with the plaintiff's injuries, surgeries, etc.

[i] Cost of Treatment

Questions should also be asked regarding the cost of past medical treatment, as well as the expected cost of plaintiff's future medical treatment (e.g., surgery, physical therapy, etc.).

§ 11.14 Summation Outline

Introduction
Parties
Scene
Instrumentalities
Weather/Lighting
What happened
Issues of Liability
Basis of Liability (don't forget proximate cause)
Corroboration
Other side and refutation
Damages (in unified, or damages only, trial)
    ambulance
    ER, hospital
    diagnostic testing
    injuries
    treatment
    surgery
    physical therapy
    loss of time from work
    residuals / prognosis
    pain and suffering
    loss of enjoyment of life
    economic losses
        past loss of earnings
        future loss of earnings
        past medical expenses
        future medical expenses
        life care
        loss of annuity, pension, health insurance
        out-of-pocket expenses
Burden of Proof – come back to Jig Saw Puzzle analogy (from opening)
Instructions (and Verdict sheet) – tell jury what questions they will have to answer and how they should answer them (and why); tell them that unless they answer yes on 1 and 2, plaintiff gets nothing
Conclusion
    amount asking for (in unified, or damages-only, trial)

§ 11.15 Settlement Worksheet

GROSS SETTLEMENT PROCEEDS: . . . . $_____

DISBURSEMENTS:

    Investigator Fees: . . . . $_____

    Film / Photos: . . . . $_____

    MV-104A / MV-104: . . . . $_____

    Last Owner Search: . . . . $_____

    Weather Records: . . . . $_____

    Big Apple Search: . . . . $_____

    Big Apple Map: . . . . $_____

    Verdict Search . . . . $_____

    Medical Records:

        Medical Records: . . . . $_____

        Medical Records: . . . . $_____

        Medical Records: . . . . $_____

        Subtotal . . . . $_____

    Process Server:

        Notice of Claim: . . . . $_____

        Summons and Complaint: . . . . $_____

        Subpoenas: . . . . $_____

        Other: . . . . $_____

        Subtotal: . . . . $_____

    Court Costs:

        Index Number: . . . . $_____

        RJI: . . . . $_____

        Note of Issue: . . . . $_____

        Jury Demand: . . . . $_____

        Motions: . . . . $_____

    Subtotal: . . . . $_____

    EBT Transcripts: . . . . $_____

    Interpreter: . . . . $_____

    Arbitration / Mediation: . . . . $_____

Experts:

    Engineer: . . . . $_____

    Medical: . . . . $_____

    Other: . . . . $_____

    Subtotal: . . . . $_____

Trial Exhibits: . . . . $_____

Miscellaneous:

    Postage: . . . . $_____

    Reproduction Costs: . . . . $_____

    Parking: . . . . $_____

    Other: . . . . $_____

    Subtotal: . . . . $_____

TOTAL DISBURSEMENTS: . . . . $_____

NET PROCEEDS: . . . . $_____

Client Gross Share (i.e. 2/3 of Net Proceeds) . . . . $_____

   Less Liens (Med, WC, Medicare, PIP, SSI, loans) $(_____)

   Less Structure (Structured Settlement) . . . . $(_____)

Client Net Share: . . . . $_____

Attorney Net Share: . . . . $_____

REFERENCES

• Association of Justices of the State of New York, Committee on Pattern Jury Instructions. *Pattern Jury Instructions - Civil.* 2008 ed. West Publishing Company, 2008.

• Brown, Frances and Ernest Goodwin, "The Right Time?" *New York Law Journal* 19 June 2006.

• Carey, Raymond. "The Kelly Formula and the Workers' Compensation Lien." *Bill of Particulars* Spring 2001.

• Chase, Oscar G. and Henry G. Miller. *New York Practice Guide*, Chapter 37 Construction Accidents. Matthew Bender & Company, Inc., 2004.

• Dachs, Jonathan. *Bender's New York Insurance Law*, Chapter 51 Uninsured and Underinsured Motorist Protection. Matthew Bender & Company, Inc., 2004.

• Donahue, Michael and Thomas Lawrence. "Health Care Liens and Personal Injury Awards." *New Jersey Law Journal* 29 September 1999.

• Farrell, Richard T. *Prince, Richardson on Evidence.* 11th ed. Brooklyn Law School, 2002.

• Hayes, J. Michael. "Subrogation Rights of Health Care Providers." *Bill of Particulars* Fall 2006.

• Kahn, Justin S. "To Rent or Not to Rent? Vicarious Liability, Negligence and Car Rental Companies." *Bill of Particulars* Fall 2006.

• Landau, Kenneth. "Nine Ways to Settle Your Cases in '99." *Nassau Lawyer* December 1998.

• Landau, Kenneth. "Nine Ways to Settle Your Cases in '98." *Nassau Lawyer* January 1998.

• Lustig, III, Carl. "The 29 Workers' Compensation Lien in Third-Party Actions." *Trial Lawyers Quarterly.* vol. 30, number 2 and number 3 (2000).

• McKeon, Hon. Douglas E. "Impanelment of Jury." *Personal Injury Practice in New York.* West Group (Bensel, Frank, McKeon, Chapter 9, West; New York Practice Series, 1997), December 2002.

• Mattei, Suzanne Y. "Update on Lead Poisoning Legislation." *Bill of Particulars* Summer 2004.

• Miller, Kirk M. *Who to Sue and What to Do, Tort Actions Under the General Municipal Law in New York City.* Looseleaf Law Publications, Inc., 1994.

• Robert, Joan Lensky. "Revisiting Medicare Claims and Personal Injury Lawsuits: 2004 Update." *Bill of Particulars* Winter 2004.

• Ryenecki, Scott and Brian J. Isaac. "Insolvency in Uninsured and Under-insured Motorist Cases." *Bill of Particulars* Summer 2004.

• Rubinowitz, Ben and Evan Torgan. "*Voir Dire* in Medical Negligence Cases: A Plaintiff's Perspective." *New York Law Journal* 24 October 2004.

• Rubinowitz, Ben and Evan Torgan. "Dealing With Monetary Damages From *Voir Dire* to Summation." *New York Law Journal* 29 November 2001.

• Schwartz, Evan S. "Third-Party Bad Faith: Still Alive in New York." *Bill of Particulars* Fall 2006.

• Siegel, David B. *New York Practice*, 4th ed., West Publishing Company, 2005.

• Taller, Y. David "Settlement Techniques in Personal Injury Cases." *New York State Bar Association newsletter* Fall 1998.

• Von Nostitz, Glenn. "Labor Law 240 Report." *Bill of Particulars* Summer 2005.

Printed in the United Kingdom by
Lightning Source UK Ltd., Milton Keynes
139268UK00001B/3/P

9 781595 941879